THE TOLERATION AND PERSECUTION OF THE
JEWS IN THE ROMAN EMPIRE

PART I

The Toleration of the Jews Under Julius Caesar and Augustus

BY
DORA ASKOWITH, A. M.
ASSISTANT INSTRUCTOR IN HISTORY IN HUNTER COLLEGE
OF THE CITY OF NEW YORK

SUBMITTED IN PARTIAL FULFILMENT OF THE REQUIREMENTS
FOR THE DEGREE OF DOCTOR OF PHILOSOPHY
IN THE
FACULTY OF POLITICAL SCIENCE
COLUMBIA UNIVERSITY

WIPF & STOCK · Eugene, Oregon

Wipf and Stock Publishers
199 W 8th Ave, Suite 3
Eugene, OR 97401

The Toleration of the Jews Under Julius Caesar and Augustus Part 1
By Askowith, Dora
ISBN 13: 978-1-62564-575-3
Publication date 1/14/2014
Previously published by Columbia University, 1915

PREFACE

Among the many ideas called to mind by the period of Julius Caesar and Augustus is the one of conflict,—a conflict of ideals, of religions and of peoples. Such a period at first sight, seems to embody the conception of warfare and to be foreign to all notions of toleration. A closer survey, however, makes evident the fact that the minds of men were engaged in solving problems other than those of military tactics and that out of the conflict of religious ideas was slowly evolving a religion whose strongest appeal was based upon its advocacy of peace and order; that despite the apparent struggle of peoples, the Jews were really being tolerated, actuated though this policy may have been by political expediency rather than by a spirit of *jus naturale* or *jus gentium*.

As we look back over the long vista of time and find the Jewish people whose history has generally become synonymous with suffering and endurance, being tolerated during a period which from the point of view of war finds many analogies in the twentieth century, there arises a distant ray of hope that the close of the present European struggle may bring about, among other things, the complete toleration of the Jews in those countries in which they are still being persecuted.

It is with considerable misgivings that I present this study on the Jews of the Roman Empire. The subject is a large and complicated one, leading into innumerable paths and ramifications to the traversing of which many scholars have devoted a lifetime. I was well advanced in my work long before the two studies of Juster, *Examen critique des sources relative à la condition juridique des Juifs dans l'empire romain* (Paris, 1911) and *Les Droits politiques des Juifs dans l'empire romain* (Paris, 1912) were announced and which have since been incorporated in his recent comprehensive work *Les Juifs dans l'empire romain leur condition juridique, économique et sociale*, 2 vols. (Paris, 1914). As the latter volumes reached me after my own dissertation was written and practically ready for the press, I did not think it advisable to change my references to Juster's earlier works, which I consulted, to correspond to his later books.

In the light of Juster's recent work, especially, the present volume makes no claim to do more than to emphasize and follow out one thread of thought from a standpoint which is perhaps of less interest to the jurist than to the student of comparative religion. If the following study leads some other student to examine the material dealing with the Jews of the Roman Empire and to traverse a field of enduring interest and value, it has served its purpose to a large extent.

To Professor James T. Shotwell of Columbia University I am not only indebted for the aid rendered me in the preparation of my dissertation and the reading of proof, but to the guidance, encouragement and counsel which I have received for several years as his student and in whose course on *Paganism and Christianity* the subject of this volume found its origin and inspiration. To the following, also, I am under great obligation for their criticism and valuable suggestions: Professor Richard J. H. Gottheil of Columbia University; Professor William W. Rockwell of Union Theological Seminary; Professor Solomon Schechter (who has read part of the manuscript), Professor Louis Ginzberg and Professor Alexander Marx of the Jewish Theological Seminary of America and Professor Cyrus Adler of Dropsie College. I should also like to take this opportunity to express my gratitude to the librarians and the staff of Columbia University, Union Theological Seminary, the Jewish Theological Seminary and the Jewish department of the New York Public Library for their kindness and ever willing aid rendered in the procuring of books, and to emphasize the fact that for errors in substance and form I hold myself entirely responsible.

DORA ASKOWITH

New York, April 26, 1915.

TABLE OF CONTENTS

CHAPTER I

INTRODUCTION

                                                                     PAGE

I. Interest in the question.................................... 1
II. Definition of terms, "toleration" and "persecution"......... 2
III. Aim of dissertation.
    1. Endeavour to prove that upon the whole the toleration of the Jews during the period of the Roman Empire was the predominant policy.
        A. Periodical massacres of the Jews popular and not official..   5
        B. Not until days of Theodosius and Justinian that we have an encroachment upon Jewish religious customs and practices 5
        C. Pagan contempt of the Jews based upon current misconceptions regarding them.
            a. Misconceptions find their origin in the pagan interpretation of the fundamental characteristics of the Jews: "religious legalism, religious fellowship, individualism, and conservatism"...................................... 6
            b. Refusal of Jews to accept or adapt themselves to pagan ideas and activities.................................... 7
        D. Tolerant attitude of Roman authorities towards the Jews based upon expediency.
            a. Repressive measures against the Jews aimed merely at preventing the further spread of Judaism; measure for the safety of Roman Empire......................... 7
        E. Repeated efforts of the Jews to overthrow Roman rule were not due to political or economic oppression but rather to the growth of a new order of religious ideas among the Jews and consequent conflict of religious and secular duties.
            a. Double phase of Judaism: yielding to influence of pagan customs together with the effort to erect a barrier against them 9

	PAGE
F. Political situation and legal position of the Jews evidence tolerant policy of Roman rule......................	10
2. Privileges conferred upon the Jews by Julius Cæsar and Augustus maintained by later pagan emperors.........	10
3. Treatment of the Jews under the Christian Emperors changed; Christianity more intolerant of the Jews than paganism.	
A. Causes	10
IV. Point of view and method of treatment of subject..........	11
V. Criticism of sources.	
1. In general..	13
2. Chief primary sources.	
A. Works of Josephus..	14
B. Rabbinical literature.....................................	15
C. Philo's works...	18
D. Greek writers..	18
E. Roman writers.	
a. Tacitus	19
F. Christian literature.	
a. Anti-Christian polemics..................................	21
b. Canon law, including decrees of Councils and letters of the popes...	24
G. Non-extant sources......................................	24
H. Numismatics	25
I. Inscriptions and evidence of papyri.	
a. Non-Jewish, Greek and Latin..........................	25
b. Hebrew	26
c. Monument at Ancyra.................................	26
J. Legal sources.	
a. Imperial decrees..	27
b. Theodosian and Justinian codes.......................	28
3 Secondary works.	
A. The more important modern historians dealing with the Jews.	
a. Jost, Grätz, S. Cassel, Derenbourg, Joel, Geiger, Salvador, Ewald, Renan, Kuenen, Schürer, and Juster............	30
4. General collections...	35
5. Encyclopædias, dictionaries and periodicals.................	35

CHAPTER II

THE DISPERSION OF THE JEWS THROUGHOUT THE ROMAN EMPIRE

PAGE

I. Causes for the dispersion.
1. Political conditions affecting the dispersion of the Jews.
   A. Forcible deportations.................................... 36
   B. Voluntary emigrations.................................. 36
2. Trade 40
3. Natural increase of the Jewish people...................... 41
4. Enfranchised prisoners of war form nuclei of Jewish communities 42
5. Increase of Jewish population through proselytism........... 42

II. Extent of the Diaspora.
1. Evidence of literary sources............................... 43
2. Epigraphic discoveries..................................... 45
3. Geographical survey within the limits of the Roman Empire.. 45

III. Numerical strength of the Jews of the Diaspora.
1. Statistics 50
2. Significance of the Jews of Mesopotamia, Babylonia, and Media as a political force within the Roman Empire.... 53

IV. Bonds of union.
1. Temple tax... 53
2. Pilgrimages to Jerusalem................................... 53
3. System of Synagogues...................................... 54
4. Communications from Jerusalem. Circular letters........... 54
5. Yearly calendar of festivals................................ 54

V. Judaism as a proselyting religion.
1. "Jewish propaganda under a pagan mask".................. 54

VI. Organization of Jewish communities.
1. Rome.
   A. First appearance of the Jews in the imperial city......... 58
   B. Settlements: Mount Vatican; Campus Martius; Subura; Valley Egeria; Trastevere............................ 59
      a. Jewish Ghetto.. 60
   C. Constitution of Jewish communities based on inscriptions found in cemeteries.
      b. Names of communities............................... 62
      c. Officials 63

CONTENTS

2. Alexandria.   PAGE
   A. Characteristics of Jewish community..................... 64
   B. Form of organization................................... 65
3. Palestine.
   A. Country districts; characteristics of people................ 66
   B. Three forms of constitutions in the towns................ 67

VII. Two tendencies apparent in the Diaspora.
  1. Expansion.
     A. Results of proselytism................................. 68
     B. Hellenism 69
  2. Exclusiveness 69

CHAPTER III

Pagan Misconceptions of the Jews

I. Opinions expressed regarding the Jewish religion in Greek and Roman literature of a disparaging character.
  1. Romans regarding Jewish religion as a tissue of superstitions and absurd fables.
     A. Expressions of Cicero, Quintilian, Horace, Tacitus, Seneca, Apuleius, Pliny... 70
  2. Judaism confounded with cult of Jupiter Sabazius; Valerius Maximus ....,................ 72
  3. Stories regarding creation, origin of Jews and Exodus from Egypt 72
     A. Idea that Jews are descendants of lepers................. 73
  4. Ideas concerning God....................................... 75
  5. Jews worshipped Heavens, clouds, sun, moon and stars; probable explanations for this belief........................ 76
  6. Jews worshipped the pig and ass; Petronius Arbiter, Tacitus, Plutarch, Diodorus Siculus, Apion...................... 78
  7. Jewish religion dedicated to Bacchus........................ 79
II. Jewish Laws derided by many Greek and Roman writers.
  1. Circumcision.
     A. Opinions of Juvenal, Tacitus, Rutilius Numatianus, Irenæus 81

PAGE
   B. Repression by Roman authorities a measure of public safety, not of religion.................................... 82
 2. Sabbath
   A. Strict observance of the Sabbath excited raillery and disdain.
      a. Ideas regarding origin of the day; Apion, Tacitus...... 83
      b. Special garments and meals source of taunts of writers.. 83
      c. As a day of solemnity, sad and austere; Ovid, Persius, Tacitus, Juvenal, and Rutilius Numatianus.
         (a) Lack of gaiety and rejoicing of pagan festivals...... 84
      d. As a fast day; Petronius, Martial, Suetonius, and Justin.. 84
      e. As a day of idleness; Juvenal, Seneca................... 86
   B. Favorable conceptions regarding the Sabbath; Dion Cassius, Nicholaus of Damascus, Philo, Aristobulus, and Fusius Aristius.. 87
 3. Year of Jubilee regarded as a period devoted to sloth........ 89
 4. Abstinence from eating pork due to fact that the pig was held to be sacred to the Jews.
   A. Opinions of Plutarch, Apion, Celsus, Juvenal, and Tacitus. 90

III. Accusations against the Jews.
 1. Contempt of Roman laws; Juvenal........................... 91
 2. Hatred of humanity; Tacitus................................ 91

IV. Roman prejudice against the Jews strengthened by uncompromising action of Jews in not tolerating gods of other nations; Tacitus, Pliny, Posidonius, and Apollonius Molo.
 1. Fact that Jews used no images a source of criticism......... 93
 2. By neglecting worship of local deities, Jews disrespectful in act and word.. 94

V. From a social standpoint, disdain rather than hatred expressed in feelings of Græco-Roman world towards the Jews.
 1. "Nation born of slavery"; Tacitus.......................... 94
 2. Occupation of the Jews source of ridicule; Juvenal, Strabo, and Pliny.. 95
 3. Poverty of Jews; Juvenal and Martial....................... 96
 4. Isolation of Jews source of aversion; Tacitus, Philostratus, and Rutilius Numatianus.................................. 97

CHAPTER IV

THE POLITICAL SITUATION

PAGE

I. Attitude of the Romans towards the Jews during the Maccabean period.
   1. Decrees and letters.................................... 99
   2. Actual value of the Roman treaties with the Jews........... 108
II. The Hasmoneans.
   1. Change in Roman policy: military intervention in Eastern affairs 110
   2. Capture of Jerusalem by Pompey. Judæa a Roman province. 112
   3. Arraignment of Gabinius................................. 117
   4. Plunder of the Temple by Crassus........................ 118
   5. The last of the Hasmoneans.............................. 119
III. The vassal king or ethnarch, Herod the Great (40 B.C-4 A.D.).
   1. Policy and government of Herod.
     A. The conflict of religious and secular duties.
       a. Introduction of foreign practices; pagan temples; theatres; Roman monuments and names; foreign retainers. 124
       b. Patron of Greek culture............................. 130
       c. Attempt to gain the favor of the people; rebuilding of the Temple...................................... 131
       d. The golden eagle as a symbol of Roman power; transgression of the Mosaic Code........................ 134
       e. Effort to separate high-priesthood from kingship........ 134
       f. Influence of the scribes upon the people............... 135
   2. The favor of Augustus and Agrippa.
     A. Resulting benefits to the Jews.......................... 140
   3. Division of his kingdom................................. 141
IV. Roman Tetrachs (4-37 A.D.).
   1. Philip, Antipas, and Archelaus............................ 142
V. The government of the procurators (6-15 A.D.).
   1. Judæa under direct control of Rome...................... 146
   2. The power of the procurators over Jewish institutions....... 147
   3. Tumults of a politico-religious kind.
     A. The census of Quirinius; objections of the Jews.......... 148
     B. The Zealots... 150
   4. Hatred of the "publicani"................................ 153
   5. General condition of the Jews under the rule of the procurators 156

CHAPTER V

THE LEGAL POSITION OF THE JEWS IN THE ROMAN EMPIRE

PAGE

I. Religious toleration.
  1. Tolerant attitude of Roman authorities towards popular charges brought against the Jews.
    A. Contempt of the gods.................................... 162
    B. Refusal to take part in imperial worship.................. 164
    C. Refusal to participate in popular festivals................ 165
  2. Privileges granted to the Jews by Julius Cæsar in deference to the requirements of the Jewish legalism.
    A. Basis of religious policy of Cæsar....................... 166
    B. Edicts in favor of the Jews............................. 166
  3. Augustus confirms privileges granted to the Jews by his predecessor.
    A. Religious policy of Augustus............................ 170
    B. Edicts in favor of the Jews............................. 172
  4. Judaism a *religio licita*..................................... 173
II. Political toleration.
  1. Jewish influence on Roman politics.
    A. Speech of Cicero.. 174
    B. Attitude of the Roman aristocracy towards the Jews...... 175
  2. Toleration and recognition of the Jewish communities by the state authorities.
    A. Forms under which Jewish communities of the Diaspora acquired political existence.
      a. Settlements of foreigners............................ 177
      b. Private societies.................................... 179
      c. Independent corporations............................ 179
    B. Right of administering their own funds; decrees.......... 179
    C. Privilege of exercising civil and criminal jurisdiction.
      a. The Jewish code..................................... 182
      b. Sanhedrin 184
      c. Local councils; official judges....................... 189
  3. Rights of citizenship.
    A. Local franchise... 191
    B. Right of Roman citizenship............................. 195
  4. Right of holding political offices.
    A. Various offices held by Jews............................ 198
    B. Semi-official professions................................ 200
    C. Jews as soldiers.. 201
III. Retrospect 205
IV. Jewish expression of gratitude to Julius Cæsar and Augustus 208

CHAPTER I

INTRODUCTION

A study of the toleration and persecution of the Jews of the Roman Empire helps to explain, indirectly, some problems which have come to the front since the usefulness and importance of the study of comparative religion have been during the last few years increasingly recognized. It serves to throw light upon the bearings of Judaism upon early Christianity and the setting of both in the pagan world. It throws light upon the following interesting questions: Does religion grow as society grows and is each of these religions, in whole or in part, an outgrowth of the other in accordance with a definite law of human progress?[1] Is a tendency towards a universal or world religion apparent during the period of the Roman Empire and how far did Judaism, the religion of our especial study, prepare the way or retard its development?

Aside from the problems of religious origins and relationships a more immediate and, to a certain degree, a more vital interest justifies a close study of the condition of the Jews of the Roman Empire.

[1] *Cf.* Toy, *Introduction to the History of Religions*, 7; 481. For further information regarding all books referred to in the foot-notes, *cf.* Bibliography *infra.* pp. 211-224.

To-day in a few countries of Europe, especially in Russia and Roumania, the Jews are often persecuted; they are denied social and political rights, confined to exclusive Jewish Ghettos, exiled, and accused of using Christian blood for ritual purposes.[1] The agitation against what has been called the "Jewish race" finds expression in the term, "Antisemitism" or "Anti-Judaism."[2] The effort to discover to what extent Anti-Judaism prevailed in the Roman Empire, in how far the Jews were persecuted at that period and the endeavour to find the causes may throw considerable light upon the causes for the modern persecution of the Jews.

To determine whether the Jews of the Roman Empire were tolerated or persecuted it is necessary to have clearly in mind a definition of the terms, "Toleration" and "Persecution." In general, by toleration we mean the allowance of freedom of action or judgment to other people. Toleration is often identified with religious liberty; but the latter term makes the definition of toleration too narrow a one and presents but one phase of toleration. In our consideration of the subject we shall include the three phases or kinds of toleration:—religious, social or ethical and political. By religious toleration we mean the right to believe, to practise certain rites, to teach freely and to propagate any characteristic beliefs in private and public. Religious toleration

---

[1] *Cf.* Strack, *The Jew and Human Sacrifice, passim.*

[2] *Cf.* Lazare, *Antisemitism, Its History and Causes, passim;* Ruppin, *The Jews of To-day,* 197-207.

would necessarily imply the existence of an official religion, or religion of the State, which admits other religions within its territory and while disapproving of them, tolerates them. This would imply, moreover, from the point of view of the pagans and Christians with whom the Jews came in contact, a policy of non-interference. This non-interference might take the form of a magnanimous indulgence although the beliefs of the adherents of Judaism are disapproved of as false, or it might take the form of a spirit of indifference.

The two phases of indulgence and indifference might be included in ethical or social toleration. To the Jews of the Roman Empire this would mean the freedom of social intercourse and trade relations with the pagans and Christians to whatever extent it was in accord with Jewish Law. It would imply, moreover, the right to put into practice the customs and traditions sanctioned by Jewish Law without having them regarded as detrimental to the maintenance of morality and civil order.

Political toleration would include the right to participate in the affairs of state; directly, by holding offices or, indirectly, by the power to express an opinion; the freedom to enjoy the rights of citizenship and to carry out its obligations. This would bring up the question of military service and jurisdiction; how far did the state sanction the jurisdiction of the leaders of Judaism over the Jews as a corporate body; how far was toleration exercised so that the demands of the state did not encroach upon the demands of Jewish Law. In considering the question of political toleration we must bear in mind that,

> where the gods are regarded as in a manner the most exalted officers of the State; where their protection is invoked on all public occasions, and religious ceremonies are intimately bound up with the outward frame and circumstances of military and civil institutions; where in short, religion is incorporated into politics, any rebellion against the established gods is apt to be regarded as equivalent to treason against the established order of government. It is not conceived as possible that those who are hostile to the gods should not be equally hostile to the laws and institutions under their protection.[1]

Under the Christian emperors, any act against the official religion was regarded as having a political bearing as well. There was a complete union between Church and State and an offense against religion was an offense against the State and had accordingly to be punished by the State. In view of this fact the magistrates of several Christian emperors, in consequence of imperial edicts, considered it a part of their work to take cognizance of Jewish matters of opinion.

By persecution we mean the coercion or punishment, whether for religious, social, economic or political purposes, whether actuated by individuals or the State, often premeditated, sometimes spasmodic; the exercise of force as a means of controlling belief and action. On the part of the State it might mean the employment of legislative, judicial or executive

---

[1] Pollock, "The Theory of Persecution" in *Essays in Jurisprudence and Ethics*, 147–148.

force or the union of all three forms to carry out the specific end in view. In trying to find out to what extent the Jews were persecuted we must bear in mind the difficulty of determining exactly the point at which repression passes into persecution. "Persecution begins when no reasonable proportion is observed between the force used in compulsion and the importance and power of the interests which it is sought to control."[1] We must, moreover, be careful to distinguish from persecution those acts of temporal police which are at times perfectly necessary and just, even though they appear to bear a resemblance to measures of persecution.

With these general definitions of toleration and persecution as criteria of judgment, we find that upon the whole the toleration of the Jews during the period of the Roman Empire was the predominant policy. It is true that, occasionally, there were periodical massacres of the Jews but for the most part they were not official but popular, and in many cases both civil and ecclesiastical authorities endeavoured to restrain the mob element which was incited often not only by superstition but by jealousy as well. At times, moreover, imperial legislation introduced certain restrictions and the Jews were subjected now and then to temporary persecution. But nothing of the nature of a material or permanent change took place in the existing condition of things until the period of the later Roman Empire. It was not until the days of Theodosius II and Justinian that we have the first

[1] Pohle, "Religious Toleration," *Catholic Ency.*, xiv, 761.

infringement upon Jewish religious customs and practices, an encroachment which finds expression in the edicts issued by those emperors.

This policy of toleration is not, however, apparent on the surface, especially in face of the attitude of the pagans toward the Jews. The feelings on the part of the Graeco-Roman world towards the Jews were by no means of a sympathetic nature. The references to them in secular literature form a collection of absurd calumnies or sarcasms. Some of the Latin authors who are commonly designated as the enemies of the Jews are Lucretius, Pliny the Elder, Quintilian, Martial, Tacitus, Juvenal, Suetonius, Varro, Horace, Ovid, Petronius, Persius, Seneca, Cicero and Rutilius Numatianus. Josephus in his work *Contra Apionem* tried to defend the Jews from the accusations brought against them by Apion and other opponents of the Jews, but his efforts did not prevent further attacks. Indeed to the very close of pagan antiquity, Greek and Roman writers disseminated and strengthened the feeling of contempt for the Jews.

The literary invectives levelled against the Jews and everything that savored of Judaism were not based upon a mere spirit of intolerance; the causes should be sought in the current misconceptions regarding the Jews which we shall endeavour to describe in a later chapter. These misconceptions find their origin in the pagan interpretation of the fundamental characteristics of the Jews:—their religious "legalism, religious fellowship, individualism, and conservatism."[1] The aversion to these characteristics, the significance of which was incomprehensible to pagan minds, amounted in individuals as Tacitus, for instance, to a contempt for the whole nation of the Jews. It was natural that the thoughts and actions of the Jews, whose very lives centered in the carrying out of the dictates of the Law with the hope of future reward, were not understood by the pagans; and then, moreover, when these same Jewish people refused to adapt themselves to prevalent pagan conceptions and activities, or at least accept them along with their own, they naturally evoked contempt for themselves on the part of the pagans.

Despite the fact that many pagans despised the Jews, Roman authorities treated them with a marked degree of toleration. We shall attempt to show that this was true even at a time when the Christians were being most severely persecuted. If the Christians were persecuted because they "formed an exclusive and potentially dangerous religious society, ... for being members of a Church and of a Church which acknowledged no divided allegiance,"[2] the question naturally arises, why did not the Romans persecute the Jews who were monotheists and exclusive; who formed a large element in the population of the empire; whose creed was regarded as a "barbarous superstition"[3] and their mode of life anti-

[1] For an interesting exposition of these characteristics of Judaism *cf.* Fairweather, *The Background of the Gospels*, 11–54.

[2] Hobhouse, *The Church and the World in Idea and in History*, 41.

[3] Cicero, *Pro Flacco*, sec. 28. It is necessary to note that the term "superstition" had a different significance from the modern use of the word. Any

social; who might be regarded as forming a "state within a state"¹ which was not in accord with Roman policy? The explanation, in a word, must be sought in expediency.

The general policy of the Roman Government was . . . one of religious toleration, but this toleration was not absolute or unconditional; it was inspired by expediency and opportunism rather than by any abstract principles of justice and liberty. Roman religion was intensely national, intimately bound up with the safety and welfare of the State; and it was therefore considered to be the duty of the Government to enforce a certain measure of external religious observance upon every citizen.[2]

From this point of view it becomes evident that

under the general principles of Roman policy a persecution of the Jews would have been perfectly legitimate, had it been thought desirable. Had Judaism existed only on a very small scale probably it would have been suppressed. On the other hand, had the Jews been more numerous and more aggressive than they were, so as to form a great and growing menace to the unity of the Empire, the Empire would have crushed them at all costs.[3]

When the spread of proselytism was at its height and its danger to the Roman Empire was imminent, some efforts were made to suppress successful propaganda, but no definite policy of persecution was adopted.

oreign cult, as Judaism, not accepted by the Roman State, was regarded as a "superstition." *Cf. Plutarch, De Iside et Osiride,* 11; Simonsen "Kleinigkeiten," in *Judaica,* 297-301.

[1] Hardy, *Studies in Roman History,* 23.
[2] Hobhouse, *The Church and the World,* 42.
[3] *Ibid.* 46.

The repressive measures against the Jews were aimed merely at preventing the further spread of Judaism; they were not a manifestation of religious intolerance on the part of the pagan emperors but a measure for the safety of the Roman Empire. If the Roman authorities had but little occasion to regard Judaism as detrimental to the Empire before the destruction of Jerusalem, much less would it be so afterwards when the Jews became more widely dispersed. Christianity, on the other hand, "was more active and aggressive, and it was not, like Judaism, a national religion, but cosmopolitan and universal."[1]

We shall try to show, moreover, that the repeated efforts of the Jews to overthrow Roman rule were not due to political or economic oppression but rather to the demands of the Torah, and the consequent conflict of religious and secular duties. In the development of Judaism two phases become apparent. On the one hand there is a yielding to the influence of pagan customs while on the other there is an effort to erect the strongest barrier against them. It was the attempt to maintain this barrier that gave rise to revolts of a religio-political kind.

The catastrophe of Judaism did not arise from the treatment of the Jewish Diaspora in the East. It was simply the relations, as they became fatefully developed, of the imperial government to the Jewish . . . state that not merely brought about the destruction of the commonwealth of Jerusalem, but

---

[1] Hobhouse, *The Church and the World*, 47.

further shook and changed the position of the Jews in the empire generally.[1]

Further proof of our contention that the policy of the Roman Government towards the Jews was one of toleration, can be found in an analysis of the actual political situation and legal position of the Jews dispersed throughout the Roman Empire. In the following chapters we deal only with the toleration of the Jews under Julius Caesar and Augustus. In the second part of our study, which we hope to complete at no distant day, we shall deal with the policy of Roman rule under the later pagan emperors. Here, too, we shall endeavour to prove that despite the temporary enforcement of repressive measures intended to check the spread of Judaism; despite the loss of Jewish independence and the suppression of revolts to restore Jewish nationality, the fundamental policy of the Roman government was one of toleration and the many privileges conferred upon the Jews by Julius Caesar and Augustus were still maintained.

This policy of the pagan emperors was changed under the Christian emperors of the fourth century. Christianity was more intolerant of the Jews than paganism. Although many passages of the Church Fathers may be found which advocate toleration in religion, as in Tertullian,[2] Lactantius,[3] Athenagoras,[4]

---

[1] Mommsen, *The Provinces of the Roman Empire from Caesar to Diocletian*, ii, 188.

[2] *Apologeticus*, c. 24, *Patr.Lat.*, 1/416; *Ad Scapulam*, c. 2, *Patr.Lat.*, 1/699.

[3] *Epit. Div. Instit.*, c. 54, in *CSEL*, iv, 728.

[4] Athenagoras, *Libellus pro Christianis*, c. 2.

and Salvian of Marseilles,[1] yet when the Christians became masters many of them forgot the maxims of toleration that they preached, and persecuted in turn the pagans and Jews. Despite the fact that Christianity announced itself as the messenger of love and peace among men it disregarded the teachings of Jesus and adopted a policy of coercion.[2] One of the most vital causes for Christian hatred of the Jews which finds its deepest expression in the writings of Chrysostom,[3] arose from the efforts of the Christians to overthrow the strong Jewish adherence to their Law. In trying to explain the attitude of the Christians towards the Jews, one thing must be borne in mind. The opposition to the Jews does not become manifest until the Christians felt that they were stronger in number than the Jews and that their own position in the empire was secure. During this period we find also that Jewish opposition to the Roman authorities is based not so much upon economic or political oppression as upon differences in religious belief and practices. That religious conceptions determined the policy of government is emphasized by the fact that when Julian the Apostate had control of affairs, the Jews were again tolerated and Judaism was utilized as a bulwark of defence for paganism against Christianity.

We shall endeavour to present our study impar-

[1] Salvian of Marseilles, *De Gubernatione Dei*, lib. v, 2, *CSEL*, viii, 104.
[2] *Cf.* Giron, "La Liberté de conscience á Rome," *EBAB*, xxv, 136; Amitai, *Romains et Juifs*, 2–6.
[3] Chrysostom, *Adversus Judaeos Orationes*, *Patr. Gr.* (1862), xlviii, 843–942.

tially from the point of view of historical investigation. New results are often gained from new points of view and perhaps the data which we have collected will merit an examination for the purpose of throwing new light upon old facts. The problem which we are trying to solve has been treated indirectly by historians and theologians but generally from the point of view of the Roman or of the Christian. The important role played by the Jews during the Roman Empire has been indicated but too often as merely that of a conquered race and the statements of pagan writers taken at face value. The strong religious prejudice of theologians succeeded to that of antiquity and has been passed along to modern times. Only in the light of scientific, historical inquiry can the story be rescued from these obscuring tendencies.

We shall try to present an evolutionary treatment of our subject and indirectly, in the course of our study of the period of the Roman Empire, to analyze the religion of the Jews from the standpoint of the comparative method. While we shall examine the polemics and apologetics of the period for information upon our subject, we shall at the same time lay emphasis upon the historical development of events and the non-religious literature. The two latter sources of information are often a better index of the actual condition of a people than are the biased polemics and apologetics and even, at times, the bare letter of the law which may prove to be an incomplete and uncertain source. We shall endeavour to show what was the feeling towards the Jews during the Roman Empire based upon actual facts whether pleasant or unpleasant; to find out whether the Jews were persecuted then, and if so, upon what grounds. We shall seek to discover whether the prejudices that exist today against the Jews are those that were prevalent during the Roman Empire or whether they have changed to meet the vicissitudes of time and place.

Upon the whole, the sources relating to the Jews of the Roman Empire,[1] especially those of Rome, throw more light upon their inner social and religious life than upon their share in the political history of the Empire. This, however, is not strange when we remember that they were generally absent from political offices or occupations. Moreover, the aristocracy was for the most parts in control of the literary marts and it was unlikely to perpetuate favorable mention of the religionists whom they detested. During the period from the death of Augustus to the coming of the Flavians, Roman literature regarding the Jews is very scarce. Comparatively little notice is taken of the Jews at the time of Alexander Severus. Most of the available information, relating to the Jews from the period of the Antonines to the succession of Constantine, deals,

---

[1] Jean Juster has examined the sources relating to the Jews of the Roman Empire, primarily, those relating to their judicial position. In his dissertation [*Examen critique des sources relatives à la condition juridique des Juifs dans l'empire Romain*] Juster has added considerably to the analysis of the sources given by Schürer in the first volume of his *Geschichte des jüdischen Volkes im Zeitalter Jesu Christi*. For Juster's recent publication *cf.* remarks in preface of dissertation and *infra*, p. 31.

primarily, with those of the eastern part of the Empire and does not concern, especially, the Jews in Rome.

Our chief primary sources are of course, apart from the Old and New Testaments and the Apocrypha, the works of Josephus, of Philo and the Rabbinical Literature upon the Jewish side, fragmentary references in the Greek and Roman literature, the Church Fathers, Roman Law, inscriptions and numismatics.

Amongst the primary sources the character of the works of Josephus[1] needs some comment. While his works are of great importance and on many points are our only sources we must be careful and weigh his evidence in the balance. Josephus is apologetic in tone and is desirous of commending himself and his people to the Romans. His vanity and self-sufficiency color his works and in his effort to glorify his nation he invests the early history of the Jews with a halo of romance. He laid his *Jewish War* before Titus, who gave him permission to present it to the public. His history varies in fulness and detail as it deals with different parts of our period. Strabo supplied Josephus with most of the material for the earlier part and Nicholas of Damascus for the time of Herod. The narrative of the *Jewish War* has the fulness and vividness of an eye-witness. The *Antiquities* which treats of the history of the Jews

---

[1] *Cf. Flavii Josephi Opera*, ed. Niese. *Cf.* also *Works of Flavius Josephus*, Whiston's Eng. tr. revised by Shilleto. For literature dealing with the life and works of Josephus *cf.* Schürer, i, 74–106; Juster, *Examen critique* 6–11.

from the earliest times down to the outbreak of the war with the Romans in 66 A. D. shows less care in preparation. His constant effort to make it apparent that his people were actually friends of the Romans and took up arms against them, unwillingly, colors the whole situation and necessitates the acceptance of his statements with caution. His *Life* which was published as a defense against Justus of Tiberias who had written a *History of the Jews* in which he characterized Josephus as the organizer of the outbreak in Galilee, is not a very reliable source of information. Josephus' *Treatise Against Apion*, an apology for Judaism, is valuable as a collection of references to ancient writers who attacked the Jews and gave expression to their prejudices against them.

The Rabbinical literature[1] is important as source material for our study but its relative value is extremely difficult to estimate. Included in this literature are the following from which we have gleaned more or less information bearing upon our field of work:—(a) The Tannaitic Literature such as (1) *Mishnah*;[2] (2) *Tosephta*;[3] (3) the *Baraitas*,[4] (quotations from Tannaitic works found in both

[1] For references to literature dealing with the whole subject, in general, *Cf.* Schürer, i, 111–165; Juster, *Examen critique*, 11–19.

[2] For the use of the term "Mishnah," *cf.* Strack, *Einleitung in den Talmud*, pp. 3–4; Mielziner, *Introduction to the Talmud*, p. 1; for different editions of text, translations and bibliography of modern works and monographs on the *Talmud*, *cf.* Strack, *op. cit.* 139–175; Mielziner, *op. cit.* 61–102; Schürer, i, 113–138.

[3] For texts and literature on the *Tosephta*, *cf.* Schürer, i, 124–125.

[4] For the *Baraitas cf.* Schürer, i, 126; Meilziner, 20–21; Ginzberg, "Baraitha," *JE*, ii, 515–521.

Talmuds and in the *Midrashim*); (4) the *halakic Midrashim*;[1] (b) The Amoraic Literature such as (1) the *Babylonian and Palestinian Talmuds*;[2] (2) the *haggadic Midrashim*; (3) the *Targums*.[3] All of these date from times considerably later than the destruction of Jerusalem and the Temple; but as they embody the teachings of the rabbis handed down from generation to generation, they help to explain the condition of the Jews during the whole period of the Roman Empire. The usefulness and importance of this literature is often disregarded, and upon the whole it is rarely consulted by historians who relate the history of the people whose intellectual product it represents. It does not give us a direct, connected story of the history of the Jews; but the large collection of laws, the discussions of the rabbis, the controversies of the schools give expression to parables, stories, maxims, proverbs, folk-lore, and fables which throw considerable light upon the general character of the Jewish people of that period, their religious customs, social and political conditions and the current abuses. If these incidental references and often fragmentary statements be regarded as reflections of actual facts, and if an investigation of their dates and places be made, they prove an abundant source of trustworthy information. On the other hand, these writings

---

[1] For literature treating of the *Midrashim*, *cf.* Schürer, i, 138–146; *JE*, viii, 548–580.

[2] For the *Talmuds*, *cf.* literature on the *Mishnah*, *supra*, note 1.

For texts and literature, *cf.* Schürer, i, 147–156.

must obviously be used with caution as sources for determining the social and religious life of the Jews.

Of the Jewish historical works the following might be mentioned as dealing more or less directly with our period, though they offer but little valuable material for our immediate subject; the *Megillath Taanith*, or the *Book of the Fasts*,[1] a record of historic anniversaries, during which there was to be no fasting; the *Seder Olam Rabba*,[2] a Jewish chronicle covering the period "from Adam down to the period of Alexander the Great, with some notices also of later times" and the *Megillath Antiochus*[3], a brief legendary account of the persecutions of Antiochus Epiphanes and the Hasmonean conquests. The *History of Pseudo-Josephus* or *Joseph Ben Gorion*[4] which is a chronicle, in Hebrew, of the Jewish people from Adam down to the destruction of the Temple by Titus bears more directly upon our work. Much of the value of this chronicle, as an independent source, is lost because it is based almost entirely upon the *Books of the Maccabees* and the work of Flavius Josephus.

[1] For different editions of Aramaic text, Hebrew scholium and explanatory notes *cf.* bibliography of dissertation, p. 216.

[2] For text *cf.* Neubauer, *Chronicles*, ii, 26–37; for literature on the subject *cf.* Schürer i, 158.

[3] Ed. in Aramaic, Hebrew and English by Filipowski, *cf.* Bibliog., *op. cit.*; Schürer, i, 158–159.

[4] This was probably written in the ninth century. For several editions of the Hebrew text and a few translations *cf.* Bibliog., p. 215; for abundant references to literature dealing with the life and work of Joseph Ben Gorion *cf.* Schürer, i, 159–161.

Unfortunately a good deal has been lost of Philo's[1] numerous works, but the bulk of them has been preserved by the Fathers and Christian theologians. The five books of Philo on the persecution of the Jews under Tiberius and Caligula would have been an important document for our thesis; but only two of these books, *Adversus Flaccum* and *De legatione ad Cajum*, are now extant. Philo, much more than Josephus, inspires confidence in the veracity of his works. For the relation of the Jews to Hellenism Philo's writings are indispensable.

Direct references on the part of classical authors to the history of the Jews during the Roman Empire are scarce. These references, for the most part, are concerned with attacks upon the Jewish customs and traditions.[2] The Roman writers give considerably more attention to the Jews of our period of study than do the Greeks. This may be attributed to the greater familiarity of the Romans with the Jews, of whom there were a large number in Rome. Among the more important Greek writers referring to the Jews were Polybius, Strabo, Plutarch and Porphyry.

[1] *Cf. Opera quae superunt,* ed. Cohn and Wendland. *Works of Philo Judaeus* tr. from the Gr. by Yonge. For other editions and translations of Philo's works and critical studies *cf.* Schürer iii, 633-716; Juster, *Examen critique* 3-6.

[2] These references have been translated into French by Reinach, *Textes d'auteurs Grecs et Romains relatifs au Judaisme.* For works dealing with attacks upon the Jews *cf.* Schürer, iii, pp. 150-151, note 1. For further bibliography of polemical writings against the Jews, *cf.* passim, Leclercq, "Accusations contre les Chrétiens," in *Dictionnaire d'archéologie chrétienne et de liturgie,* i, 265-307; *cf.* also Juster, *Examen critique* 19-27.

The Latin authors are more numerous. We might mention a few of the more important ones whose references we shall characterize as we quote from their works:—Cicero, Lucretius, Livy, Horace, Ovid, Diodorus Siculus, Pomponius Mela, Petronius, Pliny the Elder, Quintilian, Martial, Persius, Suetonius, Juvenal, Tacitus, Pliny the Younger, Seneca, Florus Apuleius, Lucian, Statius, Trogus Pompeius (in Justin), Appian, Petronius Arbiter, Dion Cassius, Theodotion, Philostratus, Spartianus, Lampridius, Vopiscus, Ammianus Marcellinus, Claudius Claudianus, Rutilius Numatianus, Cassiodorus, Eutropius. We have already indicated the disparaging tone of the writings of the classical authors in speaking of the Jews. Unfriendly, unjust, and at times naive opinions are expressed by some writers who in other cases show kindly and critical judgment.

One classical writer deserves especial notice. Tacitus is often referred to by writers as a primary source for the history of the Jews without bearing in mind the fact that he is very unreliable as an authority upon this subject. Hild has presented an interesting study of Tacitus.[1] He has picked out a few salient expressions of Tacitus regarding the Jews and gives all the sources that Tacitus used. A comparison of the source material makes evident the fact that Tacitus has taken all the opinions of the hereditary enemies of the Jews without verifying them. He has failed to verify the evident contradictions of

[1] Hild, "Les Juifs à Rome devant l'opinion et dans la littérature," *REJ* xi, 174-186.

the very sources he used when he had the information close at hand. Alleging human calamities to be the result of divine revenge[1] he is bitterly severe on Jewish irreligion because it paid no attention to omens which were said to have preceded the fall of Jerusalem.[2] The attitude of Tacitus towards the Jews has been variously regarded by different writers. C. Thiaucourt in his article, "Ce que Tacite dit des Juifs au commencement du livre V des Histories," (*REJ* xix (1889), 57-74) seems to us to have given a satisfactory explanation of this attitude. The writer says that the antipathy of Tacitus towards the Jews was justified, in a certain measure, by the time in which he lived and by the conduct of Herod and his family. One cannot prove, says Thiaucourt, that Tacitus made use only of sources hostile to the Jews. His attitude towards the Jews was that of his people, his time and his class. His ideas regarding Jewish customs were not at all strange for a Roman writer. His errors are the result of his method which was based on a common sense judgment of his sources rather than scientific analysis of them; "he followed the probable rather than the true, forgetting that sometimes the truth is the only probability."[3]

The Christian literature pertaining to the Jews of the Roman Empire is abundant and important even for the period of Julius Caesar and Augustus. The

---

[1] Tacitus, *Hist.* i, 3.

[2] Tacitus, *op. cit.* v, 13.

[3] Thiaucourt, *REJ* xix, 74; *cf.* Boissier, "Le judgment de Tacite sur les Juifs," *MLHR* i, 81-94.

New Testament[1] is a valuable source, especially the *Gospels*, for the history of Palestine, and the *Acts of the Apostles* and *Letters of St. Paul* for the Jews of the Diaspora. Indirectly, the *New Testament* gives expression to the motives for the attacks against the Jews and the anti-Jewish legislation of the Christian emperors. The anti-Jewish polemic[2] of parts of the *New Testament* is developed and amplified in the works of the Church Fathers[3] and in the monographs of several other Christian writers. From the period of Hadrian to Constantine emphasis is laid upon the fact that the punishments, forfeiture and servitude of the Jews are direct consequences of their hatred of Jesus and they call to their support, almost invariably, the law of Hadrian forbidding the Jews to remain at Jerusalem. After Constantine's reign the emphasis is shifted and the accusations made by the pagans against the Jews are utilized by the Christians in an effort to strengthen their own position. The religious worship of the Jews, especially, was made the center of attack and formed the basis of many reproaches which we shall treat in detail in the course of our dissertation.[4] The Jews were further characterized as atheists, "seditious, cruel, obstinate, wilful, insolent, sensual, prolific, vicious, slovenly, leporous, dangerous, contemptible, useless,

[1] For literature dealing with the *New Testament cf.* Juster, *Examen critique* 27-29.
[2] *Cf.* Juster, *op. cit.* 29-53.
[3] For literature on the writings of the Church Fathers relating to the Jews *cf.* Juster, *op. cit.* 34-35.
[4] *Cf. infra* ch. III.

disrespectful of the emperors, haters of mankind and 'a nation born to slavery.' "[1] One or more of these characteristics we shall see to be contained in the works of almost all of the Church Fathers, especially Origen, Eusebius, St. Jerome, St. Augustine and Chrysostom. Of such controversial literature[2] the following books are those especially important for our study: Justin Martyr's *Dialogus cum Tryphone Judaeo*;[3] Irenaeus' *Contra Haereses*;[4] Clement of Alexandria's *Stromata*;[5] Tertullian's *Liber Adversus Judaeos*;[6] Hippolytus' *Demonstratio Adversus Judaeos*;[7] Origen's *Contra Celsum*;[8] Cyprian's *Adversus Judaeos*;[9] Chrysostom's *Adversus Judaeos Orationes*, especially, the fifth oration;[10] Cyril of Alexandria's *Liber Adversus Judaeos cum quaestionibus et brevis anagoge de eis qui floruerunt ante legem*;[11] St. Augustine's *Tractus Adversus Judaeso*;[12]

[1] *Cf.* Juster, *op. cit.* 31-34, for an incomplete list of these characteristics attributed to the Jews and the references to the works of pagan and Christian writers in which they are to be found. For a general list of references to the reproaches of the Church Fathers compare Migne, *Patr. Lat., Index De Judaeis* clxxvii/990 *sqq*.

[2] *Cf.* Bibliography of dissertation; *cf.* also Juster, *Examen critique* 35-53 for literature dealing with these works.

[3] For text *cf. Patr. Gr.* vi, 471-799.

[4] *Ibid.*, vii, 438-1223.

[5] *Ibid.*, viii, 685-1382; ix, 9-602.

[6] *Ibid.*, ii, 595-642.   [7] *Ibid.*, x, 787-794.

[8] *Ibid.*, xi, 637-1632; for a better text *cf.* Koetschau, *Origenes Werke GCS ii, (1899)*. For other editions and criticisms of Origen's work *cf.* Juster *op. cit.* 23, 35.

[9] *Cypriani Opera Omnia*, ed. Hartel in *CSEL* iii, 3, pp. 133-144.

[10] *Patr. Gr.* xlviii, 843-942.

[11] *Patr. Lat.* lxxvi, 1421-1424.   [12] *Ibid.* xlii, 51-64.

and the valuable little tract, *De Altercatione Ecclesiae et Synagogae*, by an anonymous writer.[1]

The anti-Christian polemics are valuable in studying the actual condition of the Jews during the Roman Empire, especially in ascertaining the attitude of the pagan emperors towards the Jews. The pagan writers, in defending paganism against Christianity, at the same time support Judaism and give expression to the similarity in pagan and Jewish conceptions, in theory at least, if not in practise. Among those who have written, especially, against the Christians and whose writings throw some light upon our subject are the following:—Celsus, whose work has been preserved in part by Origen in his *Origen Against Celsus*;[2] Porphyry, whose writings[3] gave rise to the counter attacks of the Church Fathers, especially Eusebius[4] and Apollinaris;[5] Hierocles, fragments of whose writings are preserved in the defenses of *Eusebius*[6] and Lactantius.[7] This anti-Christian writer

[1] *Ibid.*, xliii, 1131-1140. The writing of this tract is often attributed to St. Augustine; *cf.* a discussion of this matter in Juster's *Examen critique* 42-43; 50-52.

[2] *Cf. supra* p. 22, note 8.

[3] For Porphyry's *Chronica*, *cf.* Müller, *Frag. Hist. Gr.* iii, 688 *sqq.*; *Adversus Christianos*, ed. Georgiades; *De Philosophia ex Oraculis Haurienda* ed. Wolff, Müller, *loc. cit.* iii, 712.

[4] For editions and translations of the writings of Eusebius *cf.* Bibliog. p. 6; *GCS*, 9 vols.

[5] Lietzmann, *Apollinaris von Laodicea* i, 265 *sqq.*, fragments 166 and 167. *Cf.* Juster, *Examen critique* 24.

[6] *Cf. Liber Eusebii Contra Hieroclem, Patr. Gr.* xxii, 795-868.

[7] Lactantius *Instit.* v, 2.3 *sqq.* The account of the work of Hierocles from Eusebius and Lactantius is given in Lardner's *Works*, vii (*Jewish and Heathen Testimonies To the Truth of the Christian Religion*), 471-508.

emphasizes, especially, the merits of Judaism as a national religion. In his polemics against the Christians, the Emperor Julian gives expression to his tolerant policy towards the Jews.[1]

One other field of Christian literature which is especially important for our study is the Canon Law,[2] including the decrees of the Councils[3] and the letters of the popes,[4] especially those of Gregory the Great.[5]

Among the non-extant sources,[6] that is works known to us only through quotations, the following, which are for the most part polemical writings against the Jews, deal more or less directly with our subject:—Apollonius Molon's *Diatribe Against the Jews* (συσκευὴ κατὰ Ἰουδαίων)[7] of which we have some

[1] *Cf.* Allard, *Julien l'Apostat*, 3 vols. For Julian's letters to the Jews *cf.* Lardner, *op. cit.* vii, 600-622, where the texts of the letters are given. *Cf.* Adler, "Julian the Apostate and the Jews," *JQR* v, 591-651; for other references to studies of the relation of Julian and the Jews *cf.* Juster *Examen critique* 26-27.

[2] *Cf.* Juster *op. cit.* 53-54 for references to books giving lists of manuels and treatises on the Canon Law and for a general statement of the value of the Canon Law as a source for the condition of the Jews of the Roman Empire.

[3] For the various decrees *cf.* Mansi, *Sacrorum conciliorum nova et amplissima collectio*. For references to other books giving the decrees of the councils *cf.* Juster 53-54.

[4] On the letters of the popes relating to the Jews *cf.* Viollet, *Histoire du droit francais*, 38 sqq.

[5] *Gregorii I papae regestum epistularum* ed. Ewald and Hartmann 2 vols. For exact letters referring to the Jews and their dates *cf.* list in Juster, *Examen critique*, 54, note 3.

[6] For a detailed study of these sources *cf.* Schürer, i, 40-74 Juster, *op. cit.* 20.

[7] Eusebius, *Praeparatio evangelica* 9.19.

fragments in Josephus[1] and Eusebius;[2] Alexander Polyhistor's[3] περὶ Ἰουδαίων, part of which has been preserved by Clement of Alexandria[4] and Eusebius;[5] Teucer of Cyzicus's Ἰουδαϊκὴ ἱστορία[6] in six books; the abstracts of Apion's[7] writings which find expression in Josephus' *Contra Apionen*.[8] Democritus,[9] Nicarus[10] and Philo Byblius[11] each produced a work περὶ Ἰουδαίων.

The non-Jewish inscriptions in Greek and Latin help us to understand the condition of the Jews during our period but especially important are the Jewish inscriptions found in Jewish cemeteries, particularly in Rome.[12] The large number of coins which have beem found at various times are of primary importance in placing and elucidating some events. Madden's *Coins of the Jews*,[13] the standard work on Jewish numismatics gives us the information in that

[1] Joseph. *C. Apion* ii, secs. 7, 15, 37, 38, 42.
[2] Eusebius, *op. cit.*; *Cf.* Reinach, *Textes* 60-64, nos. 26-27 for the extracts from Eusebius and Josephus.
[3] *Cf.* Freudenthal, *Alexander Polyhistor und die von ihm erhaltenen Reste judäischer und samaritanischer Geschichtswerke*; Schürer iii, 469-472.
[4] Clement of Alexandria, *Stromata* i, 21.130.
[5] Eusebius, *op. cit.* 9.17-39.
[6] Parts of the work of Teucer of Cyzicus which have been preserved can be found in *Frag. Hist. Gr.* iv, 508-509, ed. Müller.
[7] *Cf.* Schürer iii, 538-544; Juster *op. cit.* 20-21.
[8] *Cf.* Reinach, *Textes*, 123-124.
[9] *Ibid.*, *Textes*, 121.
[10] *Ibid.*, 122.
[11] *Ibid.*, 156-158.
[12] For bibliography, *cf.* Schürer iii, 1 sqq.; Juster, *Examen critique*, 55-57; Müller, *Die jüdische Katakombe am Monteverde zu Rome, passim*.
[13] *Cf.* also Reinach, *Les monnaies juives*.

field. Most of the non-Jewish inscriptions, to which we shall refer, are collected in the *Corpus Inscriptionum Graecarum* (vol. iii) and the *Corpus Inscriptionum Latinarum* (vol. iii). These inscriptions are especially valuable for information regarding the pagan districts of Palestine. Of the Jewish inscriptions, those in Hebrew have been collected by D. Chwolson in the *Corpus Inscriptionum Hebraicarum* (St. Petersburg, 1882) edited by him. One marble monument,[1] which is of especial value for the study of the Jews under Augustus, is that found at Ancyra in Galatia where was engraved on the walls of a temple, a record (in both Latin and Greek) of the chief events in the reign of Augustus. A series of papyri[2] of the Roman period referring to the lawsuits between the Greeks and Jews of Alexandria before different Roman emperors mentions, incidentally, various edicts relating to the Jews.[3] Other papyri give us valuable information regarding the social and economic condition of the Jews of Egypt,

[1] *Res gestae divi Augusti, ex monumentis Ancyrano et Apolloniensi;* cf. Bibliog. p. 11.

[2] These are collected in E. V. Dobschütz, "Jews and anti-semites in ancient Alexandria," *The American Journal of Theology,* viii (1904), 728-755 and lately again collected and re-edited by Wilcken, *Zum alexandrinischen Antisemitismus;* for other references cf. Schürer iii, 25-52; Juster, *Examen critique* 57-62; Th. Reinach, *REJ* xxxvii (1898) 219 sqq.

[3] For individual law-suits cf. Wilcken, "Alexandrinische Gesandtschaften vor Kaiser Claudius," *Hermes* xxx (1895), 485-498; cf. also Juster, *op. cit.* p. 58 for other references to the same papyrus; Wilcken, "Ein Actenstuck zum jüdischen Kriege Trajans," *Hermes* xxvii (1892) 464-480; Th. Reinach, "Juifs et Grecs devant un empereur romain," *REJ* xxvii (1893), 70-82.

and throw considerable light upon the causes of the many revolts.[1]

The legal sources,[2] which are indispensable for an adequate study of the toleration or persecution of the Jews during the Roman Empire, are quite abundant. The imperial decrees[3] relating to the Jews for the period from the Maccabees through the life time of Josephus, are to be found in the *Books of the Maccabees* and the works of Josephus. For the period extending from Josephus to the fourth century the literary and historic works say scarcely anything in regard to laws relating to the Jews. It is true that the Fathers of the Church[4] and Dion Cassius[5] mention the edicts forbidding the Jews to dwell in Jerusalem and Cyprus; that the *Augustan History* speaks of a law of Septimus Severus against circumcision[6] and against Jewish proselytism[7] and that of Alexander Severus renouncing Jewish privileges,[8] but there is no single work reproducing the text of

[1] *Cf.* Juster, *op. cit.* 61-62.

[2] *Ibid.*, 63-110; for the following section on legal sources we are indebted to Juster, whose account has been the basis of our analysis.

[3] *Cf.* Mendelssohn, "*Senati consulti Romanorum quae sunt in Josephi Antiquitatibus,*" *Acta soc. phil.* v (1875), 87-228; Krebs, *Decreta Romanorum pro Judaeis facta e Josepho collecta et commentario illustrata;* Gronovius, *Decreta Romana et Asiatica pro Judaeis;* for other works dealing with the imperial decrees relating to the Jews *cf.* Schürer i, 105; Juster, *op. cit.* 63-91.

[4] Aristo of Pella in Eusebius, *Hist. Eccles,* iv, 6.3; Tertullian, *Adv. Jud.* c. 13.

[5] *Hist.* lxviii, 32.3.

[6] Spartianus, *Hadrianus,* c. 14.2.

[7] Spartianus, *Severus* c. 17.1.

[8] Lampridius, *Alex. Severus,* 22.4.

a law relating to the Jews.[1] From the fourth century on, the authors of the *Ecclesiastical Histories* indicate or reproduce in part the anti-Jewish laws of the Christian emperors, but the notice of these historians is of little importance, for the laws are almost always found in the *Justinian Code*.[2] There is one imperial edict, however, which was not inserted in the *Theodosian Code* and which is especially important for our study. This was a decree relating to the "*aurum coronarium*" which the Jews paid to their patriarch, and was embodied in the letter of Emperor Julian addressed to the Jews.[3] Julian's letter, written in the form of a philosophical epistle, gives expression to the friendly attitude of the emperor towards the Jews.

The persecution of the Jews becomes apparent from the laws against the Jews which are contained in the *Theodosian* and *Justinian Codes*.[4] In the former there are preserved fifty-three laws relating to the Jews, thirty-three of which are contained in Title 8, "*De Judaeis, Caelicolis et Samaritanis*" of book 16, and Title 9, "*Ne christianum mancipium Judaeus habeat*" of the same book. Juster points

[1] Juster, *Examen critique*, 92.
[2] *Ibid*.
[3] This was the twenty-fifth letter of Julian, written between August 362 A.D. and March 363 A.D. For bibliography on Julian's letters *cf. supra* p. 24; *cf.* also Juster, *op. cit.*
[4] For text of *Theodosian Code cf.* bibliog. p. 214; *cf.* Juster, *Axamen critique* 95 for other editions; for chronological list of the laws relating to the Jews in the *Cod. Theod. and Just., Nov. Th. and Just. cf.* Juster, *loc. cit.* 100-103. *Cf.* Bibliog. *op. cit.* for editions of *Justinian Code*.

out that as many laws relating to the Jews have probably been lost as those which have been preserved.¹ In the *Novellae* of Theodosius, the decrees issued after the publication of the *Theodosian Code*, those against the Jews are renewed and increased in number.²

In the *Justinian Code* the laws relating to the Jews are well classified and almost all of them are contained in two titles of the first book:—Title 9: "*De Judaeis et Caelicolis*" and Title 10: "*Ne christianum mancipium haereticus vel paganus vel Judaeus habeat vel possideat vel circumcidat.*" The same attitude towards the Jews is manifested in the *Novellae*.³

The secondary works for the history of the Jews, in general, are abundant but there is no adequate study of the history of the Jews during the Roman Empire. The treatment of the Jews during the period with which we are especially concerned has usually been made a part of the universal history of the Jews with no specific object in view other than that of a direct narrative. Many excellent studies of the pagans and Christians during our period give but little attention to the Jews.

---

[1] Juster, *op. cit.* 96. Some laws are preserved in the *Constitutiones Sirmondianae* 4(336); 6(425); 12(=*C. Th.* 16.5.43, 16.10.19); 14 (*C.Th.* 16.2. 31-16.5.46).

[2] Juster, *op. cit.* 97.

[3] *Novellae* 45(537); 146(553); 37(535); 131(545). It is interesting to note that only in the *Novellae* are the Jews referred to as Hebrews. In all other official texts the term "Judaeans" is used; *cf.* Juster, *op. cit.* 103-107.

Of the modern historians who have written of the events of the period of our immediate interest or who have devoted some chapters to the history of the Jews of this time, the following merit some attention. The most complete studies are those of Jost, Grätz, S. Cassel,[1] Derenbourg, Joel, Geiger, Salvador, Juster, Ewald, Renan, Kuenen and Schürer. The first eight are Jewish historians and the others Christian writers who have produced excellent studies of the Jews, and have more or less directly, thrown considerable light upon the field of our work.

Although Jost's *Geschichte der Israeliten seit der Zeit der Makkabaer bis auf Unsere Tage*, 9 vols. (Berlin, 1820–1828) which was written at a time when but little work had been done in the field of Jewish historiography, has become antiquated, it is still, of considerable value for the period of our immediate study. More important as a secondary work, dealing with our subject, is Jost's *Geschichte des Judenthums und seiner Sekten* 3 vols. (Leipzig, 1857–59), which throws some light upon the effect of the growth and conflict of Jewish parties upon the general political position of the Jews in the Roman Empire.

Grätz has presented a very complete narrative of Jewish history but he only treats of the Jews of the Roman Empire as a part of the universal history of the Jews. Of all studies of Jewish history Grätz's *Geschichte der Juden von den ältesten Zeiten bis auf*

---

[1] Although Cassel later became a convert to Christianity, his history of the Jewish people was written while he was a Jew.

die Gegenwart, 11 vols. (Leipzig, V. P. 1895-1909), is the most sympathetic, but his treatment has often lead the author to make statements and to draw conclusions which are not substantiated by the facts. Of the eleven volumes, only the second and third deal with the period of our immediate study.

The greater part of Selig Cassel's work treating of the history of the Jewish people since the destruction of Jerusalem, ("Juden [Geschichte]" in Ersch and Grüber *Encyklopädie der Wissenschaften und Künste* 2d. ser. xxvii, 1-238 Leipzig 1850), deals with a period later than that of our immediate interest. The first section, however, on *"Die Geschichte der Juden im römischen Reiche"* because of the excellent and original research which it embodies, has been indispensable for our study.

One scholarly work of the French orientalist, Derenbourg, *Essai sur l'histoire et la géographie de la Palestine d'après les thalmuds et les autres sources rabbiniques;* i, *Histoire de la Palestine*, Paris 1867 (only one volume was published), has been especially useful in studying the condition of the Jews in Palestine. Derenbourg's work, moreover, has been of great value in opening up and indicating the importance to be attached to a large field of Talmudic sources.

In tracing the development of religious thought in the early centuries of the Roman Empire and in studying the conflict of Judaism with Paganism and Christianity the two following works of Joel, the Jewish rabbi and philosopher, are of great value:

Die Angriffe des Heidenthums gegen die Juden und Christen in den ersten Jahrhunderten der römischen Caesaren (Breslau, 1879); *Blicke in die Religionsgeschichte zu Anfang des zweiten christlichen Jahrhunderts*, 2 vols. (Breslau, 1880-1883). In both of these works we have evidence of profound research on the part of the author and a strong appeal to reason in behalf of his readers.

Geiger's works " *Das Judenthum und seine Geschichte*, 3 vols. Breslau, (1864-1871); *Die Wissenschaftliche Zeitschrift für Jüdische Theologie*: 6 vols. (V. P. 1835-1847), are especially important for the period of our study. He urged the critical study of the Torah and the Talmud from the point of view of the historian, that of evolution, development. His treatment of the Samaritans, Pharisees, and Sadducees and his studies on the origin of Christianity, give expression to his views and show at the same time the author's fervor for truth and research, his scholarly thoroughness and his power of original interpretation. In tracing the development of Paganism, Judaism and Christianity and their interrelation, Geiger's work has been a helpful guide in our study.

The French historian Joseph Salvador, treats of a very important period of the history of the Jews of the Roman Empire, in his *Histoire de la domination romaine en Judee et de la ruine de Jerusalem*, 2 vols. (Paris 1846); German tr. by Ludwig Eichler, 2 vols. (Bremen 1847). In this work Salvador deals with his subject from the point of view of universal history and looks upon the destruction of the Temple in Jerusalem as an essential stage in the spread among the peoples of what he would speak of as the Christian form of Judaism.

Ewald's *Geschichte des Volkes Israel* (Göttingen, 1843-1859) written from the standpoint of the Christian theologian has been especially valuable to us in analyzing the attitude of the Roman authorities towards the Jews.

Ernest Renan, in his *Histoire des origines du christianisme* (8 vols. Paris, 1866-1883); *Le Judaïsme comme race et comme religion* (Paris, 1883); *De l'Identité originelle et de la séparation graduelle du Judaïsme et du Christianisme* in *Annuaire de la Société des Études juives* (Paris, 1884); *Histoire du peuple d'Israel* 5 vols. (Paris, 1887-1893) and *Le Judaïsme et le Christianisme* (Paris, 1883), has given us considerable information regarding the relation of Judaism to Christianity.

Kuenen, the Dutch Christian Old Testament scholar, throws considerable light upon the significance of the Law for the Jews in his *Godsdienst van Israel* (2 vols. 1869-1870); Eng. tr. *The Religion of Israel to the Fall of the Jewish State*, 3 vols. 1874-1875). In this work he presents the view that the ceremonial law was the latest part of the Hebrew legislation. In his *National Religions and Universal Religions* (Hibbert Lectures for 1882) he gives us an interesting study of Christianity in its relations to Judaism.

Schürer's scholarly and exhaustive work [1] the *Geschichte des jüdischen Volkes im Zeitalter Jesu Christi* 4th ed. 3 vols. (Leipzig i, 1901; ii, 1907; iii, 1909 and Index, 1911) has proved to be an invaluable secondary source for our treatment of the Jews during the time of Christ. Though the book gives us very little information regarding the Jews of the later Roman Empire, the clear analysis of the fundamental characteristics of the Jews helps us to understand their later conditions. Though the German Protestant theologian is inclined at times to underestimate the sincerity of the strict Jews for their Law,[2] upon the whole his work is permeated by a marked spirit of toleration and a sympathetic feeling for Jewish institutions and ideals. In his *Die Gemeindeverfassung der Juden in Rom* (Leipzig, 1879), Schürer has thrown considerable light upon the Jewish communities in Rome during the early Roman Empire, his information being taken, for the most part, from a close study of inscriptions found in the Jewish cemeteries.

Juster in his *Les Juifs dans l'empire romain, leur condition juridique, économique et sociale*, 2 vols. (Paris, 1914), has, recently, presented a very scholarly treatment of the Jews during the period of our study. The French scholar has brought to his work the

---

[1] For an estimate and appreciation of the work of Schürer *cf.* the brief memoir of Harnack written shortly after the death of the former, April 30, 1910. *Theologische Literaturzeitung*, May 14, 1910. vol. xxxv, pp. 290-291.

[2] *Cf.* I Abrahams, "Professor Schürer on Life Under the Law," *JQR* xv, (1899) pp. 626-642.

critical acumen of a jurist and enriched his study with a wealth of references to the sources.

Of the many general collections that we have used for our work and of which a complete list is given in our bibliography, the following have been indispensable:—*Patrologiae Cursus Completus* ed. Migne, (Paris, 1844-1866); *Ante-Nicene Fathers* (N. Y., 1890-1897); *Nicene and Post-Nicene Fathers* (N. Y., 1890-1909); *Corpus Juris Civilis* ed. P. Krüger, R. Schoell and W. Kroll (Berlin, 1872-1877); Mansi, *Sacrorum Conciliorm Nova et Amplissima Collectio* (Florence, 1759-1798); *Corpus Inscriptionum Latinarum* 15 vols. (Berlin, 1863; new ed. 1893); *Corpus Inscriptionum Graecarum*, ed. A. Boeckh, 4 vols (Berlin, 1828-1827).

The various encyclopaedias and periodicals, especially those devoted to religious and, primarily, to Jewish problems, and subjects of interest, have often proved to be repositories of valuable information. Their primary importance lies in the suggestions offered for the research of original documents and the means of checking up statements often based upon unauthoritative sources. The following have been especially helpful for our study of the Jews during the Roman Empire:—*Monatschrift für Geschichte und Wissenschaft des Judenthums Breslau* 1851—); *Revue des Études juives* (Paris, 1880—); *The Jewish Quarterly Review* (London, 1888—); *Real-Encyclopaedie für Bibel und Talmud* (Leipzig, 1870-1883); *Jewish Encyclopaedia*, 12 vols. (N. Y., 1900-1906).

Chapter II

The Dispersion of the Jews Throughout the Roman Empire

The policy of the Roman government was largely affected by the dispersion[1] of the Jews throughout the Roman Empire. This dispersion had been brought about by various causes. From long before the days of Rome, there had been migration and transplantation of the Jews. The Assyrian monarchy had forcibly carried off the northern tribes in the eighth century, Tiglath-pileser III (734 B. C.) and Shalmaneser IV (721 B. C.) driving the ten tribes into Assyria. In the sixth century, Nebuchadnezzar (586 B. C.) had carried off a large part of the Jews into the " Babylonian captivity " whence, however, they were allowed to return to Jerusalem by the Persians. In addition to these forcible movements, however, there were military, commercial and, in a sense, colonizing movements, from the days of Persian control.

From papyri[2] discovered in recent years it has

---

[1] For a general treatment of the Diaspora *cf.* the following articles and the literature mentioned there:—Schürer, iii, 1-70; Th. Reinach, " Diaspora," *Jew. Ency.* iv, 561-562; Seymour de Ricci and I. Broydé, " Paleography," *Jew. Ency.* ix, 471-478; Juster, *Examen critique*, 111-140.

[2] *Cf.* Schürer, iii, 24-31 for literature dealing with these papyri.

become known that there were Jewish settlements In Egypt as early as the sixth century before Christ. Cambyses (525 B. C.) established a Jewish military colony at Elephantine.[1] About the same time a settlement of a similar character seems to have been made at Syene, modern Assuan.[2] According to Josephus,[3] Jews settled at Alexandria from its foundation in the year 332 B. C. Although the accuracy of this statement has been questioned by modern critics[4] and the visit of Alexander at Jerusalem, in the course of his conquest, during the same year, has been regarded as legendary, it is nevertheless clear that it was owing largely to his influence that Judaism was brought into touch with Hellenic thought and civilization.

With short intervals, Palestine continued throughout the third century to be under the control of the Ptolemies of Egypt. During this period, Ptolemy I, after he had taken many Jewish captives from Judea and Samaria, led them to Egypt where he put several fortresses into their hands, "believing they would hold them faithfully and valiantly for him."[5] When Ptolemy I took possession of Syria many Jews, of their own accord, asked to be permitted to go with him to Egypt and settle there.[6] The same ruler, in

[1] *Cf.* in general *Aramäische Papyrus und Ostraka aus einer jüdischen Militär-Kolonie zu Elephantine*, ed. Sachau.
[2] *Cf. Aramaic Papyri discovered at Assuan*, ed. Sayce and Cowley.
[3] *Antiq.* xix, 5.2; *Bell. Jud.* II, 18.7; *C. Apion.* ii, 4.
[4] Schürer (iii, 36) endeavours to confirm the statement of Josephus.
[5] Joseph. *Antiq.* xii, 1; *C. Apion.* ii, 4.
[6] *Cf.* Joseph. *C. Apion.* i, 22.

an effort to gain a firm hold on the government of Cyrene and other cities of Libya, sent a large number of Jews to inhabit those regions.[1]

As a result of the struggle between the Ptolemies of Egypt and the Seleucids of Syria, Palestine came under the control of Antiochus III, the Great (203 B. C.) and the Seleucids became the suzerains of the Jewish people. The founder of the Seleucid dynasty, Seleucus Nicator, had already shown his favor towards the Jews by permitting them to establish settlements in the cities which he built in Asia, Lower Syria and especially Antioch, which became famous as a Jewish center.[2] Josephus tells us that Antiochus IV, Epiphanes, thinking that the Jews would be "well-disposed guardians" of his dominions, removed two thousand Jewish families out of Mesopotamia and Babylon to Phrygia and other outlying districts where rebellions had taken place.[3]

Both the Ptolemies and Seleucids had permitted the Jews, in Judea, to form a self-governing community with a High Priest as their head. When, however, Antiochus IV, Epiphanes, who was called upon to settle a dispute between rival candidates for the High Priesthood, actuated by self-interest, plundered the treasures in the Temple at Jerusalem[4] and attempted to force upon the Jews pagan culture and ceremonies,[5] a violent reaction set in which gave

[1] Joseph. *C. Apion.* ii, 4.
[2] Joseph. *Antiq.* xii, 3.1.
[3] *Ibid.* xii, 3.4.
[4] *1 Macc.* i, 20-40; *2 Macc.* v, 1-27.
[5] *1 Macc.* i, 41-64; *2 Macc.* vi, 131; *cf.* Tacitus, *Hist.* v, 8.

rise to the Maccabean revolt (167 B. C.).[1] Through the efforts of the Maccabees the Jewish people were freed from the Syrian rule and Judaea was raised to the ranks of an independent state.[2]

Up to the period of the Maccabean revolt the expansion of the Jews had been gradual and confined for the most part to Palestine, the Tigris-Euphrates region and Egypt. The hardships inflicted upon the Jews by Antiochus Epiphanes, the discontent of the nation with the Hasmonaean princes whose struggles led to the intervention of Roman authorities, the invasion of Jerusalem by Pompey (63 B. C.),[3] and the growing political rivalry between the religious parties of the Sadducees and Pharisees may account for the increased emigration from Judaea and wider dispersion of the Jews at this time.

" The Herodian period," however, " was the golden age of the Diaspora."[4] The success of Herod the Great in gaining the favor of the Roman emperors, his visits to foreign realms and his attempt to Hellenize the Jewish people, contributed, in large measure, to the dispersion of the Jews throughout the Roman Empire. A further incentive to the migration of the Jews was the fact that Judaea, during the period of unrest following the death of Herod the Great, sank into a Roman province under the rule of a

[1] *1 Macc.* ii, 1-xvi, 24; *2 Macc.* viii, 1-xv, 36.
[2] *1 Macc.* xiii, 31-42.
[3] For a list of writers dealing with Pompey's invasion *cf.* Clinton, *Fasti Hellenici, The Civil and Literary Chronology of Greece,* iii, 176.
[4] Bousset, *Die Religion des Judenthums im neutestamentlichen Zeitalter,* 76.

procurator (6 A. D.).[1] Although for a short period of three years the Jewish kingdom was restored with Agrippa I as ruler (41-44 A. D.),[2] the continued efforts of the Jews to maintain their independence gave rise to the Judeo-Roman wars which resulted in the capture of Jerusalem and the destruction of the Temple (70 A. D.)[3]. This catastrophe, together with the fall of Bethar (135 A. D.) the last Jewish stronghold, which marked the close of the final efforts for Jewish independence, were perhaps the most vital causes for the Dispersion.

The various political changes which the Jewish people encountered in the course of their early historical development gave rise, as we have seen, to forcible deportations and voluntary emigrations. The latter were due often to the success of a ruler in attracting Jewish colonists to newly founded cities[4] or sparsely populated districts, by guarantees of important privileges, or they were actuated by the desire to follow an unsuccessful leader of a revolution to his retreat, rather than be exposed to the vengeance of the conqueror. Still other motives prompted voluntary migrations. It is possible that the prospect of pecuniary gain to be derived from trade may have induced many Jews to emigrate to countries bordering on Palestine or to more distant commercial centres of the Roman Empire, as those of Macedonia,

---

[1] Joseph. *Antiq.* xvii, 13.5; *Bell. Jud.* ii, 8.1.
[2] Joseph. *Antiq.* xviii, 6.10; xix, 5-8; *Bell. Jud.* ii, 11.5.
[3] For source material on the subject *cf.* Clinton, *Fasti Romani, The Civil and Literary Chronology of Rome and Constantinople*, i, 56-58.
[4] *Cf.* Philo, *In Flaccum*, sec. 7.

Greece, Italy and Spain. It is difficult to ascertain to what extent commercial motives fostered the dispersion of the Jews,[1] even though we know that the Jews played an important role in the commercial activities of the Roman Empire. Josephus tells us that the Jews had so strong a control of the traffic with Mesopotamia, that the great Jewish establishments in Antioch, such as the house of Saramalla, were often made use of for political purposes [2] and the same writer informs us that the Jews in Alexandria had the chief control of the corn trade and several of their number were appointed as tax collectors.[3]

Another cause of the dispersion of the Jews finds its origin in the fact that the Jewish race has always been very prolific and would naturally tend to spread to less congested districts. According to Philo, " no one country can contain the whole Jewish nation, by reason of its populousness; on which account they frequent all the most prosperous and fertile countries of Europe and Asia, whether islands or continents."[4]

[1] Friedländer in *Darstellungen aus der Sittengeschichte Roms*, iii, 505, endeavours to show that commercial motives did not prompt, to any great extent, the expansion of Jewish settlements. Schürer iii, 3, seems to take the opposite point of view, though he offers no adequate proof in support of his statement. Herzfeld, who has given us quite a complete list of Jewish settlements in the Hellenistic period (*Handelsgeschichte der Juden des Alterthums; aus den Quellen erforscht und zusammengestellt* 204), draws attention to the fact that of the settlements, 52 were in towns, and of these 39 were wealthy commercial centers.
[2] *Bell. Jud.* i, 13.5.
[3] *C. Apion.* ii, 5.
[4] *In Flaccum*, sec. 7.

Of the thousands of Jewish prisoners of war who were transplanted to various parts of the world and reduced to slavery, many were in time enfranchised. Instead of returning to their native land, they remained in the countries in which they had obtained their freedom, forming together with their co-religionists, the nuclei of Jewish communities. An inscription of Delphi gives us an instance of the enfranchisement of a Jewish slave by the payment of money.[1] According to Philo, the Jewish community in Rome owed its origin to enfranchised captives brought by Pompey.[2] Sepulchral inscriptions in Rome evidence the fact that many Jews were in the condition of slaves. As a consequence of the Jewish insurrections under Vespasian, Titus and Hadrian, Jewish captives were transported to the West, where many of them eventually formed Jewish communities in Italy, Spain and Gaul.

Despite the various factors which we have pointed out as causes for the wide dispersion of the Jews, the large numbers which we find in the Diaspora, at an early period, can only be explained by the fact that the small groups of Jewish families in different countries were augmented by numerous proselytes of other races. In Damascus, we are told, the Jewish religion made a vast number of proselytes and that almost all the women were in favor of it.[3] The

---

[1] Collitz, *Sammlung der griechischen Dialekt-inschriften*, ii, 2029.

[2] *Legat. ad Cajum* sec. 23. Philo points out the fact that their freedom was readily obtained because their fidelity to their religious customs made them inefficient slaves.

[3] Joseph. *Bell. Jud.* ii, 20.2; *cf. Acts* xiii, 50.

Jewish faith and usages were often forced upon the petty tribes bordering on the lands of Jewish sovereigns. This was true in the case of the Idumeans,[1] and Itureans[2]. Thus proselytism,[3] too, became an essential factor in the dispersion of the Jews throughout the Roman Empire.

Perhaps it is due to the fact that so many motives were at work at the same time in inducing groups of Jews to abandon their mother country, that as early as the second century, the wide extent of the Diaspora finds expression in the oracles of the Jewish Sibyl: " And every land shall be full of thee and every sea." [4] Strabo calls our attention to the fact that " even in Sulla's time a Jewish element had penetrated into every city, and there is hardly a place in the world which has not admitted this people and is not possessed by it ".[5] Exaggerated though these statements may be, as well as the remark of Josephus[6] that there is no people in the world who have not some Jews among them, they do, nevertheless, bear testimony to the wide dispersion of the Jewish people. From the first book of the Maccabeans we get indirect evidence of the early appearance of the Jews in Asia Minor.[7] According to this passage, the Romans in

[1] Joseph. *Antiq.* xiii, 9.1; *Bell. Jud.* i, 2.6.

[2] Joseph. *Antiq.* xiii, 11.3.

[3] *Cf.* Grätz, " Die jüdischen Proselyten in Römerreiche," *JJS* 1-38.

[4] *Oracula Sibyllina* iii, 271; Gr. ed. Rzach, 62; Eng. tr. in *Apacrypha and Pseudepigrapha of the Old Testament,* ed. Charles ii, 383.

[5] Strabo, fragment 6, cited by Joseph. *Antiq.* xiv, 7.2.

[6] *Bell. Jud.* ii, 16.4; vii, 3.3.

[7] *1 Macc.* xv, 15-24.

the year 139 B. C. sent out, simultaneously, to a number of kings, a letter written in the same terms, charging them to refrain from showing any hostility towards the Jews. From this letter it may be inferred that the Jews were already to be found in all the States and cities of Asia Minor mentioned in the epistle. The Roman edicts in favor of the Jews, sent out by the Roman Republic during the years 50-40, B. C. and collected by Josephus,[1] show how widely the Jews had spread over the whole of Asia Minor.

Seneca,[2] and the author of the *Acts of the Apostles*[3] also bear witness to the fact that the Jews were dispersed over the whole Roman Empire. The most complete survey of the lands inhabited by Jews is given by Philo,[4] though even this writer does not mention Italy and Cyrene which had a large number of Jewish inhabitants during the period of our immediate study.

[1] *Antiq.* xiv, 10; xvi, 6.
[2] Fragments 41-43 in Augustine's *De Civitate Dei* vi, 10.
[3] *Acts* ii, 9-11.
[4] According to Philo, in a letter of Agrippa to Caligula (*Legat. ad Cajum* sec. 36), " Jerusalem is the metropolis not only of Judaea, but of most countries. This is owing to the colonies which on suitable occasions she has sent to the neighboring lands of Egypt, Phoenicia, Syria, Coele-Syria; to the remoter Pamphylia, Cilicia, most parts of Asia, as far as Bithynia, and to the farthest corners of Pontus, as well as to Europe, Thessaly, Boeotia, Macedonia, Aetolia, Attica, Argos, Corinth, to the most and the fairest parts of the Peloponnesus. And not only is the mainland covered with Jewish settlements, but also the principal islands: Euboea, Cyprus, Crete. I leave unnamed the lands beyond the Euphrates, for, with exception of a small portion, all this district, including Babylon and the satrapies that embrace the fertile territory lying around, has Jewish inhabitants."

More concrete evidence regarding the Jewish communities of the Diaspora is to be found in the epigraphic discoveries which are constantly being made. These inscriptions, together with numerous literary texts, emphasize the wide extent of the Jewish dispersion.[1]

Within the limits of the Roman Empire, with the exception of Palestine, the largest Jewish population seems to have been in Asia Minor, Phoenicia and Syria. In Lydia[2] and Phrygia[3] the Jews had settled in large numbers. Two of the synagogues of the foreign communities in Jerusalem belonged to the Jews from Asia and Cilicia.[4] In Ionia, Ephesus[5] was the seat of a large Jewish community which during the first century obtained various privileges of synagogal communities in Smyrna[6] and Phocaea.[7]

---

[1] For a list of the places of the Diaspora inhabited by Jews and references to numerous literary texts and inscriptions concerning these Jewish settlements *cf.* Reinach, "Diaspora," *Jew. Ency.* iv, 561-562; de Ricci and Broydé, "Paleography," *Jew. Ency.* ix, 471-478; Juster, *Examen critique* 111-140. In our brief description of the expansion of the Jews we shall refer only to some of the more important texts and inscriptions which can be readily supplemented from the lists of the writers given above.

[2] *Cf.* Joseph. *Antiq.* xiv, 10.17-23; xvi, 6.6; Reinach, "Les Juifs D'Hypaepa" *REJ* x (1885), 74-78.

[3] *Cf.* Joseph. *Antiq.* xii, 3.4; xiv, 10.8,20; Cicero, *Pro Flacco* sec. 28; Ramsay, *The Cities and Bishoprics of Phrygia, passim.*

[4] *Cf.* Philo, *Legat. ad Cajum* sec. 36; *Acts* vi, 9; Friedländer, *Sittengesch.* iii, 506; *IGr.R* iii, 858.

[5] Joseph, *Antiq.* xiv, 10.11-13; 16,19.25; xvi, 6.4,7; Philo, *op. cit.* sec. 40; Hicks, *The Collection of Ancient Greek Inscriptions in the British Museum* iii, 2, pp. 262-263; nos. 676-677.

[6] *CIGr.* 3148; 9897; 9898; Reinach, "Inscription grecque de Smyrne," *REJ* (1883) vii, 161-166.

[7] Reinach, "Une nouvelle synagogue grecque à Phocée," *REJ* (1886) xii, 236-243.

Jewish communities were also found in Sardis,[1] Miletus[2] and Halicarnassus.[3] Inscriptions and coins attest the presence of Jewish settlements in Apamea.[4] From Cicero's reference[5] to the collection of Jewish money to be sent to Jerusalem, we learn of the presence of Jews in Laodicea, Adramyttium and Pergamum. Jewish communities were found at Tlos[6] in Lycia, at Antioch in Pisidia[7] and Iconium in Lycaonia.[8] Jews were numerous in the parts of Armenia under Roman control.

In Egypt,[9] the Jews settled over the whole country as far as the frontier of Aethiopia, and here they came to play an important part in the history of civilization. Alexandria[10] was noted not only for its large number of Jews, but also for their great spiritual influence. The presence of Jews in Cyrenaica[11] is evidenced by Roman decrees issued in their favor and by various inscriptions.

[1] Joseph. *Antiq.* xiv, 10.17; 24; xvi, 6.6.
[2] *Loc. cit.* xiv, 10.21.
[3] *Loc. cit.* xiv, 10.23.
[4] Cicero, *Pro Flacco* sec. 28; Ramsay, *Cities and Bishoprics of Phrygia* i, 538, No. 399a; Madden, *The Numismatic Chronicle* 173-219, pl. vi.
[5] Cicero, *op. cit.*
[6] Hula, "Eine Judengemeinde in Tlos," in *Eranos Vindobonensis* 99-102.
[7] *Acts*, xiii, 14; Ramsay, *The Cities of St. Paul* 256 sqq.
[8] *Acts*, xiv, 1; *CIGr.* 3995, 3998, 4001b; 9570.
[9] Philo, *In Flaccum* sec. 6; for various other sources *cf.* Schürer iii, 24-52; Juster, *Examen critique* 132.
[10] Besides Joseph. *Bell. Jud.* ii, 18.7; *C. Apion* ii, 4; and T. Reinach, "Sur la date de la colonie juive d'Alexandrie," *REJ* xlv (1902), 161-164, *cf.* Juster, *op. cit.*
[11] *1 Macc.* xv, 23; Joseph, *Antiq.* xiv, 7.2; *CIGr.* no. 5361.

DISPERSION THROUGHOUT THE ROMAN EMPIRE 47

In North Africa,[1] the settlement of Jews, during the Roman period, from the border of Cyrenaica to the extreme west can be easily demonstrated. In the province of Africa the Jewish community of Carthage[2] was the largest. In West Africa traces of a Jewish community at Sitifis[3] in Mauretania and of Jewish inhabitants elsewhere have been preserved.[4]

Of the Greek islands[5] Crete[6] and Melos[7] are mentioned as the homes of wealthy Jewish populations who under Augustus supported the pretender to the throne of Herod. Julius Caesar sanctioned religious unions of Jews in Delos.[8] Jewish settlements were quite numerous in Cos,[9] Paros,[10] Euboea[11] and Cyprus.[12] From the *Acts*[13] we learn of the pres-

[1] *Cf.* Monceaux, "Les colonies juives dans l'Afrique romaine," *REJ* xliv (1902), 1-28.

[2] *Cf. CIL* viii, Supple. nos. 14097-14114; Tertullian's *Adv. Judaeos* c.l., indicates the presence of Jews in Carthage.

[3] *CIL* viii, nos. 8423, 8499.

[4] Monceaux, *op. cit.*

[5] Philo, *Legat. ad Cajum* sec. 36.

[6] *1 Macc.* xv, 23; Joseph. *Antiq.* xviii, 12.1; *Bell. Jud.* ii, 7.1.

[7] Joseph, *Antiq.* xvii, 12.1; *Bell. Jud.* ii, 7.1.

[8] Joseph. *Antiq.* xiv, 10.8, 14.

[9] *Macc.* xv, 23.

[10] Joseph, *Antiq.* xiv, 10.8.

[11] Philo, *Legat. ad Cajum* sec. 36; *Acts* xviii, 1.

[12] *Cf.* Reinach, "Une inscription juive de Chypre," *REJ* (1904), xlviii, 191-196; *1 Macc.* xv, 23; *Acts* iv, 36; xi, 20; xiii, 4; Joseph. *Antiq.* xiii, 10.4.

[13] *Acts* xvi, 2 *sqq;* xvii, 1, 10,16; xviii, 4, 7. For Jewish-Greek inscriptions at Athens, *cf. Corpus inscriptionum Atticarum* (Berlin Akademie der Wissenschaften), iii, 2. nos. 3545-3547; at Thessalonica, "Les Juifs d'Hypaepa," *REJ* x (1885), pp. 77-78.

ence, in Greece and Macedonia, of the Jewish communities of Athens, Corinth, Thessalonica, Beroea and Phillippi. At an early date Jews settled on the northern shores of the Black Sea. In the Crimea two Jewish communities are known from inscriptions, one at Panticapaeum[1] (Kertch) about 81 A. D.; and the other at Forgippia [2] (Anapa) about 41 A. D.

When we turn to Italy, we find that Rome,[3] in particular, was the seat of a Jewish community the inhabitants of which could be counted by thousands. The presence of Jewish communities, outside of Rome, is not for the most part demonstrable before the period of the later empire.[4] We learn from Josephus[5] that at the beginning of the Christian era the Jews formed an important community at Puteoli which was then the principal port for trade between Italy and the East. In southern Italy[6] the Jews were especially numerous during the period of the later empire. In Apulia and Calabria difficulty was found in filling some of the communal offices because of the refusal of the Jews to accept them.[7] In northern Italy the Jews were not quite

[1] Basileus Latyschew, *Inscriptiones Antiquae Orae Septentrionalis Ponti Euxini Graecae et Latinae* 49-53, nos. 52-53.

[2] *Loc. cit.* 208-209, no. 400.

[3] *Cf. infra* pp. 58-64.

[4] *Cf.* Friedländer, *Sittengeschichte* iii, 504-505; *De Judaeorum coloniis* pp. 1-2; Schürer iii, 67.

[5] *Antiq.* xvii, 12.1; *Bell. Jud.* ii, 7.1.

[6] Neubauer, " The Early Settlements of the Jews in Southern Italy," *JQR* iv (1892), 606-625.

[7] *Cf.* decree of the emperors Arcadius and Honorius (398 A. D.) in *Cod. Theod.* xii, 1.158.

DISPERSION THROUGHOUT THE ROMAN EMPIRE 49

so thickly settled, though we find them in considerable numbers in most of the larger towns.[1]

In Spain[2] there were Jewish communities in Adra,[3] Minorca,[4] Tortosa[5] and Cartagena[6] but the testimonies for their existence at those places date from a period not earlier than the fourth century A. D. From early times we find the presence of Jews in Gaul,[7] especially Narbonne,[8] Marseilles,[9] Paris,[10] Orleans[11] and Bordeaux.[12] From an official decree we learn of the presence of Jews at Cologne.[13] In

[1] *Cf.* Schürer, iii. 68.

[2] Hubner, *Inscriptiones Hispaniae Christianae, passim.*

[3] *CIL* ii. 1892.

[4] *Cf. Epist. Severiani, Patr. Lat.* xx, 730; for a criticism of this circular letter *cf.* Juster, *Examen critique* 52-53.

[5] Hubner, *op. cit.* no. 136; Chwolson, "Die Grabschrift von Tortosa," *CIH* pp. 167-175 no. 32 and 32a. This inscription is in Hebrew, Latin and Greek.

[6] Cartagena (New Carthage) is mentioned in Jewish sources. *Cf. Jer. Shebiit* vi (beginning).

[7] In general *cf.* Gross, *Gallia Judaica: Dictionnaire géographique de la France d'après les sources rabbiniques. Cf.* also Reinach, "Inscription juive sur d'Auch," *REJ* (1889), xix, 219-223; *idem,* "Nouvelles remarques sur l'inscription juive d'Auch," *REJ* (1890), xx, 29-33; *Nouveau recueil des inscriptions Chretiennes de la Gaule, antérieures au viiie siècle, CDIF* v, no. 292.

[8] Reinach, "Inscription juive de Narbonne," *REJ* xix (1889), 75-83.

[9] Gregory of Tours, *Historia Francorum* v, 11; vi, 17. Ed. Arndt, in *MGH* i, pp. 199-200; 259.

[10] *Loc. cit.* vi, 5

[11] *Cf.* the Councils of Orleans for the years 533, 538 and 541, in Mansi, *SCC* vol. viii, tit. 19, p. 838; vol. ix, tit. 13, 30, pp. 15, 19; vol. ix, tit. 31, pp. 114, 118.

[12] *Cf.* Gregory of Tours, *De virtutibus sancti Martini* iii, 50. Ed. Krusch, *MGH* i, 644.

[13] *Cod. Theod.* iii, 16.8,3. The first official document relating to the Jews of Cologne is the decree of Constantine (Dec. 11, 321) abolishing Jewish exemptions from municipal offices.

the Danube countries inscriptions give evidence of only two Jewish settlements in lower Pannonia.[1]

The great extent of the Diaspora, instead of weakening the Jewish people as a body, tended, on the contrary, to strengthen the bonds of union. Moreover, the scattered Jewish communities were not made up of a few individuals but frequently constituted a large part of the population. It is difficult to ascertain exactly the numerical strength of the Jewish people within the Roman Empire,[2] but from various sources we can get an approximate number which in itself explains the importance of the Jews as a political factor, to be reckoned with by Roman authorities.

The estimates of Jewish populations as given by Biblical records[3] rest on slender foundations. Josephus,[4] undoubtedly, exaggerated greatly when he tells us that at the time of the siege of Jerusalem by Titus there were in that city 1,100,000 and that the estimate taken by Cestius during the reign of Nero showed that 2,565,000 Jews had come together at Jerusalem for the Passover celebration. According to Tacitus,[5] the number besieged in Jerusalem amounted to 600,000. In Syria the Jewish people

[1] *CIL* iii, 3688.

[2] *Cf.* Pressel, *Die Zerstreung des Volkes Israel*, pt. i, 20-21; ii, 5.

[3] *Cf. Exodus* xii, 37; *Numbers* i-iii; *Book of Ezra*, ii, 64.

[4] *Bell. Jud.* vi, 9.3; for criticism of Josephus' estimates of population *cf.* Chwolson, *Das Letze Passamahl Christi* 48-52.

[5] *Hist.* v. 3.

were especially numerous.[1] Reinach,[2] basing his calculation upon the amount of money confiscated by Flaccus,[3] draws the conclusion that "in Asia Minor the Jewish population numbered 45,000 males, or a total of at least 180,000 persons."

According to Philo,[4] there were nearly a million Jews of a population of eight millions[5] in Egypt. In Alexandria, especially, there was a large number of Jews.[6] Harnack[7] pointing out that of a total population of 500,000, 200,000 were Jews. Judging from the statement of Dio Cassius[8] that 220,000 "unbelievers" were put to death at Cyrene at the time of the great rebellion under Trajan, the Jews were populous in that region. In Rome, also, the Jews formed an important contingent of the inhabitants, for more than 8,000 are said to have escorted the Jewish embassy sent to plead with Augustus for the deposition of Archelaus.[9]

[1] Josephus tells us (*Bell. Jud.* ii, 20.2) that 10,000 Jews were slain at Damascus during the great war. Another reference to the same event (*loc. cit.* vii, 3.3; 8.7) gives the figure 18,000.

[2] *Jew. Ency.* iv, 562.

[3] *Cf.* Cicero, *Pro Flacco* xxviii, 68.

[4] *In Flaccum* sec. 6.

[5] Mommsen, *Provinces of the Roman Empire*, ii, 280. Old Egypt is said to have had seven millions while under Vespasion, Mommsen thinks, there were at least a population of eight millions.

[6] *Ibid,* viii; *cf.* Strabo in Joseph. *Antiq.* xiv, 7.2; *CIGr*, no. 5361.

[7] *Die Mission und Ausbreitung des Christentums in den ersten drei Jahrhunderten* 5, n. 1; Eng. tr. by Moffatt, i, 6, n. 2.

[8] *Hist.* lxvii, 32; *Cf. loc. cit.* lxix, 14, in which he makes the statement that 580,000 Jews lost their lives in Palestine at the period of Barcochba's rebellion.

[9] Joseph. *Antiq.* xvii, 11.1; *Bell. Jud.* ii, 6.1. According to Hausrath

From the figures of Beloch and Harnack, an interesting though probably excessive estimate of the total Jewish population in the Roman Empire can be drawn. According to the former writer,[1] there were in Syria more than a million Jews out of a population of seven million at the time of Nero.[2] Estimating, according to Harnack,[3] the number of Jewish people in Palestine at 700,000 and in the remaining districts of the empire, excluding Egypt and Syria, at about one million and a half, we have a total of about four and a half million Jews living within the limits of the Roman Empire. If, according to Beloch, the total population of the Roman Empire at that period was fifty-four millions, the Jews made up about one-twelfth of the whole population.

The strength of the Jews was due not only to their

(*Neutestamentliche Zeitgeschichte* iii, 384-385), there were, at the time of Augustus, forty thousand Jews in Rome, and this number increased to sixty thousand during the reign of Tiberius. Although we know that Tiberius decreed that four thousand Jews be deported to Sardinia (Tacitus *Annals* ii, 85; Suetonius, *Tiberius* xxxvi), we have no means of definitely proving the calculation of Hausrath. Harnack in "Christianity and Christians at the Court of the Roman Emperor, Before the Time of Constantine," *Princeton Review*, July, 1878, pp. 252-253 and note 8, once estimated that "the number of Jews in Rome in the post-Augustinian period may be reckoned in round numbers as over twenty thousand," but in his later work (*Ausbreitung des Christenthums* 5; Eng. tr. i, 7), in speaking of the Jewish community at Rome at the time of Tiberius, sets the number at upward of 10,000 persons. *Cf.* Renan, *L'Antichrist* 7, n. 2, who puts the number between twenty and thirty thousand, including women and children.

[1] *Dei Bevölkerung der griech. römisch. Welt* 248.

[2] Under Augustus, Beloch estimates the population at about six million. *Cf. loc. cit.* 242 sqq; 507.

[3] *Ausbreitung des Christentums* 6; Eng. tr. i, 8.

numbers within the Roman Empire. Three other factors were at work in increasing this strength and making Judaism a force which made itself "felt in the imperial palace, no less than in the poorest quarter of Rome or the remotest valleys of the province."[1] Outside the limits of the Roman Empire, in Mesopotamia, Babylonia and Media were millions of Jews under the sovereignty of rulers, many of whom were avowed enemies of the imperial government. There was always the possibility that these Jews might join with their co-religionists within the empire against Roman rule, or what was more likely, the Roman Jews might join the enemies of Rome. Added to this was the fact that the Jews were greatly united among themselves. Five things served as links in the chain which bound the Jews of the Diaspora to their mother country, especially to the religious and national capital.[2] The paying of the Temple tax[3] which was collected annually in certain designated cities and sent through representatives to Jerusalem, was actuated by a common motive. No less effective in uniting the people was the desire of each Jew to make at least one pilgrimage to Jerusalem. In the words of Philo:[4]

innumerable companies of men from a countless variety of cities, some by land and some by sea, from east and from west, from the north and from the south came to the temple at every festival, as if to some common refuge and safe asylum from

[1] Hausrath, *Hist. of New Testament Times*, i, 2d ser. 104.
[2] *Cf.* Bousset, *Die Religion des Judentums* 82-83.
[3] *Cf.* Joseph. *Antiq.* xiv.
[4] *De Monarchia*, ii, 1.

the troubles of this most busy and painful life, seeking to find tranquillity, and . . . forming a friendship with those hitherto unknown.

Like a network spread throughout the Diaspora and connected by threads of thought, finding expression in the Sabbath prayers, was the system of synagogues[1] situated on the hill-top, on the banks[2] of the river, or in the heart of the cities. The synagogues were thus not only the centers of unity within each community but served to bind together the members of the Diaspora and those of the mother country. The connection between Jerusalem and the Diaspora was also maintained by regular communications, sometimes in the form of circular letters dealing with matters of general concern which were read aloud in the synagogues. Not only did these letters, which often proceeded from the Sanhedrin at Jerusalem, in consequence of some legislative act, serve to unite the people, but also the yearly calendar of festivals[3] sent out by the same judicial body and participated in by all the Jews of the Diaspora.

Aside from its numerical strength, and the unity of the Jewish people, Judaism became a power within the empire by reason of the role which it played as a proselyting religion. While on one hand it gained strength because of the number of those

[1] *Cf.* Philo, *De Vita Mosis*, ii, 168. In general *cf.* Elbogen, *Der jüdische Gottesdienst in seiner geschichtlichen Entwicklung*. Sometimes the term *Proseucha* was used to designate a synagogue; *cf. loc. cit.* 445.

[2] *Cf.* Joseph. *Antiq.* xiv, 10.23; for discussion regarding the building of synagogues near the water, *cf.* Elbogen, *op. cit.* 448-449.

[3] *Cf.* Schürer, i, 749-751.

who embraced Judaism, on the other hand it gave rise to considerable opposition on the part of some government authorities and those anti-Jews who looked askance at the influence exercised by those engaged in finding proselytes, especially the Pharisees, among all ranks of society. The medium of the strong appeal upon the minds of the people was the monotheistic conception and the Messianic hope;[1] an appeal which led many from the imperial palace to seek the most obscure recesses of the Ghetto.

The Graeco-Roman world, which had already begun its syncretizing process of religion through the introduction of many Oriental cults,[2] was a favorable field for Jewish propaganda. In many respects[3] Judaism, although beset with difficulties as a proselytizing religion, had a stronger appeal and met with more success than the various mystery cults. Once it gained adherents, it had a stronger hold upon the proselytes because of its stringent requirements, its marked tendency toward exclusiveness and the character of the Jewish people as a whole. Those embracing Judaism became in all respect Jews. This was contrary, for instance, to the followers of Cybele, Sabazius, Serapis, Mithra, Isis or other Oriental deities. While accepting these cults, those initiated still remained essentially

[1] *Cf*. Elbogen, "Die messianische Idee in den alten jüdischen Gebeten," *Judaica*, 669-679.
[2] *Cf*. Cumont, *Les religions orientales dans le paganisme romain*, *passim*.
[3] *Cf*. Bousset, *Die Religion des Judentums*, 90-92.

Romans or Greeks.¹ Jewish propaganda was made especially effective by adopting the device of setting forth Jewish conceptions and ideals in the words of the ancient Sibyl, Orpheus the mythical bard of Thrace or some person as Hecateus, Aristeas or Phocylides, who were regarded as authorities in the pagan world.² The main object of this literature as well as the *Wisdom of Solomon*³ and some of the works of Josephus and Philo was to show that embodied in the Pentateuch⁴ were "the universal laws of reason, love and morality";⁵ to bring Hellenism and Judaism into intimate touch by showing their interrelation and thereby gain adherents to Judaism throughout the Diaspora.

Many of these proselytes became important members of the Jewish communities which were organized, wherever there were any considerable number of Jews living together, for the purpose of common worship, protecting their interests and maintaining the privileges accorded to them. These Jewish communities were of varying magnitude and importance, their internal organization differing according to the political rights and privileges which they possessed and the degree of culture attained by the

¹ *Loc. cit.* 91.

² For "Jewish propaganda under a pagan mask" and for a general discussion of the literature dealing with attempts at Jewish proselytism *cf.* Schürer, ii, 553-629; Bousset, *Die Religion des Judentums* 92-95.

³ *Cf.* ed. Charles, *Apocrypha*, i, 518-568.

⁴ *Cf. The Holy Bible Containing the Old and New Testaments,* American Standard Version 1-212.

⁵ Hausrath, *Hist. of New Testament Times;* i, 2d ser. 118.

Jews in the various localities where they had settled. Despite local differences, there were many common features in the various constitutions of the communities of the Jewish Diaspora.

There is hardly any source-material dealing with the constitution of the Jewish communities in the Euphrates districts during the period of our immediate study. A considerable amount of information dealing with the internal organization of the Jewish communities of Rome and of Italy in general has been obtained from the epitaphs that have been found in the cemeteries of Rome, Venosa and a few other towns of Italy. About five hundred texts referring directly to Jews, besides a certain number of pagan inscriptions relating to Jewish affairs, have been found throughout the ancient world. Of these the greater number come from Italy, especially from the various catacombs which have been discovered at different times.[1]

A careful study of the internal organization of the Jewish communities of the Diaspora has been made by Schurer.[2] We shall endeavor to indicate a few results of his work so far as it deals with typical

[1] For a geographical list and criticism of Jewish inscriptions in Greek, Hebrew and Latin and a description of the Jewish catacombs in Italy where many of the texts have been found *cf.* the article " Paleography " by de Ricci and Broydé in *Jew. Ency.* ix, 471-479; *cf.* also Schürer, iii, 65-68, where a copious bibliography dealing with the whole subject can be found. Several inscriptions are included in the recent monograph on *Die jüdische Katakombe am Monteverde zu Rom,* by N. Müller.

[2] *Gesch. des jüdischen Volkes* iii, 71-96 (*ibid.*, Hasting's *Dict. of the Bible,* extra vol. 99-102); *Die Gemeindeverfassung der Juden in Rom in der Kaiserzeit.*

Jewish communities, such as those of Rome, Alexandria and Palestine, the centers of our field of study; to point out a few characteristics of the Jewish population of these districts, characteristics which throw light upon the subject of our immediate interest, the policy of the Roman government towards the Jews.

It is during the Maccabean period that we hear of the first settlement of the Jews in Rome. We have no contemporary document affirming the statement but we are able to infer from some lines of Valerius Maximus[1] that the Jews were in Rome in 139 B. C. According to this writer, the praetor who sent out of Rome the Chaldeans because of their magical practices, also "forced the Jews who sought to corrupt the Roman usages with the rites of Jupiter Sabazius, to return to their country."[2] It is possible that this statement of Valerius Maximus may refer to some Jews who accompanied the ambassadors sent by

---

[1] These lines were in a work entitled *Factorum et dictorum memorabilium libri*. This has been almost entirely lost, but two extracts have been preserved, by Julius Paris and Januarius Nepotianus. *Cf.* the edition of Kempf, *Valerii Maximi factorum et dictorum memorabilium libri novem, cum Iulii Paridis et Januarii nepotiani epitomis,* pp. xxiv; 672.

[2] For an interpretation of this passage which identifies the God of the Jews with Sabazius, a Phrygian deity, the confusion of the two arising perhaps from the fact that the Greek Jews pronounced the name Zebaoth as Sabaoth, and for a criticism of the various texts of the works of Valerius Maximus, many of which omit entirely the term Jews ("*Judaeos*") which appears in the extracts of Paris and Nepotianus, *cf.* Reinach, *Textes*, 258, note 2; 259 note 2-3; Schürer, *Geschichte* iii, 58-59; *Gemeinderverfassung* 5; Hild *REJ* viii, 5; Marquardt, *Römische Staatsverwaltung* iii, 82 note 1.

Judas Maccabeus to Rome in 140–139 B. C.[1] and while at the imperial city they may have been engaged in seeking proselytes to Judaism. At any rate, there was probably only a temporary settlement made at this time. The permanent settlement of a large number of Jews in Rome dates from the time of Pompey.[2] After his conquest of Jerusalem he brought many Jewish prisoners of war to Rome, where they were sold as slaves. When, at a later period, they received their freedom and were given the rights of Roman citizenship, they settled on the right bank of the Tiber, forming the nucleus of an autonomous Jewish community.[3]

This settlement was on the slope of Mount Vatican and the Bridge of St. Angelo leading across the Tiber, was known for a long while as the "*Pons Judaeorum.*" Later, many Jews settled in the Campus Martius[4] and north of the Forum in the valley called the Subura.[5] The latter place, which was a busy center of commerce, was one of the most thickly settled, and unclean sections of the city. A settlement of Jews was also made in the Valley Egeria,[6] near the

[1] *1 Macc.* xiv, 24; xv, 15-24.

[2] *Cf.* Schürer, *Gemeinderverfassung* 5; *cf.* also Levy, "*Epigrapische Beiträge zur Geschichte der Juden,*" *JGJ* ii, 277 *sqq.* regarding the statement that there were many Jews in Rome before the time of Pompey.

[3] Philo, *Legat. ad Cajum* sec. 23: " And they were mostly Roman citizens having been emancipated; for, having been brought as captives into Italy, they were manumitted by those who had bought them for slaves, without ever having been compelled to alter any of their hereditary or national observances."

[4] *Cf.* Orelli, *Inscr. Lat.* nos. 2522; *CIGr.* 9905, 9906.

[5] *Cf. CIGr.* 6447.

[6] *Cf.* Dezobry, *Rome au siècle d'Auguste* ii, 400-401.

Porta Capena, where was the so-called "Wood of the Muses." It is here that Juvenal says the Jewish fortune-tellers dwelt while engaged in that particular occupation.[1]

The most important Jewish quarter was the one on the right bank of the Tiber at the base of the Janiculum, called Trastevere.[2] As many of the Jews were engaged in commerce, it was convenient for them to live on the quay where the merchandise brought from Ostia on flat-boats was unloaded. Their ware-houses and residences occupied a large part of the water-front not far from the Porta Portuensis. The Trastevere corresponded to what was later spoken of as the Roman Ghetto.[3] In respect to the question of settlement we find greater toleration exercised towards the Jews during the period of Caesar and Augustus than in the interval between the sixteenth and nineteenth centuries when the Jews were forced to dwell within a few, narrow, overcrowded and unhealthy streets. The Jewish settlements of the period of our immediate study gave rise to ample adverse criticism by the Roman writers; but no compulsory laws, in regard to sections where the Jews must live, were passed.

Although the Jews of imperial Rome were confined to no special quarter, yet the majority lived in

[1] *Cf.* Juvenal, *Satires* iii, 10-20.

[2] Basnage in his *Histoire des Juifs* xi, 210-211, suggests that this Jewish settlement was on the Island Tiber near the Fabritian Bridge and the one on the Janiculum was possibly another.

[3] For the origin of the term and literature dealing with the Roman Ghetto *cf. JE* v, 652-653.

Trastevere. They created, as it were, a voluntary Ghetto[1] which has been graphically reconstructed for us by the imaginative touch of a modern author, whose account we have good precedent in adapting to our use.[2] The Ghetto was a low lying place enclosed within a circuit of a few hundred yards which the Jews preferred to more spacious districts elsewhere. Here several thousand human beings crowded together in buildings centuries old and built upon ancient drains and vaults that were continually exposed to the inundations of the Tiber river. Here the pale-faced but eager-eyed people worked on, hoped on, looking forward to the ever brightening future. Labouring for small gain amid unhealthy surroundings, against the dangers of which they were strangely proof, the elders, half doubled with toil, mechanically put aside their work on Friday night when they heard the old crier's melancholy voice re-echoing in the darkening alleys, "the Sabbath has begun." Then in the rich synagogue, the center of communal life, earthly cares were forgotten and all united in the worship of God. After the Sabbath was over, the Jews of Trastevere went back to the daily routine of life which was but little disturbed by the pagan world without. The very contempt which the Jewish quarter inspired served to protect it and its inhabitants were not sensitive to the mockeries of more fashionable people, many of whom found a

[1] *Cf.* Gregerorius, *Wanderjahre in Italien,* vol. i, *Der Ghetto und die Juden in Rom.*
[2] *Cf.* Spence, on Crawford in *Early Christianity and Paganism,* 32-33.

strong appeal in the religion of those whom they denounced.

The general character of the various Jewish communities can best be obtained from the many inscriptions found in the Jewish cemeteries[1] at Rome. From these inscriptions we learn that each community had its own synagogue, *gerousia*, and public officials. Unlike the Jews of Alexandria, who formed a large political corporation, those of Rome were not united into a corporate body but organized into separate religious societies or *collegia*.[2] These various communities had different names which appear on the inscriptions:[3] (1) a συναγωγή Αὐγουστησίων; (2) a συναγωγή Ἀγριππησίων; (3) a *synagoga Bolumni* (*Volumni*). These three, Schürer says, took their names from Augustus, his friend and adviser M. Agrippa, and Voluminus, either because these distinguished personages were patrons of the Jews or because these communities were made up, primarily, of their slaves or those freed by them. Other communities took their names from the particular section of the city in which their members happened to live, as for example, (4) the Καμπήσιοι from the Campus Martius, and (5) the Σιβουρήσιοι from the Subura. Besides these there was (6) a συναγωγή Ἑβρέων, probably that of such of the Jews as spoke their native language in

---

[1] *Cf. supra* p. 57.

[2] *Cf.* Schürer, *Gemeinderverfassung* 10; 15, and the literature mentioned there.

[3] *Cf.* Schürer, *op. cit.* 15-17 and *Geschichte* iii, 82-84, for a copious list of books in which the texts and criticisms of these inscriptions can be found.

contradistinction to those of them who had ceased to speak it, and (7) a συναγωγὴ Ἐλαίας, so called from the symbol of the olive.

Among the officials[1] of the communities the γερουσιάρχης and the ἄρχοντες are especially noteworthy. The title γερουσιάρχης which occurs not only on the Roman inscriptions, but also on those at Venosa and elsewhere seems to have referred to the president or head of the γερουσία. The ἄρχοντες were not ordinary members, but the committee of the γερουσία. Only the offices properly so called, Schürer indicates, were mentioned by name upon the epitaphs, whereas the "elders" were not looked upon as officials in the technical sense of the word. The latter were merely representatives and advisers of their community with no specific functions. The title ἄρχων occurs frequently in the Roman inscriptions and often upon epitaphs found outside of Rome. Tertullian[2] groups together in the same class, the priests, Levite, and archon. In each of the Roman communities there were several ἄρχοντες who acted as the managing committee of the γερουσία. The archons were appointed for a definite period, judging from the title δὶς ἄρχων. Chrysostom tells us in a *Homilia in S. Johannis Natalem*[3] that the archons were always elected in September, the beginning of the civil year of the Jews. Some archons were appointed for life.

Another officer was the ἀρχισυνάγωγος or archi-

---

[1] Cf. Schürer, *Gemeindeverfassung* 18-32.
[2] *De corona* ch. ix, quoted in Schürer iii, 86, note 39.
[3] The passage is given in Schürer, *Gemeindeverfassung* 23.

synagogus who was not only the president of the community, but had besides, the special function of conducting and supervising the meetings for religious purposes. Upon the Roman inscriptions is mentioned the synagogue officer, the ὑπηρέτης, an official who had certain duties to perform in connection with meetings for public worship. The titles *pater synagogae* and *mater synagogae*,[1] which often are mentioned on the inscriptions, probably do not denote any office, but simply indicate honourable positions in the community.

One of the most important of the Jewish communities of the Diaspora, at this time, was that at Alexandria, where there were a large number of Jews[2] who were able to exercise political influence. According to Philo, of the five districts of the town which were named after the first five letters of the alphabet, two were called "the Jewish"[3] because the majority of the population there were Jews. Despite this division there were many Jews living in the other three sections[4] and there were synagogues in all parts of the city.[5] The specifically Jewish quarters were advantageously situated beside the eastern harbor and the Campus canal. This accounts for the fact that they were able to get control of the

[1] *Cf.* Wesseling, *Diatribe de Judaeorum archontibus ad inscriptionem Berenicensem* 1-20.
[2] *Cf. supra* p. 51.
[3] *In Flaccum* sec. 8.
[4] *Ibid.*
[5] Philo, *Legat. ad Cajum* sec. 20.

corn trade¹ and to have also the harbor police chosen from their own numbers.²

Alexandria had become the mart of three corners of the world. The merchants of Italy and Spain, the trader from India and Babylon, and those whose homes were in the Nubian desert, found their way amongst the Greeks and the native Egyptians.³ With this mixture of nations mingled the Jews and often the force of a Roman proconsul was necessary to curb the quarrels which arose amongst the rivals of the motley populace. In time, however, the Jews of Alexandria acquired an advantageous position and by a gradual process of Hellenization became united with the civilization of the Roman Empire.

In Alexandria the Jews were organized as a single great corporation with a sort of monarchical head. According to Strabo,⁴ "'there is also an ethnarch allowed them, who governs their nation, and dispenses justice and sees to their contracts and laws, as if he were the ruler of a free republic.'" In their efforts to maintain independence the Jews of Alexandria had an advantage over those of other Jewish communities for from the period of the Ptolemies down to the reign of Septimus Severus, Alexandria, unlike almost all the Hellenistic towns, had no city Senate.⁵ During the period of Augustus a change in

¹ *Cf.* Joseph. *C. Apion.* ii, 4.5; *Bell. Jud.* ii, 18.7-8; *Antiq.* xiv, 7.2; 10; 1; xix, 5.2.
² Joseph, *C. Apion.* ii, 25.
³ *Cf. Strabonis Geographica* xvii, 1; Pliny, *Nat. Hist.* v, 10.
⁴ Strabo, in Joseph. *Antiq.* xiv, 7.2.
⁵ *Cf.* Spartian, *Severus* 17; Dio Cassius, *Hist. Li,* 17.

the constitution seems to have been enacted. A *gerusia* was chosen by Augustus but whether this *gerusia* was substituted for the monarchical authority of the ethnarch, or whether it was appointed to manage Jewish affairs side by side with the ethnarch cannot clearly be ascertained from the sources dealing with the subject.[1] The former view is maintained by Philo[2] while in a decree of Claudius as given by Josephus[3] it is pointed out that "when the Jewish ethnarch was dead, Augustus did not prohibit making ethnarchs." The main object of Claudius in this edict is to emphasize the fact that as early as the period of Augustus the political rights and the religious freedom of the Jews in Alexandria were assured.

Quite different from the Jewish communities in the large cities as Rome and Alexandria were the settlements of the Jews in the country districts[4] of Palestine. The predominant occupation of the Jewish inhabitants in Palestine was agriculture which was carried on by means of simple instruments of husbandry. The entire country was well cultivated with the exception of the mountainous and stony regions of Judaea. On this high plateau were many

[1] *Cf.* a somewhat vague reference to the *gerusia* or council of elders in the *Letter of Aristeas* 35-53 as given in Charles, *Pseudepigrapha* pp. 98-100.

[2] *In Flaccum* sec. 10.

[3] *Antiq.* xix, 5.2.

[4] For an interesting account of Jewish life in the country districts *cf.* Stapfer, *La Palestine au temps de Jesus Christ,* pp. 216-230; Eng. tr. pp. 218-245; *cf.* also Schwalm, *La Vie privée du peuple juif à l'époque de Jesus-Christ* 1-193.

desolate villages tenanted by a few shepherds or by the great proprietors whose sheep grazed on the hillsides or in the valleys. Aside from the peasant who worked in the fields one might find the Jewish village artisan who accounted himself neither rich nor poor. Earning his living from day to day, he suffered no privation and was content with his calling which in time was taken up by his son. In less congested quarters than those of their co-religionists of the cities those Jews led simpler, freer and perhaps healthier lives. The daily routine of work was broken by the observance of the Sabbath or the occasional journey to Jerusalem for the feasts.

Several country districts were usually grouped around one large town which served as its political center. The political constitution varied in the different towns of Palestine. There existed three different forms.[1] In some places the Jews were deprived of all civic rights; in others, they enjoyed them equally with non-Jews. In several towns, civic rights were limited only to Jews. The first two possibilities were found in towns where the population was mixed or where it was predominatingly Greek. In such cases, because of their religious requirements, the Jews would form a sort of self-organized religious community. In Caesarea, for instance, the Jews and pagans were in possession of the same civic privileges and had the same right to offices in the town senate, down to the time of Nero.[2]

[1] *Cf.* Schürer, ii, 222; 501-502.
[2] *Cf.* Joseph. *Antiq.* xx, 8.7, 9.

In towns where the inhabitants were entirely or in greater part, Jewish, the civic authorities were Jews and the comparatively small non-Jewish population were not permitted to have representatives in the college of elders or town senate. This was the case in Jerusalem, and other towns of the strictly Jewish territory[1] which included the three provinces of Judaea, Galilee and Peraea. As the local authorities were often called upon to deal with religious matters, for the Jewish law includes both the religious and the civil, they had practical jurisdiction over affairs of the synagogues. It is therefore, probable, that it was only in towns where the population was mixed that we can speak of the congregation of the synagogue as forming a community distinct from that of the political body.[2] In places inhabited entirely by Jews, the elders of the town were at the same time the elders of the synagogue.

The importance of the Jewish community at Jerusalem was due not so much to its organization as to the fact that it was the cynosure of the eyes of the Jews throughout the Diaspora. Whatever motive had induced each successive group of Jews to abandon its mother country, it still clung to the outward symbols of its nationality, wherever it happened to be settled. In looking at the dispersion as a whole, we can already discern, at the beginning of the period of the Roman Empire, two powerful currents running through the widespread ramifications

---

[1] *Cf.* Schürer, ii, 223-236.
[2] *Cf. loc. cit.* ii, 504.

of the Diaspora; the tendency to expansion on one hand and the tendency to exclusiveness on the other. It is the constant interaction of these two forces which gave rise to problems the solution of which affected the general policy of the Roman government towards the Jews. Carried along in the stream of expansion, were the efforts at Hellenization, proselytism and, indirectly, some contributions to the blending of religions. Embodied in the attempts at propaganda, the tendency of Judaism to become a world religion finds its highest expression. But at the period of our immediate study this object was not attained; Judaism was not a universal religion, nor did it in fact remain, as we shall see, a national religion, for Jewish nationality was destroyed. Although it became identified with a single people and became as it were, a religion of observance and an exemplification of perseverance, it still made a strong appeal; it still had something to offer to the world without and its heritage was taken up by Christianity. But at this period we still see the two tendencies in conflict. The barriers of exclusiveness are too powerful to overcome. The tendency of the Jews to form exclusive communities, to avoid all contact with the pagans, and the desire to cling to their traditions and customs provoked the hatred of the pagans. This hatred, based on misconceptions of the Jewish religion, finds expression in the writings of the Graeco-Roman world.

CHAPTER III

PAGAN MISCONCEPTIONS OF THE JEWS

The ancient world, as shown by Josephus in his *Contra Apionem*, was unfamiliar with the life and customs of the Jews. Although we find, among the learned Greeks, expressions of sympathy with the monotheistic conceptions of the Jews and a friendly disposition towards them; as early as the third century before Christ there is apparent, among Greeks and Romans alike, a spirit of enmity which has continued, to a certain extent, to be the heritage of modern times. The origin of this feeling of contempt and scorn is due, in large measure, to the isolation of the Jews and their apparent contempt of the pagan beliefs. The opinions expressed regarding the Jewish religion, in Greek and Roman literature, are of a disparaging character.[1]

A large number of the Romans regarded the Jewish religion as a tissue of superstitions and absurd fables. These conceptions find expression in both poets and prose writers. Cicero characterized the Jewish religion as a "barbaric superstition."[2]

[1] For literature dealing with pagan conceptions of the Jews *cf.* Schürer, iii, 150-151 note 1; for the texts of Greek and Roman writers referring to the Jewish religion *cf.* Reinach, *Textes,* under names of authors.

[2] Cicero, *Pro Flacco* sec. 28; for significance of the term "superstition," *cf. supra.* ch. i, p. 7, note 3.

Quintilian, who makes but one reference to the Jews in his works, in an effort to illustrate his general statement that "ignominy follows some men after death," proceeds to remark that "it is a disgrace to the founders of cities to have drawn together any race of people hurtful to others, such as the chief author of the Jewish superstition and the hateful laws of the Gracchi."[1] In speaking of some superstitious belief of the inhabitants of the city of Gnatia in Italy, Horace says with apparent contempt: "That the Jew Apella may believe not I."[2] Tacitus makes the following statements: "Their other institutions are tainted with execrable knavery";[3] "Prodigies had occurred which that race, enslaved to superstition, but opposed to religion, held it unlawful, either by vows or victims, to expiate."[4] Seneca bears his testimony to this "most outrageous nation" as he calls the Jews. He adds further, "They are in the dark as to the principles upon which their own ceremonial is founded, and the greater part of the people do that for which they can assign no

---

[1] *Inst. Orat.* iii, 7; *cf.* Reinach, *Textes* 285, note 1; Hild, *REJ* xi, 166.

[2] *Sat.* i, 5.100. There have been various interpretations of this verse of Horace. The commentator Porphyrio (ed. W. Meyer, Leipzig, 1874) attempted to show by an analysis of the term "Apella" that Horace alluded to the circumcision of the Jews. Reinach (*Textes,* 245, note 3) regards this etymology as absurd and adds, however, that the passage is a contemptuous allusion to the theodicy of the Jews rather than to their superstition or credulity (*loc. cit.* note 4). Hild (*REJ* xi, 36 sqq.) on the other hand, regards the statement of Horace as an illusion to the credulity of the Jews.

[3] *Hist.* v, 5.

[4] *Ibid.* v, 13.

reason."[1] Apuleius, while characterizing the Egyptians as learned, calls the Jews, "most superstitious,"[2] and regards Moses among the Magi.[3] Pliny, also, considers the Jews adepts in the magic art.[4]

Judaism was sometimes confounded with other cults, especially that of Jupiter Sabazius.[5] Valerius Maximus tells us that those Jews who sought to corrupt the Roman manners by the cult of Jupiter Sabazius were forced to return to their country.[6]

Celsus characterizes "the Mosaic cosmogony as extremely silly"[7] and alleges "that Moses and the prophets, from ignorance, have woven together a web of sheer nonsense."[8] He adduces instances of alleged great antiquity put forth by other nations and asserts that the Jews wove together some of the most incredible and stupid stories, regarding the creation of man, the formation of woman, the issuing of certain commands by God, who is thus shown to have been weak at the very beginning of things and unable to persuade a single individual to obey His will.[9] The question of the origin of the Jews and the

[1] In *De Civitate Dei* vii, 36. *Cf.* Reinach, *Textes*, 263, note 1.
[2] *Florida* c. 6; *cf.* ed. Helm, *Apulei Opera Quae Supersunt* ii, 2, p. 6.
[3] *Apologia* c. 90. *cf. loc. cit.* ii, 1, p. 100.
[4] *Nat. Hist.* xxxi, 11.
[5] *Cf.* Hild, *REJ* viii, pp. 5-6; xi, 35; Orelli's inscription, 1259, which associates the name of Sabazius with that of Jupiter. Plutarch, *Sympos.* iv, 6.12; *De Iside et Osiride* 31, 36.
[6] Valerius Maximus, i, 3.2. *Cf. supra*, ch. 11, pp. 58-59. *Cf.* also Reinach, *Textes*, 258-259, notes 1-2; 1-3.
[7] Origen, *C. Celsum* ii, 6.49.
[8] Origen, *C. Celsum* ii, 6.50-51.
[9] *Ibid.* ii, 4, 36-40.

Exodus from Egypt brought forth many ridiculous stories which for the most part were due to ignorance and not to malignity.[1] Celsus asserts that

> the Jews, accordingly, endeavoured to derive their origin from the first race of jugglers and deceivers, appealing to the testimony of dark and ambiguous words, whose meaning was veiled in obscurity, and which they misinterpreted to the unlearned and ignorant, and that, too, when such a point had never been called in question during the long period.[2]

He again asserts that the Jews were "fugitives from Egypt, who never performed anything of note and were never held in any account."[3]

Woven together with the stories of the Exodus from Egypt was the fable that the Jews were the descendants of lepers and unclean persons. The story seems to have originated with Manetho.[4] It was then taken up and developed with various alterations by Chaeremon,[5] Lysimachus,[6] Apion,[7] Diodorus Siculus,[8] and later by Tacitus,[9] and Justin.[10] The

[1] *Cf.* Goldschmidt, " De Origine Iudaeorum Quid Censuerint Romani," in *De Iudaeorum apud Romanus Condicione*, pp. 5-9; Meier, *Judaica seu Veterum Scriptorum Profanorum de Rebus Judaicis Fragmenta*, pp. 11-16; Gill, *Notices of the Jews and their Country by the Classic Writers of Antiquity;* Reinach, *Textes*, 14; 21-34; 57, 116, 118, 125, 253, 303.
[2] Origen, *C. Cels.* ii, 4, 33, 34, 35.
[3] Origen, *C. Cels.* ii, 4, 31, 32.
[4] Joseph. *C. Apion.* i, 14, 15, 16, 26.
[5] In *loc. cit.* i, 32.
[6] In *ibid.* i, 34.
[7] In *ibid.* ii, 2.
[8] *Bibliothaeca Historica*, Frag. of Bk. xl.
[9] Tacitus, *Hist.* v, 3.
[10] *Hist.* xxxvi, 2.

substance of the story as told by Manetho is that the Egyptian king Amenophis forced all the unclean persons and lepers, numbering eighty thousand, to work with criminals in the stone quarries along the Nile. After a while they were permitted to leave the quarries and were given the city of Avario for their habitation. Among them there happened to be a priest Osarsiph, who afterwards changed his name to Moses. Under his leadership the walls of the city were repaired and the inhabitants of Jerusalem, who were the shepherds expelled from Egypt, came to the aid of the followers of Moses. They made war upon Egypt and reigned there for thirteen years, after which the fugitive king, returning with a large force, defeated the shepherds and lepers and drove them into Syria.[1] According to the version of Lysimachus:

> In the reign of Bocchoris, king of Egypt, the Jewish people, being infected with leprosy, scurvy, and some other diseases, took refuge in the temples, and begged for food; and in consequence of the vast number of persons who fell into the sickness there was a failure of crops in Egypt.

Upon consulting the oracle of Ammon the king was told, "to cleanse the temples from all impure and impious men, and to cast them out from the temples into the desert places, but to drown those who were affected with scurvy and leprosy." Those afflicted with leprosy and scurvy having been wrapt in sheets of lead and drowned, "the rest were sent in a body

[1] *Cf.* Joseph. *C. Apion.* i, 26-27.

to the desert and exposed to perish." The latter, however, took counsel among themselves and selected a priest named Moses as their leader. After enduring many hardships they reached Judaea which they conquered and named Hierosyla from their disposition (to rob temples). Later they changed the name to Hierosolyma.[1]

Special accusations against Judaism were in respect of its religious worship and the idea that the Jews entertained concerning God. Celsus, expressing his opinion regarding the Jews, says:

It is not probable that they were in great favor with God, or are regarded by Him with more affection than others, or that angels are sent by Him to them alone, as if to them had been alotted some region of the blessed. For we may see both the people themselves and the country of which they were deemed worthy.[2]

Their doctrine concerning heaven is not peculiar to them, but, to pass by all others, is one which has long ago been received by the Persians, as Herodotus somewhere mentions. "For they have a custom," he says, "of going up to the tops of the mountains, and of offering sacrifices to Jupiter, giving the name of Jupiter to the whole circle of the heavens."[3] And I think that it makes no difference whether you call the high-

---

[1] In Joseph. *C. Apion.* i, 34; *cf.* Milman, *History of the Jews*, 74-75, for precautions taken against leprosy by the Hebrews. While Milman indicates the fact that leprosy was prevalent among the Hebrews owing largely to the vicissitudes of environment which they were enforced to undergo, he does not in any way support the theory that they were expelled on this account.

[2] Origen, *C. Cels.* ii, 5.1.

[3] *Cf.* Herodotus, *Hist.* i, 131.

est being Zeus, or Zen, or Adonai, or Sabaoth, or Ammon like the Egyptians, or Pappaeus like the Scythians.[1]

It was commonly believed that the Jews reverenced not only God, but worshiped the Heavens, Clouds, Sun, Moon and Stars.[2] Juvenal affirms that the Jews, "worship nothing but the clouds and the deity of heaven."[3] Celsus makes the statement that:

> the first point relating to the Jews which is fitted to excite wonder, is that they should worship the heaven and the angels who dwell therein, and yet pass by and neglect its most venerable and powerful parts, as the sun, the moon, and the other heavenly bodies, both fixed stars and planets, as if it were possible that, "the whole" could be God, and yet its parts not divine.[4]

Origen in refuting his statement declares that had Celsus investigated the practices of the Jews he would have found that the Jews could not worship the Maker of the Heaven and Heaven at the same time, for one of the commandments of the Law was "(Thou shalt) worship nothing else than the Supreme God, who made the Heavens, and all things besides."[5] Petronius contemptuously connects the taboo on pork with the worship of Heaven.

[1] Origen, *C. Cels.* ii, 5.41.

[2] *Cf.* Geiger, "Juden u. Judenthum nach d. Auffassung d. Schriftsteller d. Alterthums," *IM* ii (1865), p. 13; Schuhl, *Les préventions des Romains contre la religion juive;* "Le Dieu des Juifs," pp. 24-30.

[3] *Sat.* xiv, 97.

[4] Origen, *C. Cels.* v, 6; *cf.* also, for statement regarding the worship of angels, i, 26.

[5] Origen, *C. Cels.* v, 6.

"Let Jews adore their guardian swine,
And pray to heavenly 'ears' divine."[1]

In the Theodosian Code, Jews are called plainly "worshippers of Heavens."[2] The origin of this belief can be easily accounted for by the fact that the Jews in praying to God look up to the Heavens, and because the prophetic God is always seen in clouds.[3] Moreover, the term "Heaven" is frequently used by the Jews as an expression for God.[4]

The cult of an incorporeal God was at variance with the popular notions of the pagan world. It was claimed that the Jews concealed the inner secrets of the Temple of Jerusalem. Pompey when he entered the Temple had not found any statue or

---

[1] *Petronii Arbitri Satirae et Liber Priapeorum tertium,* ed. Buechler. Frag. xxxvii, 1-2, p. 117.

"*Iudaeus licet et porcinum numen adoret,
At coeli summas advoce auriculas*"

The expression "summas auriculas" may have been suggested to Petronius by the habit of the Jews to address their prayers towards the Unseen above, or raising the eyes to heaven. (*Cf.* Yeb. 105b; *Luke* xvii, 13; Ginsberg, "Adoration," *JE* i, p. 211.) Vitringa, in his *De Synagoga Vetere,* 228-229, suggests that the expression refers to the Jewish custom of praying in the open air (*sub dio absque tecto*). It is more probable, however, that Petronius' allusion is based upon the following passage in Philo's writings in which the angels are referred to as the "ears" of God:—"There are others (souls or angels) again, the purest and most excellent of all which have received greater and more divine intellects . . . as though they were the eyes and *ears* of the great King (God), beholding and listening to everything." *De somniis* i, 22.

[2] *Cod. Theod.* lib. xvi, tit. viii, lex. 19.

[3] Geiger, "Juden u. Judenthum," *IM* ii, p. 14.

[4] Dalman, "*Aramaisch-Neuhebraisches Wortebuch zu Targum, Talmud und Midrash* p. 179.

image[1] nor at a later period did the soldiers of Titus find any representation of the deity. These facts, however, did not prevent the Romans from believing that the Jews worshiped animals.

Among the animals, the pig and the ass[2] were supposed to receive divine honors. Petronius Arbiter is convinced that the Jews worshipped the pig.[3] Apion had declared that the Jews were accustomed to pay honors to an ass's head.[4] Tacitus makes the same statement, attributing this custom to the fact that while the Jews were in the wilderness a herd of wild asses had led the Jews to copious springs of water.

Whatever (says Tacitus) is held sacred by the Romans, with the Jews is profane; and what in other nations is unlawful and impure, with them is permitted. The figure of an animal, through whose guidance they slaked their thirst, and were unable to terminate their wanderings, is consecrated in the sanctuary of their temple, while in contempt of Jupiter Ammon, they sacrifice a ram. The ox, worshiped in Egypt for the god Apis, is slain as a victim by the Jews.[5]

Plutarch remarks, "that as they honour the ass which showed them a fountain of water, so also they reverence the swine which was their teacher of sowing and ploughing."[6] Diodorus Siculus indi-

---

[1] *Cf.* Tacitus, *Hist.* v, 9.
[2] *Cf.* Tertullian, *Apology* 11; *Ad Nationes* i, 11; Minucius Felix, *Octavius* c. 9; 28, in which we find statements that the Christians, also, were accused of worshipping the ass.
[3] *Cf. supra* p. 77; *cf.* also *infra* p. 89.
[4] Joseph. *C. Apion.* ii, 8.
[5] *Hist.* v, 4.
[6] *Symposium* iv, 5; *cf. De Iside et Osiride* 31.

cates the reverence paid to the ass: "For Antiochus, surnamed Epiphanes, having overcome the Jews in war, entered into the unenterable shrine of their God where it was lawful for the priest alone to enter. Finding therein a stone image of a man with a thick beard, sitting on an ass, and having a book in his hands, he supposed this was of Moses."[1] Apion, Josephus tells us:

presumed to say that the Jews placed an ass's head in their holy place and worshipped it and made it worthy of so great a religion, and he affirms that it was discovered when Antiochus Epiphanes despoiled the temple, and found the ass's head there made of gold and worth a great deal of money.[2]

Because of the famous golden vine in the temple[3] and certain observances at the feast of Ingathering,[4] the idea arose that the Jewish religion was dedicated to Bacchus. In Plutarch's *Symposium*, we have a long discussion of the bacchanalian rites participated in by the Jews:

. . . Adonis is said to have been killed by the swine, and

---

[1] *Bibl. Hist.* ii, Eclog. xxxiv, i. *Cf. supra* p. 77. Strabo in his *Geog.* xvi, 2, directly contradicts the statement that any image was found. Hecateus in his *Antiquities of the Jews*, the fragment of which is quoted in Joseph. *C. Apion.*, declared that "there is no image or suffering at all." Dion Cassius, moreover, made the statement (*Hist.* xxxvi, 17) that "there never was any image in Jerusalem."

[2] *C. Apion.* ii, 7. *Cf.* also Reinach, *Textes* 31, note v; Simonson "Kleinigkeiten" in *Judaica. Festschrift zu Hermann Cohen's Siebzigsten Geburtstage* 297-298.

[3] *Cf.* Joseph. *Antiq.* xv, 11, 3; *Bell. Jud.* v, 5.4; *Mishnah*, "Middoth," iii, 8; Tacitus, *Hist.* v, 5; Florus, *Epit.* iii, 5; Reinach, *op. cit.* 334, note 2; Gill, *Notices of the Jews* 168, note 1.

[4] *Cf. Mishnah*, "Sukkah," iv, 1; *Lev.* xxiii, 34; *Ex.* xxiii, 16; xxxiv, 22.

they think that Adonis was no other than Dionysus (Bacchus), and many of the rites performed to each in the feasts confirm the account. . . .

Do you, O Lampriae, ascribe and suggest under the mysteries of the Hebrews, Bacchus the " Erian woman-exciting deity, blooming with mad honors?" . . .

In the first place, says he, the season and the mode of the greatest and most perfect feasts among them is applicable to Bacchus. For at the fast which is so-called when the vintage is at its height, they put forth tables of every kind of fruit, under tents and cabins platted for the most part out of vine-twigs and ivy, and name it the first tent of the feast. A few days afterwards, they celebrate another feast, not in allegories, but openly in the name of Bacchus. But there is also a feast of cup-bearing and a feast of thyrus-bearing among them, in which they enter the temple holding thyruses. But what they do, when they are inside, we do not know, but it is likely that their doings are of a bacchanalian character. For they use small trumpets, as the Argives use those of Bacchus, calling on the name of the deity, and others come up playing the harp, whom they call Levites, a name derived either from the word Lysion or rather from Erian; but I think also that the feast of the Sabbaths is not wholly unconnected with the worship of Bacchus. For even now, also, many persons call the Bacchanals Sabbai, and they shout this name when they perform the orgies to the god.

But the men themselves bear witness to this account, when they honour the Sabbath, mostly exhorting one another to drink and be drunken, and, when any greater things prevent them, being accustomed to taste wine wholly unmixed. . . . First the high-priest tests it, coming forth with a mitre on his head at the feasts, and clothed with a fawn-skin spangled with gold, and wearing a vest reaching to his feet and buskins. But great bells hang from his garment, which ring as he walks.[1]

[1] Plutarch, *Sympos.* iv. 6.1-2.

Tacitus presents much the same picture:

> Because their priests performed in concert with the pipe and timbrels, were crowned with ivy, and a golden vine was found in the temple, some have supposed that Bacchus, the conqueror of the East, was the object of their adoration; but the Jewish institutions have no conformity to the rites of Bacchus. For Bacchus has ordained festive and jocund rites while the usage of the Jews are dull and repulsive.[1]

The Jewish laws which especially astonished the Romans and which became a source of the jeers of the educated world of the time, were those regarding circumcision, the sabbath and the abstinence from eating pork. Juvenal in his satire on the force of education points out the characteristics which were considered at that time the distinguishing marks of a Jew.

> Certain persons (he says), happening to have a father who is afraid of breaking the Sabbath, worship nothing but the clouds and the deity of Heaven, and they believe there is very little difference between human flesh and the flesh of swine, from which they have been taught to abstain. The next thing they do is to practise circumcision. But though they adhere to the Jewish fashion in their eating, and carefully keep every precept handed down by Moses in his secret volume, not even showing the way to a traveller unless he follows their religion, or guiding any but the circumcised to a fountain if they can help it, yet they generally treat the Roman laws with indifference. But the fault was the father's with whom every seventh day was one of idleness, on which he did not perform a single duty of life.[2]

---

[1] *Hist.* v. 5.

[2] *Sat.*, xiv, 96-106; *cf.* Reinach, *Textes*, 293, note 1; Gill *Notices of the Jews* 94-95; Allard, *Histoire des persécutions pendant les deux premiers siècles d'après les documents archéologiques*, 7.

The practice of circumcision[1] was looked upon by many Romans with contempt. The efforts directed against the rite of circumcision and castration were generally regarded as measures in behalf of public safety not as the repression of religious custom.[2] According to Tacitus the Jews had established the practice of circumcision in order that they might be known by a distinctive mark.[3] He seems to be unaware of the fact that the same custom prevailed among the Egyptians.[4] Petronius alludes "to the rigour with which they enforced the law of circumcision, and the effect of this bigoted attachment to a mere outward rite in driving some of their own race, who had not been properly initiated into their community, to forsake both their people and their religion."[5] Rutilius Numatianus, declared that circumcision was not only a ridiculous but a disgraceful practice.[6]

The strict observance of the Sabbath, the seventh day of the week, as a period of rest, excited raillery

[1] *Cf.* For literature on the subject of "Circumcision" [Semitic], *ERE* iii, 679-680.
[2] Wagner, *Bulletins de l'academie royal de Belgique* xxvi, p. 318.
[3] *Hist.* v, 5.
[4] *Cf.* Herodotus, *Hist.* ii, 37; Strabo, *Geog.* xvii, 2.5; Diodorus Siculus, *Bibl. Hist.* i, 28.
[5] *Sat. Frag.* xxxvii, 3-6.
[6] *Claudii Rutilii Numatiani, De Reditu Suo Libri II,* ed. Müller, i, 387-388, p. 11. It is needless to emphasize the fact that the Christians were against circumcision; *cf.* for Christian attitude, Irenaeus, *Against Heresies, ANF* i, 480-481; *cf.* also Bacher, *Die Agada der Palästinensischen Amoräer* i, p. 92, and Diestel, *Geschichte des alten Testaments in der Christlichen Kirche* 37, regarding the disputations held between Origen and the Jewish Rabbis concerning circumcision. Origen declared that the laws concerning circumcision were as impossible as those in regard to the keeping of the Sabbath.

and disdain on the part of the Romans.[1] In order to explain the origin of this Jewish institution, strange and fantastic reasons were invented. Apion gives us a very strange origin for the name Sabbath. He tells us that when the Jews had travelled for six days, they had a certain malady and so they rested on the seventh day, having reached, safely, the country which was called Judaea. They called that day Sabbath, preserving the language of the Egyptians.[2] The great exertions of the Jews to honor the Sabbath by special garments and special meals,[3] characteristic features of the Jews, excited the taunts of both Greek and Roman writers.[4]

According to Tacitus:

the seventh day was given up to rest because after marching for six days through the desert they were enabled on the seventh day to take possession of a fertile country where they dedicated a city and temple.[5] They say that they instituted a rest on the seventh day because that day brought them rest from their toils; but afterwards, charmed with the pleasure of idleness, the seventh year also was devoted to sloth. Others say that this honour was rendered to Saturn either because their religious institutes were handed down by the Idaeans, who, we are informed, were expelled from their country with Saturn, and were the founders of the nation; or else because among the seven planets, by which men are governed, the star of Saturn moves in the highest orbit, and exercises the great-

[1] *Cf.* Vogelstein and Rieger, *Geschichte der Juden in Rom* i, 69.
[2] In Joseph. *C. Apion,* ii, 2.
[3] *Cf. Book of Jubilees* ii, 21, 31 in ed. Charles, *Pseudepigrapha* ii, pp. 17, 21.
[4] *Cf.* Plutarch, *Sympos.* vi, 2; Persius Flaccus, *Sat.* v. 183.
[5] *Hist.* v. 3.

est influence; and most of the heavenly bodies complete their effects and course by the number seven.[1]

One of the prevalent errors among the Roman poets was the belief that the Sabbath was a day of solemnity, sad and austere. Ovid refers to the Jewish Sabbath in his *Art of Love* where he offers advice to the youth seeking an object for his affections. He tells him not to forget the Temple of Venus when the Roman women, following the custom of the Syrians,[2] bewailed Adonis, and "the seventh day kept holy by the Syrian Jew."[3] Persius speaks of the fear that the Sabbath inspires amongst certain Romans.

"You mutter secret prayers, by fear devised,
And dread the Sabbaths of the circumcised!"[4]

Many of the ancient writers who speak of the Jews regard the Sabbath as a fast day when all Jews abstained from nourishment.[5] Petronius alludes to "their sabbath-fasting law."[6] Martial speaks of "the fasting breath of the Sabbath-keepers," in a long list of the most offensive odours that he could think of.[7]

Not only the poets regarded the Sabbath as a day of fast but the same idea finds expression in the writings of Suetonius and Justin. According to

[1] *Hist.* v, 4.
[2] *Cf. Ezekiel* viii, 14.
[3] *Art. Amat.* i, 75-76.
[4] *Sat.* v, 183-184.
[5] *Cf.* Geiger, *IM* ii, 20-22.
[6] *Sat.* Frag. xxxvii, 6; *cf.* Reinach, *Textes* 266, note 4.
[7] *Epig.* iv, 4; *cf.* Reinach, *op. cit.* 287.

Suetonius, Augustus, in a letter to Tiberius wrote, "No Jew, my dear Tiberius, keeps his fast on a Sabbath so strictly as I have held it today."[1] Justin, the abridger of Trogus Pompeius' *History of the World*, in relating the experiences of Moses says, "Moses having returned to Damascus, the country of his ancestors, took possession of Mount Sinai, where, on his arrival with his people, wearied by a fast of seven days in the desert, he set apart the seventh day, called the Sabbath according to the custom of the nation, to be observed as a fast day in all ages, because that day had brought their wandering and their hunger to an end."[2]

It is difficult to explain exactly the origin of these conceptions regarding the Jewish Sabbath. It is possible that the Sabbath was confused with the Day of Atonement. Schuhl offers another hypothesis. It is known that in the early days of Christianity the adepts of the new religion fasted on Saturday.[3] The Romans who often confused the Christians with the Jews may have concluded that the Sabbath was a day of fasting for all Jews.[4] Geiger, is inclined to attach but little significance to the suggestion of Frankel that the idea of the Jews abstaining from

[1] *Octavianius* 76.

[2] Justin, xxxvi, 2.

[3] *Cf.* Schuhl, *Les Préventions des Romains* 20; Johns, art. "Sabbath," *Ency. Brit.* 11 ed. xxiii, 960:—"In the Roman Church a practice of fasting on Saturday as well as on Friday was current before the time of Tertullian." *Cf.* also Carleton, "Festivals and Fasts" (Christian), Hastings' *ERE* v, 844.

[4] Schuhl, *Les Préventions des Romains*, 20.

all nourishment arose from the fact that the Jews did not do any cooking on the Sabbath.[1]

The fact that the Romans considered the Sabbath to be a day of sadness is not astonishing when we compare the Jewish with the pagan festivals. On the Sabbath the Jews remained quietly at home giving up part of the day to study and prayer. All manual work was suspended until evening and perfect quiet reigned throughout the Jewish quarter.[2] To the Romans, on the contrary, the festivals were always occasions of gaiety and rejoicing. Tacitus strikes the keynote of the current pagan conception of the difference between the religious ceremonies of the Jews and the pagans when he says that the rites of the former are "dull and repulsive" in comparison to the "festive and jocund rites of Bacchus."[3]

The hatred of the Romans for the Sabbath of the Jews which was unaccompanied by any buoyant demonstration of joy finds expression in the words of Rutilius Numatianus:

> "That rod of folly, worshipping cold sabbaths,
> Whilst colder still their heart than their religion,
> Each seventh day is condemned to shameful sloth,
> Like the soft image of a wearied God.[4]

[1] *Cf. Exod.* xxxv, 3; *Num.* xv, 32 *sqq.; cf.* also Felten, *Neutestamentliche Zeitgeschichte* i, 467.

[2] On the solemn celebration of the Sabbath *cf.* Ginzberg, "Eine unbekannte jüdische Sekte," *MGWJ* lvii (1913), 158-160; Reynier, *Die l'Economie publique*, 249-263.

[3] *Cf. supra* p. 80 for a quotation from Tactitus, *Hist.* v, 5; *cf. Virgil Aeneid*, viii, 717.

[4] *De Reditu Suo* i, 389-392. For Eng. tr. *cf.* Giles, *Heathen Records to the Jewish Scripture History; containing all the extracts from the Greek and Latin writers in which the Jews and Christians are named.*

Juvenal had only aversion for the Jewish Sabbath. To him it was a day of sadness[1] because as he tells us, the kings of Palestine celebrated this day bare-footed.[2] Using the term Sabbath, indiscriminately, as referring to all festivals, Juvenal is probably thinking of the Day of Atonement, when it is customary for some of the Jews to offer prayer bare-footed. To Juvenal, also, the Sabbath is a day of idleness for which,

> "Their father is to blame, who passed in sloth
> The seventh day and therein would do no work." [3]

Augustine says of Seneca,

> this man censures, among other things, even the sacred observances of the Jews, and especially their Sabbaths, affirming that there is no use in such an institution. By taking out every seventh day they lose almost the seventh part of their own life in inactivity, and many matters which are urgent at the same time suffer from not being attended to.[4]

In his ninety-fifth epistle Seneca says, "Let us forbid a man to light a candle on the Sabbath day, for the gods do not want a light, and neither do men take pleasure in smoke."[5]

Many, however, looked upon the Sabbath from a more favorable point of view. To Dion Cassius

[1] *Sat.* vi, 159.
[2] *Cf.* Martha, *Les Moralistes sous l'empire romain,* 318, who points out that this singular explanation, proves how little effort is made on the part of a satirical poet to examine and understand what he dislikes.
[3] *Loc. cit.* xiv, 106-107. *Cf.* Reinach, *Textes* 293, note 1.
[4] *De Civitate Dei,* vii, 11. Augustine refers to a treatise of Seneca, *Against Superstitions,* which is not extant.
[5] *Epist.* 95; *cf.* Reinach, *Textes* 264, note 1.

the Sabbath was only a day of rest.[1] Nicholas of Damascus, who often pleaded for the cause of the Jews, declares that the Sabbath was dedicated to learning, sacred rites, religious customs and meditation on the law of Moses, not idleness.[2] According to Philo the day was really intended for God, a part of whose divine happiness it is to enjoy perfect peace and rest. Divine rest, Philo explains, "does not mean inactivity, but unlabored energy."[3] Aristobulus, in his treatise on the Sabbath, fragments of which are extant, endeavors to point out that the observance of the day is both reasonable and profitable.[4] "He (God) has also plainly declared that the seventh day is ordained for us by the Law, to be a sign of that which is our seventh faculty, namely, reason, whereby we have knowledge of things human and divine. . . . And its name 'Sabbath' is interpreted as meaning 'rest'." Aristobulus, by quoting verses from Homer, Hesiod[5] and Linus attempts to show that even these writers had the same respect for the Sabbath.

Horace in whose satires we find several ironical passages referring to the Jews, alludes also to the Jewish Sabbath. In one verse[6] he speaks of meeting his friend the poet Fuscus Aristius who had some

[1] *Hist.* xxxvi, 16.
[2] In Joseph. *Antiq.* xvi, 2.4.
[3] *De Cherubine* 26. Cf. *De Decalogo*, 20; *De Migratione Abrahami*, 23; *De Septenario*, 6.
[4] In Eusebius, *Praeparatio Evangelica*, xiii, 12.9-16.
[5] *Work and Days* 770. Gifford asserts that the other verses quoted by Aristobulus are spurious. Cf. *ibid*, i, p. 667.
[6] *Sat.* i, 9.69-72.

message to give him but decided to defer communicating it because of the Sabbath day. Aristius remarks, "This is the thirtieth Sabbath.[1] Would you slight the circumcised Jews?" Horace answers, "I have no scruple of conscience about that." "But," rejoins Fuscus, "I have; I am a bit weaker; one of the many."[2] It is evident from this passage that Aristius[3] as many other pagans who were not converts to Judaism, commonly showed great respect for the Sabbath of the Jews.[4]

Not only the Sabbath but the seventh year also, according to Tacitus, "was devoted to sloth."[5] He is here undoubtedly referring to the septennate or seventh year, during which the land is to lie fallow. The Jubilee,[6] or celebration of the fiftieth year after seven Sabbatical cycles, finds its origin, according to Tacitus, in the desire of the Jews to be free from work.

The abstinence from the use of swine's flesh was according to most ancient writers, due to the fact that divine honors were paid to this animal which was considered to be one of the gods of the Jews.[7] Instead of explaining the abstinence from eating pork by the fact that swine are enumerated among unclean

[1] *Cf.* Reinach, *Textes* 246, note 2.
[2] *Cf. ibid.* note 3.
[3] Basnage in his *Histoire des Juifs* xi, 212, speaks of Aristius as a Jewish poet, but there are no sources to affirm the statement.
[4] *Cf.* Gill, *Notices of the Jews,* 56.
[5] *Hist.* v, 4.
[6] *Cf. Leviticus* xxv, 1.
[7] *Cf. supra* p. 77, *cf.* also Schuhl, *Les Préventions des Romains* 24-25.

animals,[1] the use of which as food was prohibited by the Law,[2] the Romans thought the Jews would not touch this animal because it was sacred.[3] The contempt in which the animal was held by the Jews[4] finds expression in the proverbial use of its name.[5]

Plutarch[6] raises the question as to whether the Jews abstain from eating pork owing to the reverence for swine or abomination of that animal. Apion reproaches the Jews with the fact that they do not eat pork.[7] Celsus declares that the Jews need not consider themselves more holy than others because they abstain from swine, "for the Egyptians do this also and moreover from both goats and sheep, and both oxen and fishes."[8] Strabo affirms that "abstaining from meats arose from superstition"[9]

[1] *Lev.* xi, 7; *Deut.* xiv, 8; *cf. Berachoth*, 43b; *Shabbath*, 155b.

[2] Reynier, "Des bestiaux et les lois qui les concernent," in *De l'Economie publique*, pp. 487-511.

[3] Goldschmidt, *De Iudaeorum Apud Romanos Condicione*, 20-21; Geiger, *IM* ii, 16.

[4] *Cf.* Cassel, *De Iudaeorum Odio et Abstinentia a Porcina Eiusque Causis, passim.*

[5] *Proverbs* xi, 22. The abhorrence to swine is shown, in later times, by the endeavour in the Talmud to avoid mentioning it by name, using instead a Hebrew word signifying "another thing" ("dabar ahar"). *Cf. Berakot*, 43b; *Shabbat*, 129b. In the Talmud we find, moreover, that the breeding of swine was forbidden (*Baba Kamma*, 82b; *Menakoth*, 64b; *Sotah*, 49b; *Jer. Shekalim*, 47c), and the Jews were prohibited from keeping them among the flocks (*Mishnah* "Baba Kamma" vii, 7). Cunaeus, in his *De Republica Hebraeorum* 204, gives the Gentile explanation of the reason for the Jews not pronouncing the name and for their supposed worship of the pig by saying that the Jews regarded this animal as among unlucky things and productive of all evil.

[6] *Sympos*, iv, 5, 1, 2.

[7] In Joseph. *C. Apion.* ii, 13.

[8] Origen, *C. Cels.* v, 43.

[9] *Geog.* xvi, 2.

and Juvenal points out that they "deem swine's flesh as sacred as a man's,"¹ while he bestows a contemptuous notice upon the indulgence they show to swine in permitting them to reach a good old age.² Tacitus explains that the Jews "abstain from the flesh of swine, from the recollection of the loathsome affliction which they had formerly suffered from leprosy, to which that animal is subject."³

Another accusation brought against the Jews was voiced by Juvenal who declared that they held the Roman laws in contempt while they learnt and kept and feared every precept handed down by Moses in his secret volume.⁴ Tacitus goes a step further and accuses them of the hatred of humanity. Among the Jews, this writer declares, "faith is inviolably observed and compassion is cheerfully shown towards each other while the bitterest animosity is harboured against all others." ⁵

The Roman prejudice against the Jew was undoubtedly strengthened by the uncompromising action of the Jews themselves in not tolerating the gods of other nations.⁶ The Romans had willingly admitted into their Pantheon the gods of conquered nations; they had added strange divinities to theirs and worshipped them in the same spirit as the ancient

¹ *Sat.* xiv, 99.
² *Loc. cit.* vi, 160.
³ *Hist.* v, 4.
⁴ *Sat.* xiv, 100-102.
⁵ *Hist.* v, 5.
⁶ *Cf.* Giron, *Bulletins de l'academie royale* 118-121; Schuhl, *Les Préventions des Romains* 5-8.

gods of Rome and even raised temples to them at the expense of the public treasury.[1] Equally on the other hand, the Gauls, the Egyptians, the Syrians and all the other conquered nations, the Romans pointed out, found no scruples in reconciling themselves to the gods of Rome. These subject nations worshipped their own local divinities but admitted other gods as well. Not only did they worship them all but they built temples to the Roman gods with whom the strange gods were often identified or who added the Roman to their own.[2] But the Jews, on the contrary, would not accept any of these gods nor conform to any of the practices or beliefs in regard to the Roman gods. In fact, the Jews went further and claimed that their religion was superior to all the others and looked with disdain upon all the Roman gods. " The Jews " says Tacitus, " consider as profane whatever is held sacred by the Romans." [3] " The first thing instilled into their proselytes is to despise the gods."[4] Pliny characterizes the Jews as " a nation remarkable for their contempt of the divinities."[5] Posidonius and Appolonius Molo, " accuse the Jews of not worshiping the same gods whom others worship."[6]

The Romans would, indeed, according to their

[1] *Cf.* Boissier, *La Religion romaine, d'Auguste aux Antonins* i, 334.

[2] *Cf.* Julius Cæsar, *Commentarii de Bello Gallico* vi, 17; Boissier, *La Religion romaine* i, 340-341; Cumont, *Les Religions orientales dans le paganisme romaine, passim.*

[3] *Hist.* v, 4.

[4] *Loc. cit.* v, 5.

[5] *Nat. Hist.* xiii, 4.9.

[6] In Joseph. *C. Apion.* ii, 7.

PAGAN MISCONCEPTIONS OF THE JEWS 93

policy have been willing to give a place in the Pantheon to the God of the Jews in whom they thought they recognized Bacchus[1] but they soon realized that the Jewish religion differed essentially from their own and that their gods were not analogous to the one God whom the Jews worshipped and of whom no material image was permitted to be made. It was the idea that the Jews made no use of images,[2] that aroused so much adverse criticism. Some still persisted in believing that they used them in concealment even though none had ever been found.[3] Tacitus says, "the Jews acknowledge one God only, and conceive of him by the mind alone, condemning, as impious, all who, with perishable materials, wrought into the human shape, form representations of the Deity. That being, they say, is above all, and everlasting, neither susceptible of likeness nor of decay. They therefore allow no resemblance of him in their city, much less in their temples."[4]

To some educated Romans of the time, the Jews were successful in showing the advantages of accepting the monotheistic and spiritual nature of God. The Roman scholar Varro remarked that, "the ancient Romans, for more than a hundred and seventy years worshipped the gods without an image. 'And if this custom,' he says, ' could have remained till now, the gods would have been more purely

[1] *Cf.* Tacitus, *Hist.* v, 4.
[2] *Cf.* Glover, *The Conflict of Religions in the Early Roman Empire*, 14.
[3] *Cf. supra* p. 77.
[4] *Hist.* v, 5.

worshiped.' In favor of this opinion, he cites as witness among others the Jewish nation."[1] But the masses were not to be influenced by such conceptions. Theoretically it might work but not practically; the Jews might think as they pleased but not act as they pleased. By neglecting the worship of the local deities they must still meet the reproach that they were disrespectful in act and word. Moreover, it was declared that the curse of the angry god would strike those who defended the offender. It was the duty of each member of the state to promote its welfare by religious observances. It was incumbent upon every citizen to worship the gods or some of the gods whom the city worshipped, and if he failed to do so, he was exposing himself to the reproach of atheism.[2]

From a social standpoint the intolerance of the pagans toward the Jews took the form of expressions of disdain rather than that of adverse legislation.[3] The feelings cherished towards the Jews were not so much those of hatred as of pure contempt. Cicero characterized the Jews along with the Syrians as " nations born for slavery."[4] Many of the occupa-

[1] In St. Augustine's *De Civitate Dei* iv, 31. *Cf.* Plutarch's *Numa* 8, in which the statement is made that the temples and the churches were without images for 170 years; Hild, *REJ* viii, pp. 25-26.

[2] *Cf.* Joseph. *C. Apion.* ii, 6; A. Linsenmayer, *Die Bekaempfung des Christentums durch den römischen Staat bis zum Tode des Kaisers Julian* (München, 1905), p. 29, A. 3; Schürer, iii, 415; Hobhouse, *The Church and the World* 12.

[3] *Cf. Bibliotheca Latino-Hebraica*, 142-144; *cf.* also Kautsky, " Der Judenhass," in *Der Ursprung des Christentums*, 273-279.

[4] *Oratio de Provinciis Consularibus* c. 5.

tions of the Jews, as many of their customs and traditions, were an incessant butt for the wit and wrath of the Roman writers. The Jews were often spoken of as fortune-tellers and connected with Chaldaeans, Mathematici, Astrologers and Soothsayers. Juvenal calls attention to those who, he says, practiced this art:

> " Leaving her hand and basket,[1]
> The trembling Jewess whispering begs her bread,
> Interpretress of Salem's law, and priestess
> Of trees,[2] and faithful go-between of heaven.
> She fills the hand, too, but with smallest coin.
> Those Jews will sell you any dreams you please." [3]

According to a statement of Strabo, Moses pointed out to his people that those who were felicitous in their dreams were to be permitted to sleep in the Temple where thy might receive inspirations for themselves and for others.[4] Pliny makes the remark,

[1] For an explanation of the term "*copinus*" as referring to baskets which the Jews were accustomed to carry about with them for their daily food, *cf.* Gill, *Notices of the Jews* 93, note 2.

[2] *Cf.* Meier, *Judaica* 52, note 27, who says that the phrase "*magna sacerdos arboris*" alluded to the fact that the Jews were accustomed to tie their horses at night to some trees in the sacred grove where they slept before going into the city as fortune tellers.

[3] *Sat.* vi, 542-547. *Cf.* Origen *C. Cels.* ii, 4.31,32, who calls the Jews "jugglers and vagabonds"; *cf. supra* p. 73.

[4] *Geog.* xvi, 35. While as Reinach (*Textes* 100, note 1) points out, the practice of sleeping in the pagan temples for the purpose of dreaming was current in some places, there is no other evidence besides that of Strabo, to the fact that the practice prevailed in the Jewish temple of Jerusalem. *Cf.* also Gill, *Notices of the Jews,* 31, note 1. *Cf.* Gray, " Incubation," Hastings' *ERE* vii, 206-207. Sleeping in the Temple was prohibited by law; *cf. Middoth* i, 2, where a severe punishment is given for those who fell asleep in the temple.

"There is another sect, also, of adepts in the magic art, who derive their origin from the Jews, Moses, Jannes and Lotapa."[1]

The poverty of some of the Jews at Rome is ridiculed, especially, by Juvenal and Martial. The former declares that at his time the place where Numa used to meet his mistress and where there was once a sacred fountain and the temples, had been let out to Jews who were so poor that their only furniture was a basket and a bundle of hay. "For every single tree is bid to pay a rent to the people and the Camonae (the prophetic deities of the wood) having been ejected, the wood is one mass of beggars."[2] In the same satire, Juvenal describes an encounter at night with a drunken Roman gentleman whom he thus addresses: "Where do you hang out? In what Proseucha[3] may I expect to find you?"[4] Martial makes a contemptuous remark about "the poor Jew-boy brought up to begging by his mother."[5] and referring to a rival

[1] *Natur. Hist.* xxx, i, sec. 11; *cf.* Reinach, *Textes* 282, note 1, 363.

[2] *Sat.* iii, 13-17.

[3] *Cf. Acts* xvi, 13; *Luke* vi, 12; for the use of the term "proseucha," *cf.* Elbogen, *Der jüdische Gottesdienst* 445 and Vitringa, *De Synagoga Vetere* 228 for a description of a *proseucha*. *Cf.* also Bernard, *The Synagogue and the Church* (condensed from the original Latin work of Vitringa) Appendix, note A, p. 238.

[4] *Sat.* iii, 13-17.

[5] *Epig.* xii, 60. The reference of Martial to the hawker on the other side of the Tiber, "who sells matches for broken glass" (i, 41, *transtiberinus ambulator Qui pallentia sulphurata fractis Permutat vitreis*), had been regarded by some writers (Gill, *Notices of the Jews* 63; Hild, *REJ* xi, 171; 184) as a scornful reproach of the Jews. Reinach, on the other hand, thinks that Martial as well as Statius who speaks

Jewish poet whom he accuses of tampering with his verses[1] he says " may he wander through town after town, an outcast on the bridge and hill, and lowest among the craving mendicants, may he entreat for mouthfuls of the spoilt bread reserved for the dogs."[2]

The isolation of the Jews was a source of aversion to the Romans. The fact that they would neither eat, drink nor pray with other men[3] seemed sufficient proof that the law of the Jews was hostile to man and calculated to inspire the Jew with hatred and opposition of mankind.[4] Philostratus in his *Life of Apollonius of Tyana* declared:

> The Jews have long fallen away, not from the Romans alone, but from all mankind; for a people that devises an uncompanionable life, declines to associate at table with others, as well as partake in drink-offerings, prayers and incense-offerings, stands further removed from us than Susa and Bactra, and the yet more distant dwelling Indians.[5]

The aversion of the Romans to Jewish customs and manners reaches its height in the words of Rutilianus Numatianus who has been called "the bitterest and most abusive of all writers against the unsocial habits of the Jews."[6] In describing a journey which of the " ambulant sellers of brimstone for bits of broken glass " (*Silvae* i, 6, *Illic agmina confremunt Syrorum, Hic plebs scenica, quaeque comminutis Permutat citreis gregale sulfur*) have not the Jews, but the Syrians in mind.

[1] Martial, *op. cit.* xi, 94.
[2] *Ibid.* x, 5.
[3] Tacitus, *Hist.* v, 5.
[4] *Ibid.*
[5] *Vita Apollonii Tyaneii* v, 33.
[6] Gill, *Notices of the Jews* 105-106.

he had taken from Rome into Gaul at the close of the fourth century, he speaks of meeting a Jew who complained if his trees were touched or a drop of water taken from his tanks. He adds that in the lying slave-cage of Judaea insane practices go on which he believes even some boys would not credit. Then he winds up with the wish that Judaea had never been conquered in the wars of Pompey, for "though the excrescence has been cut off, the virus creeps through the veins, and the conquered nation overcomes its conquerors."[1]

[1] *De reditu suo* i, 381-398. *Cf.* Remarks of Seneca in Augustine's *De Civ. Dei* vi, 2, "the conquered have given laws to the conquerors." *Cf.* also, Reinach, *Textes* 359, note 3-4; 360, note 1.

Chapter IV

The Political Situation

As early as the Maccabean period the friendly attitude of the Romans towards the Jews became evident. When the Selucids under Antiochus Epiphanes attempted to force the Greek worship and practices upon the Jews,[1] prematurely and with violence,[2] their efforts were finally foiled by the work of the Maccabeans. Owing largely to internal dissensions, in the Seleucid dynasty, which broke out upon the death of Antiochus, Judas Maccabeus was able to obtain complete religious freedom for the Jews.[3] The Maccabean struggle now became a contest for political freedom and the attainment of independence. The Jewish nation had become divided within itself and the question at issue was whether the Hellenists or the national party should have control.

As a result of a complete victory over his opponents, Judas found himself at the head of the Jewish Commonwealth. In order to maintain the supremacy of his party and realizing that he could not compete with the imperial armies, Judas determined to seek

[1] *Cf.* 1 *Macc.* i, 11-15; 2 *Macc.* iv, 10-15; Tacitus, *Hist.* v, 8.

[2] *Cf.* 1 *Macc.* i, 21-25; Joseph. *Antiq.* xii, 5.4. In regard to the plundering of the Temple, *cf.* Josephus in *C. Apion,* ii, 7.

[3] *Cf.* 1 *Macc.* iii, 1-9; 25; iv, 48-59, Joseph. *Antiq.* xii, 9.7.

the aid of Rome in freeing his people from the Syrian yoke.[1] Eupolemus and Jason were sent as ambassadors to Rome where they were readily granted an audience.[2] According to the statements of the *First Book of Maccabees*, the Senate sent an epistle in "tablets of brass" to Jerusalem where they might have by them "a memorial of peace and confederacy."[3] Inaccuracies which have been found in this book of the Maccabees, when explaining foreign relations and details of information, have raised the question as to the reliability of this treaty. But all circumstances seem to lead to the acceptance of the treaty itself with certainty.[4] The treaty as given in the eighth chapter of the *First Book of Maccabees* is as follows:

Good success be to the Romans and to the nation of the Jews, by sea and by land for ever; the sword also and the enemy be far from them. But if war arises for Rome first or for any of their confederates in all their dominion, the nation of the Jews shall help them as confederates as the occasion shall prescribe to them, with all their heart; and unto them that make war they (*i. e.*, the Jews) shall not give, neither supply, food, arms, money or ships, as it hath seemed good unto the Romans; and they (*i. e.*, the Jews) shall observe their obligations, receiving nothing (in the way of a bribe). In the same manner, moreover, if war comes first upon the nation of the Jews, the Romans shall help them as confederates with all their soul, as

[1] 1 *Macc.* viii, 1-16.
[2] 1 *Macc.* viii, 17-21.
[3] 1 *Macc.* viii, 22; cf. Joseph. *Antiq.* xii, 10.6.
[4] *Cf.* Niese, *Kritik der beiden Makkabäerbücher* 88-89; Grimm, "Ueber 1 *Macc.* viii und xv, 16-21," *ZWT*, xvii (1874), 231-238 Mendelssohn, *Acta soc. phil.* v (1875) 91-100; Schürer i, 220, note 32.

the occasion shall prescribe to them; and to them that are confederates there shall not be given corn, arms, money, or ships, as it hath seemed good unto the Romans; and they shall observe these obligations and that without deceit.¹

At the same time as this treaty was concluded the Romans issued an epistle to Demetrius, wherein they ordered him to desist from every sort of hostile proceeding against the Jews, who were allies of the Romans.

According to these words have the Romans made (a treaty) with the people of the Jews. But if hereafter the one party or the other² shall determine to add or diminish anything, they shall do it at their pleasure; and whatsoever they shall add or take away, shall be established. And as touching the evils which king Demetrius doeth unto you, we have written to him, saying: "Wherefore hast thou made thy yoke heavy upon our friends (and) confederates the Jews? If, therefore, they plead any more against thee, we will do them justice, and fight with thee by sea and by land." ³

This missive failed of its purpose, for the overthrow of Judaea had been already completed before the Romans could interfere. Not only were the Jews completely defeated by Demetrius but Judas himself was killed.

With the death of Judas the cause of the Jewish national party seemed lost. The party friendly to the Greeks had control of the country.⁴ But the

---

¹ 1 *Macc.* viii, 23-30.

² The Greek text of 1 *Macc.* viii, 31, is corrupt. It is inconceivable that one party can break a treaty. The original Hebrew read as follows: ואלו אלו אם אבל which is to be translated: "But if hereafter the one party as well as the other shall. . . ."

³ 1 *Macc.* viii, 31, 32.

⁴ *Cf.* 1 *Macc.* ix, 23-27; Joseph. *Antiq.* xiii, 1.1.

nationalists in their effort to regain power elected Jonathan, brother of Judas, civil and military leader of Judaea (143 B. C.).[1] The success of Jonathan was due rather to his shrewd political policy than to his abilities as a warrior. In order to strengthen his position Jonathan entered into diplomatic negotiations with foreign nations. He sent ambassadors to Rome and Sparta and other places. No material aid was sought, but simply a renewal and confirmation of the friendship shown to the Jews in the days of Judas.[2] The Roman Senate confirmed what had been formerly decreed concerning their friendship with the Jews and "gave the ambassadors letters unto (the governors of) every place, that they should bring them on their way to the land of Judah in peace."[3] The Spartans also, we are told, received the ambassadors kindly and sent a letter of greeting in which there was a claim of brotherhood on the ground that the Lacedaemonians were of the stock of Abraham.[4]

[1] *Cf.* 1 *Macc.* ix, 28-31.

[2] *Cf.* 1 *Macc.* xii, 1-4; Joseph. *Antiq.* xiii, 5.8; *cf.* Mendelssohn *Acta soc. phil*, v, 101-104.

[3] 1 *Macc.* xii, 4; Joseph. *Antiq.* xiii, 5.8.

[4] 1 *Macc.* xii, 21. For letters from Jonathan and King Areus of Sparta *cf.* 1 *Macc.* xii, 6-23; Joseph. *Antiq.* xiii, 5.8. The Greek legend that the Spartans were descendants of the Phoenicians may account, in some measure, for the claim of relationship between the Jews and the Spartans. As it has been pointed out in Charles, *Apocrypha and Pseudepigrapha of the Old Testament* i, 112, note 21, "the probability is that while the details can scarcely be regarded as historical, the broad fact of diplomatic relations of some kind between the Jews and the Spartans is to be accepted as true." For literature upon the subject *cf.* Charles, *loc. cit.*

The support of the Romans was again sought by Simon who upon the death of his brother Jonathan[1] was appointed high priest, military commander and ethnarch over his people.[2] He sent ambassadors to Rome to renew the bonds of friendship of the Romans with the Jews. The Senate received the embassy courteously and gave a decree granting all that they sought. Letters regarding the contents of this decree were sent to Egypt, Syria, Pergamum, Cappadocia, and Parthia, and to many of the smaller independent states and cities of Greece and Asia Minor. The contents of the letters is indicated in the one sent to Ptolemy:

> Lucius, consul of the Romans, unto king Ptolemy, greeting: The Jews' ambassadors came unto us (as) friends and confederates, to renew the old friendship and confederacy, being sent from Simon the high priest, and from the people of the Jews; moreover, they brought a shield of gold of a thousand pound. It pleased us, therefore, to write unto the kings and unto the countries, that they should not seek their hurt, nor fight against them, and their cities, and their countries, nor be confederates with such as fight against them. And it seemed good to us to accept the shield from them. If, therefore, any pestilent fellows should have fled from their country unto you, deliver them unto Simon the high priest, that he may take vengeance on them according to their law.[3]

[1] *Cf.* I *Macc.* xii, 41-53; Joseph. *Antiq.* xiii, 6.1-3.
[2] *Cf.* I *Macc.* xiii, 1-11; xiv, 8-15; Joseph. *Antiq.* xiii, 6.3.
[3] *Cf.* I *Macc.* xv, 16-21; *cf.* Schürer, i, 250-251, who points out that the relations indicated in I *Macc.* xiv, 24 and xv, 15-24, are exactly the same as the terms in the "*Senatus consultus*" communicated by Josephus in *Antiq.* xiv, 8.5, which, however, the latter assigns to the time of Hyrcanus II. *Cf.* Mendelssohn, *De senati consulti Romanorum ab Josepho Antiq. xiv, 8, 5, relati temporibus* 1-36; Mendelssohn and

Holtzmann points out that in these letters we have the first great attempt to restrict the blending of the Jews with the nations among which they were dispersed, on the ground of a jurisdiction which pertained to them as well as to those in Judaea, and which was to be recognized by foreign peoples. Not only a religious but also a legal bond was to hold them in inseparable connection with the fatherland.[1] The recognition by the Romans seemed to make evident the unity of this widely scattered people, and at the same time gave a Jew in foreign lands a feeling of security.

As a result of Simon's negotiation with the dethroned king of Syria, the Jewish people were delivered from Syrian rule and Judaea was raised to the rank of an independent nation. Demetrius wrote Simon a letter to this effect:

> King Demetrius unto Simon the high priest, and Friend of kings, and unto the elders and nation of the Jews, greeting: The golden crown and the palm-branch, which ye sent, we have received; and we are ready to conclude a lasting peace with you; and to write to the officers, to grant immunities unto you. And whatsoever things we (have now) confirmed unto you they are confirmed; and the strongholds which ye have builded, let them be your own. As for any oversights and faults (committed) unto this day, we forgive (them); and the crown which ye owed (we remit); and if there were any other toll exacted in Jerusalem, let it no longer be exacted. And if

---

Ritschl, "Nochmals der römische Senatsbeschluss bei Josephus Antiq. xiv, 8.5," *RMP* xxx (1875), 419-435; Ritschl, "Eine Berichtigung der republicanischen Consularfasten," *RMP* xxviii (1883), 586-614.

[1] Holtzmann and Weber, *Geschichte des Volkes Israel und der Entstehung des Christenthums* ii, 378.

(there be) some of you meet to be enrolled among those round about us, let them be enrolled; and (thus) let there be peace betwixt us.[1]

The independence acquired found expression in the fact that the Jews dated their documents and treaties according to the year of Simon as high priest and prince of the Jews.[2] The independence of Judaea was further emphasized by the right which Simon acquired from the son of Demetrius to coin money, a right which was generally recognized in antiquity as a mark of sovereignty.[3] The position of Judaism was strengthened by driving out the remaining Hellenists from their stronghold and endeavouring to remove all traces of Heathenism. From this time the Hellenistic party ceased to exist.

The successor of Simon sent an embassy to remind the Romans of a previous decree in which they warned the nations against making war upon Judaea.[4]

When the Senate received his letter, they made friendship with him in the following manner. " Fanius (the son of Marcus) the praetor gathered the Senate together on the eighth day before the Ides of February in the Comitia, in the presence of Lucius Manlius, the son of Lucius, of the Mentine tribe, and Caius Sepronius, the son of Caius, of the Falernian tribe, to discuss what the ambassadors sent by the people of the Jews,

---

[1] 1 *Macc.* xiii, 36-40. As to the genuineness of this letter *cf.* Charles, *Apocrypha und Pseudepigrapha* i, 63 (e).

[2] 1 *Macc.* xiii, 42; *cf.* xiv, 27. In Justin's *Hist.* xxxvi, 1-10; 3.9, the freedom of the Jews is made to date from the time of Demetrius I.

[3] *Cf.* 1 *Macc.* xv, 6; *cf.* also Grätz, *Gesch. der Juden* iii, 59; Schürer, i, 242-243.

[4] *Cf. supra*, p. 103.

namely, Simon, the son of Dositheus, and Apollonius the son of Alexander, and Diodorus the son of Jason, all three good and virtuous men, came to treat about, namely the league of friendship and mutual alliance which existed between them and the Romans, and about the other public affairs. For example, they desired that Joppa and its havens, and Gazara and its springs, and the several other cities and places of theirs which Antiochus had taken from them in war contrary to the decree of the Senate, might be restored to them, and that it might not be lawful for the king's troops to pass through their country, or the countries of those that were subject to them, and that whatever had been decreed by Antiochus during the war, without the consent of the Senate, might be made void, and that the Romans would send ambassadors, who would take care that restitution should be made to them of what Antiochus had taken from them, and that they would make an estimate of the country that had been laid waste in the war, and that they would grant them letters of protection to kings and commonwealths for their security on their return home. It was decreed then as to these points to renew the league of friendship and mutual alliance with these good men, who were sent by a good and friendly people." [1]

Although the Jewish ambassadors were treated kindly by the Roman praetor, the desired letters were not received and a final decision of the Senate was deferred. It seems evident, however, from a later decree of the Roman senate, that a second embassy sent by Hyrcanus was successful in obtaining the desired results. According to this decree which Josephus has, erroneously, inserted in a decree

[1] Joseph. *Antiq.* xiii, 9.2; *cf.* Bonnetty, *Documents historiques sur la religion des Romains et sur la connaissance qu'ils ont pu avoir des traditions bibliques, par leurs rapports avec les Juifs* i, 12-13.

of the Pergamenes[1] Antiochus, the son of Demetrius,[2] received peremptory orders to restore all towns taken from the Jews. In the words of the decree of the people of Pergamus

. . . Antiochus, should do no injury to the Jews, the allies of the Romans; and that the fortresses and havens and territory, and whatever else he had taken from them, should be restored; and that it should be lawful for them to export their goods out of their havens; and that no king or people should have leave to export any goods, either from the country of Judaea or from their havens, without paying customs, except Ptolemy the king of Alexandria, because he is our ally and friend; and that, according to their desire, the garrison that was in Joppa should be expelled. . . .

Antiochus gave up the cities but demanded tribute and hostages.[3] After the death of Antiochus the taxes imposed upon Judaea were not paid to any of the following Syrian kings.[4] The yoke of Syria was thrown off and the Jewish kingdom maintained its independence until it was compelled to acknowledge the Roman dominion, first under the Hasmonean dynasty, then under the House of Herod.

[1] *Antiq.* xiv, 10.22; *cf.* Schürer i, 26-262, and note 7; Mendelssohn, " De senati consultis Romanorum ab Josepho Antiq. xiii, 9.2; xiv, 10.22, relatis commentatio," *Acta soc. phil.* v (1875), 123-158.
[2] The text reads " Antiochus, son of Antiochus," but according to Schürer and Mendelssohn *op. cit.* the text is corrupt and the king referred to can hardly be any other than Antiochus VII Sidetes, son of Demetrius.
[3] *Cf.* Joseph. *Antiq.* xiii, 8.2-3; Diodorus, *Bibl. Hist.* xxiv, 1; Porphyry in the fragments collected by C. Müller, *Fragm. Hist. Graec.* iii, 712; Justin, *Hist.* xxxvi, 1.
[4] *Cf* Joseph. *Antiq.* xiii, 10.1; Schürer i, 258.

With the independence of Judaea apparently secured we may endeavour to find out to what extent the various treaties of Rome helped to gain this independence and what were the effects of the Roman policy upon the Jews. While the friendly attitude of the Romans towards the Jews during the Maccabean period becomes evident from a study of the alliances, it is doubtful whether they really helped the Jews to attain independence. Some of these treaties rest on slender historical foundations.[1] According to Ewald, the Jews sought to obtain these alliances with the Romans for the purpose of furthering their commercial and trade development rather than the securing of their political independence.[2] This idea seems to be strengthened by the fact that John Hyrcanus endeavoured to get possession of the city of Joppa in order that he might obtain the right of ingress and egress of his ships free of toll. An effort to develop trade and commerce may perhaps be one of the motives underlying some of the alliances sought by the Jews, but it certainly is not the main nor only one. Documents which many historians think Josephus has erroneously placed at a later date in his narrative,[3] show us that the inhabitants of many

[1] On the State papers used by Josephus *cf.* Judeich, *Caesar im Orient* 119-141; *cf.* also Justin, *Hist.* xxxvi; Berliner, *Gesch. der Juden in Rom* i, 1; Vogelstein, *Gesch. der Juden in Rom* i, 4; Grätz, *Gesch. der Juden,* iii, 655-671.

[2] *Hist. of Israel,* v, 363.

[3] *Cf. Antiq.* xiv, 10.22-25. *Cf.* also Schürer iii, 67-68; Ewald, *op. cit.* v, 364, note 2.

Greek cities granted certain requests to the Jews dwelling amongst them primarily because they were allies and friends of the Romans.

While the alliances of the Romans with the Jews during the Maccabean period, undoubtedly, were of some indirect advantage to the Jews, as expressions of toleration, none of them seem to have been of great material benefit. "Roman professions of friendship were never backed up by arms."[1] The main motive of the Roman policy of friendship towards the Jews, was an effort to overcome the power of Syria. The Jews, who were trying to throw off the Syrian yoke, were encouraged in their revolts by the Romans. In fact, the Jewish state could maintain its position and finally gain complete independence from the Syrian suzerainty only because of the internal weakness of the Syrian empire. The encouragement of the Jews, on the part of the Romans, took the form of verbal alliances, not the sending of armies, for Rome was not desirous of making additional conquests in the East. In other words, Roman interference on behalf of the Jews was diplomatic and not military. The Romans continued to befriend the Jews for many years after they gained independence. When the power of the Roman Senate was lost and the main control was in the hands of military chiefs, and when the Roman Empire began to extend its boundaries into Asia, a change was made in the policy of Roman rule in the East. Instead of merely making friendly

[1] Morrison, *The Jews Under Roman Rule* 19.

alliances with the Jews, Rome herself took control of affairs in Judaea with the aid of military forces.

As a result of an alteration of the balance of power in the Republic, Rome gave up her policy of non-intervention in Eastern affairs. The loss of Roman possessions in the East as a result of the revolt of the Asiatic provinces (88 B. C.), aroused the hostile factions in Rome, and Sulla was sent to put down the revolt. A war was waged by Sulla against Mithridates with varying success on both sides until Pompey arrived with a large army and completely defeated the eastern monarch.[1] In an effort to extend the Roman frontier to the banks of the Euphrates, Pompey determined, if possible, to subjugate Palestine. The task of Pompey would have been a difficult one, had the Jews been able to organize themselves into a homogeneous nationality. But the strife of Jewish parties within Judaea made such a union impossible. Under the Hasmonean princes who were at first high priests and then kings, the Jewish state prospered and succeeded in annexing several territories. But the discord which soon arose in the royal family and the growing discontent of the pious, the soul of the nation, with rulers who no longer showed any appreciation of the real aspirations of their subjects, made the Jewish nation a comparatively easy prey for the ambition of the Romans.

[1] *Cf.* de Champagny, *Rome et la Judée au temps de la chute de Néron*, i, 53; Mommsen, *Roman Hist.* iv, 409; Clinton, *Fasti Hellenici* iii, 174-180 (*ad. ann.* 60-62).

Scaurus, the general of Pompey, had scarcely reached the boundaries of Judaea when he was met by ambassadors from the rival Jewish princes, Aristobulus and Hyrcanus, both seeking the Roman aid and support and both bringing gifts of money.[1] When Aristobulus was assured of his position, he made every effort to gain the good will of Pompey and sent him a beautifully wrought golden vine, valued at five hundred talents, which Strabo found still on view in the temple of Jupiter Capitolinus at Rome.[2]

The arrival of Pompey, himself, at Damascus,[3] was made the occasion of three embassies from Jerusalem. Beside the representatives of the rival princes, there were ambassadors from the Jewish people, who expressed the desire for which some Pharisees had long contended. "We do not wish," they declared, "to be under kingly government because the form of government we received from our forefathers was that of subjection to the priests of that God whom they worshiped."[4] Pompey

---

[1] *Cf.* Joseph. *Antiq.* xiv, 2-3; *Bell. Jud.* i, 6.2-3.

[2] Joseph. *Antiq.* xiv, 3.1; Josephus might possibly have seen it himself on his visit to Rome in the year 64 or 65 A.D., but as Schürer i, 295, points out, if Josephus did see it at that time he would not have failed to mention that this was before the great fire in which the Capitol was burnt down. *Cf.* also Tacitus, *Hist.* iii, 71-72; Suetonius, *Vitellius* 15; Dio Cassius, lxv, 17.

[3] *Cf.* Dio Cassius xxxvii, 7; Joseph. *Antiq.* xiv, 3.2.

[4] Joseph. *Antiq.* xiv, 3.2; *cf.* Diodorus, xl. By taking away the independence of Judaea and stripping the high-priesthood of civil authority, Rome fulfilled the desire of this embassy and "the first and most important stage of the battle between the Pharisees and the Sadducees came to an end." (Wellhausen, *Israelitische und Jüdische Geschichte* 307.)

promised to give a decision as soon as he returned from his expedition against the Nabatians[1] but upon discovering that Aristobulus was preparing to resist him, he turned at once from his proposed expedition and marched into Judaea.[2] Aristobulus, vacillating between negotiations and preparations for defence,[3] finally promised to give up Jerusalem to Pompey but endeavouring to exact the fulfillment of these promises, the Roman general met with resistance from the Sadducees who composed the garrison. As a result of this supposed treachery, Aristobulus was thrown into prison and Pompey prepared to take the city by force.[4]

No resistance was offered by the followers of Hyrcanus who regarded Pompey as their confederate, but the adherents of Aristobulus gathered together on the Temple mount and for three months defied the efforts of the Romans to affect an entrance.[5] The siege might have continued longer, had not the besiegers taken advantage of the strict observance of the Sabbath day[6] In accordance with a strict interpretation of the Law, the besieged pointed out that they were not permitted to interfere with their enemies unless the latter made an actual assault.[7]

[1] *Cf.* Joseph. *Antiq.* xiv, 3.3.
[2] *Cf.* Grätz, "Zur Topographie Palastina's" *MGWJ* (1882), 14-17.
[3] *Cf.* Joseph. *Antiq.* xiv, 3.3-4; *Bell. Jud.* i, 6.4-5.
[4] *Cf.* Joseph. *Antiq.* xiv, 4.1; *Bell Jud.* i, 6.6-7.1; v, 12.2.
[5] *Cf.* Joseph. *Antiq.* xiv, 4.2; *Bell. Jud.* i, 7.2.
[6] *Cf.* Joseph. *Antiq.* xiv, 4.2-4; *Bell. Jud.* i, 7.3-5.
[7] Joseph. *Antiq.* xiv, 4.2; *cf.* Grätz, *Gesch. der Juden* iii, 161; *cf.* Herzfeld, *MGWJ* (1855), 109-115.

As soon as the Romans learned of this distinction, they refrained from throwing missiles but worked steadily at demolishing the walls. Finally a breach was effected in the walls on the Sabbath day and troops were hurried into the enclosure where the priests were still ministering at the altar. In the massacre which ensued, no less than twelve thousand Jews are said to have lost their lives.[1] Pompey, in order to satisfy his curiosity as to the nature of Jewish worship, forced his way into the Holy of Holies where he was surprised to find that there were no images of any kind.[2] The treasures of the Temple were left untouched "on account" as Josephus says, "of his regard to religion."[3] The exact motive of Pompey's policy cannot be definitely ascertained. It may be as Grätz suggests, because "he was penetrated by awe at the sublime simplicity of the Holy of Holies" or because "he did not wish to be designated as the robber of sanctuaries."[4] His respect for the religion of the Jews seems to be emphasized by the fact that he took great care to see that the priests continued the services without interruption.[5]

The attitude of a large section of the Jewish people towards these events finds expression in the *Psalms of Solomon*. In the words of the Psalmist:

[1] *Cf.* Joseph. *Antiq.* xiv, 4.4; Duruy, *Hist. of Rome,* ii, 831; iii, 231.
[2] *Cf. supra* ch. iii, pp. 77-78.
[3] *Antiq.* xiv, 4.4; *cf.* Cicero, Pro Flacco 28.
[4] *Gesch. der Juden* iii, 163.
[5] Joseph. *op. cit.*

Therefore God mingled for them a spirit of wandering;

  *   *   *   *   *

He brought him that is from the end of the earth, that smiteth mightily;
He decreed war against Jerusalem, and against her land.

The princes of the land went to meet him with joy; they said unto him:
Blessed be thy way! Come ye, enter ye in with peace.
They made the rough ways even, before his entering in;
They opened the gates to Jerusalem, they crowned its walls.

As a father (entereth) the house of his sons, (so) he entered (Jerusalem) in peace;
He established his feet (there) in great safety.
He captured her fortresses and the wall of Jerusalem;
For God Himself led him in safety, while they wandered.
He destroyed their princes and every one wise in counsel;
He poured out the blood of the inhabitants of Jerusalem, like the water of uncleanness.
He led away their sons and daughters, whom they had begotten in defilement.

They did according to their uncleanness, even as their fathers (had done):
They defiled Jerusalem and the things that had been hallowed to the name of God.

To the pious of this period, especially, the bloody chastisement was the work of God, the Romans being regarded as the medium for carrying His vengeance into effect. The Hasmoneans were justly punished for assuming kingly titles which did not rightly belong to them and the people were punished for upholding the transgressions of their princes and falling with them into sin.[1]

These sentiments, current among a large part of the population, aided Pompey, considerably, in his final disposition of affairs, especially, in his effort to establish a form of government which would be satisfactory alike to the Jews and to Roman authorities. The leaders of the war were beheaded, and Aristobulus and his children retained to grace Pompey's triumph in Rome.[2] A large number of Jewish prisoners, who were taken to the Capitol and later set at liberty, formed an important element in the development of the Jewish community in Rome. They were treated as *libertini* or freemen.[3]

The hierarchical constitution of the Jews remained unimpaired and Pompey gave the people, as their high priest, Hyrcanus II, who was strongly supported by the Pharisees. But the high priest was a vassal of the Romans for Judaea was made tributary to Rome and her independence lost forever.[4] The territory which she had gained during her period of

[1] *Cf. Psalms of Solomon* ii, viii, xvii.

[2] *Cf.* Joseph. *Antiq.* xiv, 4.4; Plutarch, *Pompeius* 45; Appian, *Mithridates* iv, 27; Pliny, *Nat. Hist.* vii, 98; Schön, *Das capitolinische Verzeichniss der römischen Triumphe* 57 sqq.; Grätz, *Gesch. der Juden* iii, 164; Schürer, i, 300.

[3] Philo, *De legat. ad Cajum* c. 23. For a discussion of the question as to whether these Jews formed the first settlements in Rome *cf. supra*, ch., iii; Vogelstein, *Die Juden in Rom* i, 5-6.

[4] *Cf.* in general the *Megillat Ta'anit* which seems to have been composed during the year when Judaea was made a Roman province. This calendar of victories was, undoubtedly, intended to arouse the spirit of liberty in the hearts of the Jewish people by presenting to their mind former victories such as those of the Maccabees.

independence, along the coast, beyond the Jordan and in Samaria was taken from her and placed under the control of the governor of the Roman province of Syria.[1] The reduced province of Judaea was given to Hyrcanus who received the civic title of Ethnarch, the name applied to his predecessors before they assumed the title of king.[2] The Jews were permitted to manage their own internal affairs and to live according to their own laws.

While on one hand, the Pharisees were grateful to the Romans for upholding the cause of Hyrcanus against Aristobulus, on the other hand, the memory of Pompey's desecration of the Temple served to strengthen their feeling of ill-will towards the Romans. There was soon apparent amongst the Pharisees a spirit of patriotism which owing to Sadducean control had lain dormant for some time. But now every appeal to strike for freedom was met with an immediate response. Hithertofore, the Sadducees stood out as the party strongly opposed to the Romans. This, however, was due to the fact that the political leaders were the aristocratic Sadducees while the Pharisees lacked political influence. Once the Pharisees gained political control, patriotism became for them the popular religion and the impelling force[3] which later found expression in the work of the Zealots.

[1] Cf. Joseph. Antiq. xiv, 4.4; Bell. Jud. i, 7.7.
[2] Cf. loc. cit.; Mommsen, History of Rome iii, 145; Marquardt, Römische Staatsverwaltung i, 405.
[3] Cf. Wellhausen, Israelitische und Jüdische Geschichte, 307-308.

For a few years after Pompey's departure for Rome there was peace in Palestine but there soon arose a number of futile attempts on the part of the Sadducees to restore the Hasmonean rule. As a result of a revolt led by the son of Aristobulus, the proconsul of Syria, Gabinius, made an important change in the government of Palestine for the purpose of destroying, if possible, the spirit of national unity. Hyrcanus was deprived of his political administration and restricted to his priestly functions. The country was divided into five juridical or fiscal districts, each with its own council made up of leading citizens and directly responsible to Rome.[1] Many towns which were old Hellenic centers of influence and had been destroyed by the Jews were ordered to be rebuilt and were re-populated.[2] Although, as Josephus says, "the Jews were now freed from kingly rule, and were governed by an aristocracy,"[3] the new arrangement did not in any way serve to disintegrate the national unity or lessen the importance of Jerusalem as the center of influence. After a brief duration, the political constitution drawn up by Gabinius was set aside by the ordinance of Julius Caesar.[4]

[1] *Cf.* Joseph. *Antiq.* xiv, 5.4; *Bell. Jud.* i, 8.5; Strabo, Geog. xvi, 2.29. Jerusalem, Gazara, Jericho, Amathus and Sepphoris were made the capitals of the five districts, the first three being in Judaea proper; cf. Kühn, *Die städtische und burgerliche Verfassung des römischen Reichs* ii, 365-367; Schürer i, 338-341; Marquardt, *Römische Staatsverwaltung* i, 500 sqq.; Rudorff, *Römische Rechtsgeschichte* ii, 5, 13.
[2] *Cf.* Joseph. *Antiq.* xiv, 5.4.
[3] *Ibid.*
[4] Schürer i, 341.

In consequence of the agreement of the Triumvirate of Caesar, Pompey and Crassus, the latter was sent to Syria as proconsul instead of Gabinius. While Pompey and Gabinius offended the religious sense of the Jews, they left the temple treasures untouched. Crassus, on the other hand, pillaged the Temple at Jerusalem and carried away everything of value that he could find.[1] The Jews were soon relieved from any further rapacity of Crassus for he lost his life in the war against the Parthians. Cassius, the legate of Crassus, led back the remnant of his army to Syria where he was confronted by an insurrection of the Jews occasioned by the robbery committed by Crassus. The leader of the rebels, at the instigation of Antipater, was executed and thirty thousand Jewish warriors were sold into slavery.[2]

Thus, within a period of five years, four insurrections had given expression to the restless spirit of the people. This restlessness was due partly to the provocation of the Romans, themselves, and partly to that spirit of patriotism which was so easily enkindled by some inspiring word of a member of the Hasmonean house.

While the Jews were endeavouring to maintain control in Palestine, the series of civil wars had begun which resulted in transforming Rome from a republic to an empire. These struggles affected, especially,

---

[1] *Cf.* Joseph. *Antiq.* xiv, 7.1; *Bell. Jud.* i, 8.8. According to Josephus, Crassus took away a golden beam worth 10,000 talents, upon the receipt of which he solemnly swore not to touch anything else, 2000 talents in pure gold, other articles of value of 8000 talents.

[2] *Cf.* Joseph. *Antiq.* xiv, 7.3; *Bell. Jud.* i, 8.9.

the provinces which had to bear the heavy expenses incurred by the contesting parties in carrying on their operations.¹ After Pompey and the Senate fled from Rome to Macedonia, Caesar released Aristobulus from prison in order to make use of him against Antipater who had declared for Pompey. The adherents of Pompey, however, succeeded in poisoning Aristobulus and at about the same time his son Alexander was beheaded in the East.² After the defeat of Pompey by Caesar at Pharsalia in 48 B. C., Hyrcanus and his friend Antipater immediately espoused the cause of Caesar³ and proceeded to show their ability to serve him. Upon Caesar's arrival in Alexandria, where he learnt of Pompey's death, Antipater came to his aid with three thousand Jewish troops. He succeeded, moreover, in arousing a general zeal among the petty Syrian and Arabian princes who hastened to help Caesar with a large number of picked troops and by his bravery he contributed materially, in the Egyptian struggles, to the ultimate victory.⁴ For their effective service, Caesar highly rewarded the Jews.

Hyrcanus was confirmed in the high-priesthood which was declared hereditary and he was reinstated in his political position as Ethnarch.⁵ The plea of

---

¹ *Cf.* Schürer i, 342.
² *Cf.* Joseph. *Antiq.* xiv, 7.4; *Bell. Jud.* i, 9.1-2; Dio Cassius xli, 18.
³ *Cf.* Joseph. *Antiq.* xiv, 8.3.
⁴ For the service rendered by Antipater to the cause of Rome, for the period 63-48 B.C., *cf.* Josephus, *Antiq.* xiv, 5.1-2; 6.2-3; 7.3; *Bell. Jud.* i, 8.1, 3, 7, 9. In the decree of Caesar (*Antiq.* xiv, 10.2), the number of Jewish auxiliary troops is given only as 1500.
⁵ Other details with respect to the proceedings of Caesar from docu-

Antigonus, for the recognition of his claims was met by Caesar with an ignominious dismissal. Antipater was made procurator of Judaea,[1] Galilee and Samaria, after being raised to the rank of a Roman citizen and granted immunity from taxation.

Many privileges were granted to the Jews generally and the Jewish State obtained the most favored position which could possibly be granted to a province subject to Rome. In their own country the Jews were permitted to live according to their own laws and customs, and justice could be administered by their own tribunals. The five divisions of Gabinius were abolished and Jerusalem remained the center of the jurisdiction of the land.[2] Religious liberty was

ments given us by Josephus (*Antiq.* xiv, 10.2-10) are so meagre and fragmentary, that in regard to many particulars no definite conclusion can be reached. As Schürer (i, 345) points out, the letter of Caesar to the Sidonians (*Antiq.* xiv, 10, 2), was without question written in the year 47 B.C., and the formal decree of Caesar appointing Hyrcanus was issued in that same year. *Cf.* in regard to these documents, Mendelssohn in Ritschl's *Acta soc. phil.* v (1875), 191-246; Rosenthal, " Die Erlasse Cäsars und die Senatsconsulte im Josephus Alterth. xiv, 10, nach ihrem historischen Inhalte untersucht," *MGWJ* (1879), 176 *sqq.;* 216 *sqq.;* 300 *sqq.;* Mommsen, *The Provinces of the Roman Empire* i, 190-191; Grätz, *Gesch. der Juden* iii, 660-671. For discussion regarding decrees, *cf.* Schürer, *op. cit.* i, 344-348 and notes.

[1] The objection of Morrison (*The Jews Under Roman Rule* 57), to the statement that Antipater was made procurator, is not substantiated by Josephus (*Antiq.* xiv, 8.3; *Bell. Jud.* i, 10.3), Schürer, Grätz, Ewald, and Hausrath among the many historians who support the fact, nor is it proven to be untrue, as Morrison says, by Mommsen in his analysis of the treaties of Josephus. If he were not procurator, it would be unlikely that he would have the power to divide the territory amongst his sons whom he appointed as governors.

[2] *Cf.* Kuhn, *Die städtische und bürgerliche Verfassung des röm. Reichs* ii, 14-41; Mommsen, *The Provinces of the Roman Empire* i, 190; Marquardt, *Römische Staatsverwaltung* i, 69-80.

assured not only at home but also throughout the East.¹ They were exempt from paying the tribute imposed upon them by Pompey, from military service in the legions and relieved from supporting the Roman garrisons.² The Jews were allowed to rebuild the walls of Jerusalem.³ The important sea-port of Joppa, "which the Jews had originally, when they made a league of friendship with the Romans,"⁴ was made over to them. It was also decreed, that the villages in the great plain which they had formerly possessed should be restored to them. Moreover, it was ordained that "the Jews retain those places, lands, and farm-steads, which belonged to the kings of Syria and Phoenicia, the allies of the Romans, and which they had bestowed on them as their free gift."⁵ The privileges conferred by Caesar were not limited to Palestine. The Jews of Alexandria had the privilege of citizenship bestowed upon them and were permitted to be governed by a prince of their own.⁶ The Jews of Asia Minor were assured the undisturbed exercise of their religion.⁷

Although Antipater had aided the Jews consider-

¹ *Cf.* Joseph. *Antiq.* xiv, 10.8, 20-24.
² *Cf.* Joseph. *Antiq.* xiv, 10.5, 6.
³ *Cf.* Joseph. *Antiq.* xiv, 8.5; Mommsen, *op. cit.*, i, 190-191.
⁴ Joseph. *Antiq.* xiv, 10.6.
⁵ *Ibid.* Who the "kings of Syria and Phoenicia, the allies of the Romans" were, cannot be definitely ascertained. Possibly, the statement refers to the princes to whom Pompey had given Jewish lands. As Schürer (i, 347, note 25) suggests, this obscurity may be due, like others, to the corrupt text.
⁶ Schürer i, 348; iii, 80; Grätz, *Gesch. der Juden* iii, 215; *cf.* Joseph. *Bell. Jud.* ii, 18.7.
⁷ *Cf.* Joseph. *Antiq.* xiv, 10.8, 20-24.

ably in securing these concessions, and endeavoured to govern the province under the protection and according to the will of Rome, the adroit and active diplomatist received but little from the people in Judaea. The Jewish aristocracy realized that Hyrcanus was but a tool in the hands of the Idumaean who endeavoured to strengthen his control of the reins of government by appointing his two sons, Phasael and Herod, governors, the one in Jerusalem and the other in Galilee.[1]

The assassination of Caesar involved Palestine in political confusion and made that country again the center of rivalries, intrigues and war. When the republicans gained the upper hand in the East, Antipater was the first to submit to the stronger power, and immediately set to work to gain the good will of Cassius who became master of Syria. In order to raise money for the support of his army, Cassius imposed heavy taxes upon the cities and provinces and the inhabitants of those places that were unable to contribute their share were sold as slaves.[2] By furnishing, immediately, the quota falling upon Galilee, of the fine of seven hundred talents imposed upon Palestine, Herod gained the reappointment of the governorship of Coele-Syria and the promise of the kinship of Judaea.[3]

In the meantime the leaders of the republican party were defeated at Phillipi and all Asia fell into

[1] Cf. Joseph. *Antiq.* xiv, 9.2; *Bell. Jud.* i, 10.4.
[2] Cf. Joseph. *Antiq.* xiv, 11.2; *Bell. Jud.* i, 1-2.
[3] Cf. Joseph. *Antiq.* xiv, 11.4; *Bell. Jud.* i, 11-4.

the hands of Antony who was soon confronted by deputations from opposing parties at Jerusalem. Upon the request of one of these embassies, Antony liberated the Jews sold into slavery by Cassius and restored the places in Galilee that had been conquered by the Tyrians.[1] Upon his return to Rome, Antony cordially welcomed his Jewish ally Herod[2] who soon succeeded in gaining the favor of Octavius and having himself declared king of Judaea by a formal meeting of the Senate. In accordance with the custom of Roman officials on their entrance upon office, Herod offered sacrifice in the temple of Jupiter on the Capitol and Antony, to celebrate the event, held a banquet in honor of the Jewish king.[3] Within a short time Herod succeeded in having the last of the Hasmonean rulers executed at the command of a Roman general[4] and with no apparent obstacles to

[1] *Cf.* Joseph. *Antiq.* xiv, 12.1-2; *Bell. Jud.* i, 12.3. For the letter of Antony to Hyrcanus and two letters to the Tyrians, *cf. Antiq.* xiv, 12.3-5. One of the letters to the Tyrians refers expressly to the restoration of the conquered places; the other (*Antiq.* xiv, 12.5) refers to the emancipation of Jewish slaves. Similar letters were also sent to the cities of Sidon, Antioch, and Aradus (*Antiq.* xiv, 12.6). In reference to these documents *cf.* Mendelssohn in Ritschl's *Act. soc. phil.* v (1875), 254-263; Schürer i, 352.

[2] *Cf.* Joseph. *Antiq.* xiv, 14.1-3; *Bell Jud.* i, 14.1-3.

[3] *Cf.* Joseph. *Antiq.* xiv, 14.4-5.

[4] This was the first time that a king was put to death by the stroke of a Roman lictor. *Cf. Antiq.* xiv, 16.4; xv, 1.2, where Josephus also quotes a passage from the historical work of Strabo, which is now lost; *Bell. Jud.* i, 18.3; Dio Cassius xlix, 22; Plutarch, *Antony* 36; *cf.* Salvador, *Gesch. der Römerherrschaft im Judas und der Zerstörung Jerusalems* i, 300, who deplores the want of indignation in Josephus. The latter speaks of the death of Antigonus as a just reward for his cowardice and timidity.

overcome, he became the head of a city in ruins[1] and the king of a people that hated him.[2]

The two unvarying principles of Herod's policy in his government were the safeguarding of his own power and the strengthening of the friendship with the Romans.[3] The impulse of his every action arose from one or the other of these guiding principles. He was keen enough to realize the fact that under the circumstances of the time nothing could be gained except through the favour and by the aid of the Romans to whom he owed his position in Palestine.[4] The Romans, on the other hand, were aware of the fact that the military energy and fidelity of Herod and his successors constituted the best available fortress of the eastern frontier of their empire which was so easily accessible to the Arabs and Parthians.

The reorganization of a kingdom in which for the last thirty years all the various powers had been in confusion, and for the most part in open conflict with one another, was no easy task.[5] Herod was soon confronted with the various adversaries at whose expense he had won the crown, but he succeeded, eventually, in establishing the authority of his government. He was considerate towards the Jews from the point of view of their religious demands

---

[1] *Cf.* Joseph. *Antiq.* xiv, 15.3; *Bell. Jud.* i, 15.4

[2] *Cf.* Joseph. *Antiq.* xvii, 6.5; *Bell. Jud.* i, 33.6.

[3] *Cf.* Schürer i, 376; Riggs, *A Hist. of the Jewish People* 180; Muirhead, *The Times of Christ* 15.

[4] *Cf.* Schürer, *op. cit.*

[5] *Cf.* Hausrath, *Neutestamentl. Zeitgesch.* i, 211.

for he realized that he could only win over his people by respecting their Law. Yet here there was an apparent contradiction, for this very Law condemned his position. He endeavoured to show favour towards the Rabbis, but their schools were his determined adversaries.[1] Despite the interest which Herod manifested in his country, despite his influence with the Romans which assured the religious liberties of the people, he could find love and fidelity only in Idumaea and Samaria but not in Judaea. In the latter place he was only tolerated with deep aversion for in Herod the Judaeans saw not so much the man upon whom the guilt of blood rested, but the Idumaean, the half-Jew, the foreigner.[2] This toleration was based to a certain extent upon what was regarded as a judgment of God that a foreigner should hold dominion over them, a judgment which found expression in the words of Sameas.[3]

After the decisive battle of Actium and the consequent suicides of Antony and Cleopatra,[4] Herod promptly espoused the cause of Augustus.[5] Before

[1] *Ibid.*

[2] *Cf.* Joseph. *Antiq.* xiv, 15.2; xiv, 1.3; *Bell. Jud.* i, 6.2; Justin Martyr, *Dialogue with Trypho* c. 52; Sulpicius Severus *Hist. sacra* ii, 27; Julius Africanus, *Epist. ad Aristidem*, in Eusebius, *Hist. Eccles.* i, 7.11.

[3] *Cf.* Joseph. *Antiq.* xiv, 9.4; *cf.* also xv, 1.1, and xv, 10.4, where Josephus refers again to Sameas in conjunction with Pollion (Abtalion or Ptollion). Since, as it has been pointed out (Ginzberg "Abtalion," *Jew. Ency.* i, 136), the Pollion referred to in *Antiq.* xv, 10.4, is probably Hillel, Josephus may have had Shammai in mind when he wrote Sameas.

[4] *Cf.* Joseph. *Antiq.* xv, 6.7; Plutarch, *Antony* 74 *sqq.;* Dio Cassius li, 9.14; Suetonius, *Octavianus*, xvii; Horace *Odes*, i, 87.

[5] *Cf.* Joseph. *Antiq.* xv, 6.7; *Bell. Jud.* i, 20.2; Dio Cassius li, 7.

seeking an audience with Augustus,[1] Herod contrived to have the aged Hyrcanus murdered lest, during his absence, he might become an aspirant for the crown and the object of an uprising.[2] In a long address Herod sought the good-will of Augustus. "Antony," he declared, "adopted a counsel more fatal to himself, more advantageous to you. If, then, attachment to Antony be a crime, I plead guilty; but if, having seen how steady and faithful I am in my friendships, you determine to bind me to your fortunes by gratitude, depend on the same firmness and fidelity."[3]

Augustus, aside from any personal considerations, was glad to accept the allegiance of Herod. The former realized the advantage of having a staunch and cautious friend of the Romans between Egypt, Arabia and Syria, whose rulers were always ready to conspire with the Parthians.[4] Herod was confirmed in his royal rank and obtained from the Senate a decree making his kingship secure. Augustus restored to the king the territory of Jericho, with all the surrounding districts which had been taken from him by Cleopatra, and, in addition, the maritime towns of Gaza, Anthedon, Joppa, and Straton's tower,

---

[1] Suetonius, *Octav.* xvii.

[2] *Cf.* Joseph. *Antiq.* xv, 6.1-4; *Bell. Jud.* i, 22.1. Herod endeavoured to give as a motive the attempt of Hyrcanus to conspire with the Arabian king. This cause is recorded in Herod's journals; contemporary writers have expressly indicated his innocence; *cf.* Joseph, *loc. cit.* xv, 6.3; Müller, *Frag. hist. graec,* iii, 350, for *Commentaries of Herod. Cf.* also Schürer i, 384.

[3] Joseph, *Antiq.* xv, 5.4.

[4] *Cf.* Hausrath, *Neutestamentl. Zeitgesch.* i, 230.

which Antony had bestowed upon Cleopatra. Samaria, which hitherto Herod had administered in the name of the Syrian proconsul, was incorporated with his kingdom. Gadara and Hippos, with the adjoining district of the Decapolis, fell to him at the same time, "so that the territories of the Maccabean crown were once more united."[1] The king was also presented with the body-guard of Cleopatra, consisting of four hundred Gauls.[2] Herod as a mark of gratitude made elaborate preparations for the march of the Romans through Syria and himself accompanied the emperor as far as Antioch.[3]

Although Herod had met with great success in his political relations with Rome, upon his return to his own kingdom he found in his household confusion and strife.[4] By a series of executions he was able to maintain his position but he still had to overcome, if possible, the great opposition of his subjects. This opposition was due primarily to the fact that he was an Idumean, a foreigner, and to the efforts on the part of the Roman vassal king to Hellenize his realm. In his effort to imitate his imperial master and establish in Judaea an Augustan age of civilization, Herod introduced various foreign practices. The Jews regarded this work as a deliberate attempt to estrange them from the customs of their fathers.

The wrath of the people was especially enkindled by the erection of pagan temples, dedicated to

---
[1] Joseph. *Antiq.* xv, 6.5-7; cf. *Bell. Jud.* i, 20.1-3.
[2] *Cf.* Hausrath, *Neutestamentl. Zeitgesch.* i, 231.
[3] *Cf.* Joseph. *Antiq.* 7.4; cf. xv, 6.5; 7.1-2.
[4] *Cf.* Joseph. *Antiq.* xv, 7.9-10.

Caesar, for the purpose of celebrating the emperor-cultus.[1] In order to hold the festal games[2] in honor of Augustus, Herod built amphitheatres and introduced Roman spectacles, prize-fights, gladiatorial contests, combats of animals, the very things for which "the Maccabees had once drawn the sword against the Syrians."[3] These games were held every five years, at Caesarea[4] and Damascus,[5] where were erected amphitheatres and gymnasiums. To the pious the very style of the architecture of the amphitheatres in which they beheld with grief, human life fall a sacrifice in the struggles with wild beasts,[6] expressed the contempt for the Law.

The theatres built within the holy city was another source of indignation. In the Roman trophies and eagles, displayed in the theatres, the Jews recognized the introduction of Roman deities.[7] Plays were unfamiliar to the Jewish people and as there were no Hebrew dramas, the contents of these plays were

[1] *Cf.* Suetonius, *Octavianus* 59-60.

[2] These were the Actian games held every five years in remembrance of Augustus' victory over his rival Antony. *Cf.* Suetonius, *op. cit.* 59; Dio Cassius, li, 1. Schürer's statement that the games were held every four years (i, 387) is not supported by any other authority. There is a vague, legendary, reference to these games in the *Talmud., cf. Abodah Zarah* 116.

[3] *Cf.* Hausrath, *Neutestamentl. Zeitgesch.* i, 236.

[4] *Cf.* Joseph. *Antiq.* xv, 9.6; *Bell. Jud.* i, 21.8; *cf. Corp. Inscr. Graec.* p. 158.

[5] For coins upon which are mentioned the games in honor of the emperor, held there *cf.* De Sauley, *Étude chronologique de la vie et des monnaies des rois juifs, Agrippa I et Agrippa II,* 42 sqq.

[6] *Cf.* Hausrath, *op. cit.* i, 236.

[7] *Cf.* Joseph, *Antiq.* xv, 8.2.

readily regarded as blasphemous.[1] Although Herod endeavoured to convince the discontented members of the Sanhedrin that there was nothing unlawful in the decorations which they regarded as offensive, by inviting them to examine them in person in the theatre, the effort was of no avail. The scribes continued to proclaim the fact that God would in time send punishments as retribution for such abominations. The teachings of the pious aroused ten zealots who conspired to put Herod to death in the theatre. The conspiracy was soon discovered and resulted only in the death of all who took part in the attempt.[2]

Along the military roads Herod placed many Roman monuments. Palaces, towns, cities and public edifices received Roman names. The old Samaria was reconstructed and received the name of Sebaste,[3] and Straton's Tower became Caesarea. Many cities were built and named in honor of members of his family.[4] Beyond the limits of Palestine the architectural works gave expression to the liberality of Herod. In Rhodes, Nicopolis, Chios, Tyre and even Athens and Lacedaemonia, Herod aided in the erection of public edifices.[5] In the non-Jewish cities

[1] *Cf.* Hausrath, *Neutestamentl. Zeitgesch.* i, 236.
[2] *Cf.* Joseph. *Antiq.* xv, 8.2.
[3] *Cf.* Joseph. *Antiq.* xv, 8.5; *Bell. Jud.* i, 21.2.
[4] Antipatris for his father, Phasaelis for his brother. *Cf.* Joseph. *Antiq.* xvi, 5.2; *Bell. Jud.* i, 21.9.
[5] On the buildings of Herod, *cf.* Hirt, "Ueber die Baue Herodes des Grossen überhaupt, und über seinen Tempelbau zu Jerusalem insbesondere," *Abhandlungen der. histor. philolog. Klasse der Berliner Akademie aus den Jahren,* 1816-1817, pt. iv, pp. 1-24; van der Chijs, *de Herode Magno* 55-57; Schürer i, 387-395.

of his territory and in the province of Syria, the king erected numerous temples such as he built in honor of Caesar and embellished them with beautiful statuary.[1] The reconstructed cities of Sebaste and Caesarea contained each a temple of Augustus.[2] Parks and magnificent gardens were laid out about the palace of the king at Jerusalem. Walks and water canals, fountains decorated with iron works of art near which stood dovecots with tamed pigeons, adorned the surroundings of the palace.[3] It is only in reference to Herod's fondness for pigeon-breeding that his name appears in the *Mishnah*.[4]

To maintain his position as the patron of paganism and to introduce western methods into his realm, Herod employed foreign mercenaries from Galatia, Germany and Thrace and in his court he placed foreign retainers who could satisfy the demands of an Augustan age in Judaea. Jerusalem became the focal point of the social and literary interest of a foreign culture. In order that he might appear to the Graeco-Roman world as a patron of culture, Herod surrounded himself with Greek orators, sophists, historians and artists. Notable members of this coterie were the two brothers Ptolemaeus and Nicholas of Damascus. The former was a trusted councillor of

[1] *Cf.* Joseph. *Antiq.* xv, 9.5; *Bell. Jud.* i, 21.4.

[2] A description and sketch of the ruins of a temple of the Herodian era is given by C. de Vogüé in his *Syrie centrale, architecture civile et religieuse,* i pl. 2 et 3; ii, 31-33; *cf.* Le Bas and Waddington, *Inscriptions Grecques et Latines,* t. iii, n. 2364.

[3] *Cf.* Joseph. *Bell. Jud.* v, 4.4.

[4] *Cf.* Shabbath xxiv, 3; *Chullin* xii, 1.

the kings in state affairs. The talent of Nicholas, a man of wide and varied scholarship, a naturalist,[1] poet,[2] philosopher, and historian[3] lent an air of marked intellectual splendour to the court of Herod.[4] Nicholas was, moreover, a skilled lawyer[5] and orator and to him was entrusted all important diplomatic missions. He was the chief agent of Herod in his relations with Augustus and Roman officials. He had pleaded for the Asiatic Jews against the Hellenistic cities before Agrippa, and it was at that time that he made that collection of Roman edicts which constituted the main source for Josephus' records.[6] Beside such counsellors as Nicholas and Ptolemaeus there were Hellenic syncophants of a less worthy character,[7] who only deepened the lack of harmony which existed between the court and the aims and interests of the Jewish people.

Conscious of the fact that his material success and the favor shown him by his imperial master did not temper the hatred of his subjects and anxious, on the other hand, to be regarded by the Romans as a popular sovereign, Herod devolved upon a new

[1] *Cf.* Strabo, *Geogr.* xv, 1. Concerning his discovery of a new species of date, *cf.* Pliny, *Nat. Hist.* xiii, 9.4; Athenaeus, *The Deipnosophists* xiv, 22.

[2] *Cf.* Suidas, *Lexicon Graece et Latine* iii, 623.

[3] He wrote a history of the world in 144 books which seems to have concluded with a life of Augustus. *Cf. Antiq.* xii, 3.2; Athenaeus vi, 249; Müller's *Fragm. Hist. Graec.* iii, 356.

[4] *Cf.* Hausrath, *Neutestamentl. Zeitgesch.* i, 240-241.

[5] *Cf.* Hild, *REJ* xi, 26.

[6] Joseph. *Antiq.* xv-xvii; *cf.* Niese, " Bemerkungen über die Urkunden bei Josephus," *Hermes* xi, 478.

[7] *Cf.* Joseph. *Antiq,* xvii, 9.4.

scheme. He suddenly called an assembly of the people and proposed to them the building of a new Temple. Various motives have been assigned to Herod's attempt to rebuild the Temple. According to a somewhat doubtful statement in the *Talmud*, Rabbi Baba Ben Buta had advised Herod to atone for his deeds of violence towards the teachers, whom he had persecuted, by undertaking a work of this kind.[1] Herod was, undoubtedly, actuated by a desire to ingratiate himself with his people to whom, according to Josephus, he made the following address:

I think I need not speak to you, fellow countrymen, about such other works as I have done since I came to the kingdom, although I may say they have been performed in such a manner as to bring more security to you than glory to myself: for I have neither been negligent in the most difficult times about what tended to ease your necessities, nor have the buildings I have erected been so much to preserve me as yourselves from injuries; and I imagine that, with God's assistance, I have advanced the nation of the Jews to a degree of prosperity which they never had before. And as for the particular edifices belonging to your own country, and your own cities . . . we have erected and greatly adorned, and so augmented the dignity of your nation, it seems a needless task to enumerate them to you. But as to the undertaking which I have a mind to set about at present, and which will be a work of the greatest piety and excellence in our power. . . . Our fathers, . . . when they returned from Babylon, built this Temple to Almighty God, yet, does it want sixty cubits in height compared with the first Temple which Solomon built. But let no one condemn our fathers for negligence or want of piety

---

[1] *Baba Batra* 36; *Bamidbar-Rabba* 12; *cf.* Derenbourg, *Histoire de la Palestine* 152.

herein. . . . But since I am now, by God's will, your governor, and have had peace a long time, and have gained great riches, and large revenues, and, what is the principal thing of all, am at amity with and favourably regarded by the Romans, who, if I may so say, are the rulers of the whole world, I will do my endeavour to correct that imperfection which has arisen from necessity and the slavery which we were under formerly, and to make a thankful return in the most pious manner to God, for the blessings I have received from him in giving me this kingdom, by rendering His Temple as complete as I am able.[1]

Herod's proposition was met with a storm of indignation, for the people feared that the king's only purpose was the destruction of the old Temple and by an endless protraction of the work he would deprive them entirely of their sanctuary. Herod allayed their fears by promising them that the old Temple would remain standing until all the workmen with their material were at hand ready to construct the new one. The Temple service was carried on at the same time that the new Temple was being constructed. Herod punctiliously observed the law which forbade a foreigner entering the inner courts.[2] When the sanctuary was nearly completed, Herod appointed the anniversary of his accession as the day of consecration and henceforth this day was to be celebrated as a Jewish festival.[3] With imposing ritual and amid great rejoicing the new Temple was dedicated to the worship of God.[4]

[1] Joseph. *Antiq.* xv, 11.1; *cf.* Gfrörer, *Geschichte des Urchristenthum* i, 46 *sqq.*
[2] *Cf.* Joseph. *Antiq.* xv, 11.5.
[3] *Loc. cit.* 11.7; *cf.* Persius, *Sat.* v. 180.
[4] *Cf.* Joseph. *Antiq.* xv, 11.2, 6.

Scarcely had the glamour of the dedication passed away when Herod again aroused the consternation of the pious Jews by placing a large golden eagle, the symbol of Roman power, above the principal entrance of the new Temple, thus transgressing the commandments of the Mosaic Code.[1] Their indignation was not tempered by the fact that Herod expected a visitor from Rome, probably, Agrippa.[2] An insurrection eventually followed in which the eagle was destroyed and the devotees who tore it down lost their lives.[3] The tension in the relations between the people and the king was increased when the latter published a law by which thieves who had been convicted were to be sold abroad as slaves.[4] Such a proceeding, the teachers of the law declared, was contrary to natural feelings as well as the dictates of the Law.[5]

Herod, moreover, was at variance with the people in regard to the matter of the priesthood. At the very beginning of his reign he was called upon to settle the question of filling the office of high-priest. Hitherto the office of high-priest and of prince had been held by the same person. Unable to hold the position of high-priesthood himself and unwilling to appoint an illustrious person who might become

[1] Joseph. *Antiq.* xvii, 6.2.
[2] *Cf.* Hausrath, *Neutestamentl. Zeitgesch.* i, 252.
[3] *Cf.* Joseph. *Antiq.* xvii, 6.1-4; Mommsen, *Provinces of the Roman Empire* ii, 197.
[4] *Cf.* Joseph. *Antiq.* xvi, 1.1; *cf.* Kahn *L'Esclavage selon la Bible et le Talmud, pt. ii* of *Rapport sur la situation morale du Séminaire Israélite* 73.
[5] *Cf. Exodus* xxii, 3; *Kiddushin* 18a.

his political rival, Herod sent for an obscure priest from Babylon and conferred the high-priesthood upon him.[1] The bestowing of the dignity of high-priesthood upon a foreigner aroused the indignation of the people and even the members of Herod's own family. Owing to the strong oppostion exerted, Herod finally appointed Aristobulus, the grandson of Hyrcanus, to the office.[2] After the death of this youthful incumbent of the office of high-priesthood, other priests were appointed by Herod, but, contrary to what had been the usual custom, the dignity was no longer held for life. This king's example was followed by his successor and subsequently by the Romans. The frequent changing of the high-priests brought about a noted decrease in their power. They had now to hold their office by the grace of the king, to discharge their duties in accordance with his wishes, and their influence could only be exercised within limits set by their ruler.[3]

A strong reaction against the unfavorable tendencies of Herod was being exerted, at this time, by the schools that were paying increased attention to the study of the Torah and the teachers who were strengthening their influence upon the people. Both Hillel and Shammai fostered the development of Jewish culture which, necessarily, was in conflict with Roman or pagan culture. While Hillel advo-

---

[1] *Cf.* Joseph. *Antiq.* xv, 2.4.
[2] Joseph. *op. cit.* xv, 3.1.
[3] *Cf.* the strict censure of the Talmud on this question and the sarcastic remarks concerning high-priests buying offices from the Roman government; *Yoma* 9a.

cated the kind treatment of the pagans and while a broad, humanitarian spirit finds expression in his numerous sayings[1] and anecdotes, yet he made strenuous efforts to offset the attempt of Herod to Hellenize his realm. The various principles advocated by Hillel and Shammai, who continually urged a strict interpretation of the Law, tended only to intensify the conflict between the dictates of the Jewish conception of life and the demands of the Roman authorities.

Despite the opposition of the teachers of the Law and the apparent breach between himself and the people, Herod did not relax his efforts to keep them under his control. He strengthened the defences of Jerusalem which served not only to protect the capital but, as Josephus says, to prevent any possible insurrections.[2] For the same purpose he established a fortress in Samaria. Realizing the hatred of the people for their king, Herod endeavoured to keep order and curb disaffections by maintaining a system of espionage. It was the function of the net-work of spies to inform the king of all seditious opinions or adverse criticisms upon his government and to ascertain the true state of affairs, the king would himself, disguised, mingle with the people at night.[3] To further safeguard himself against conspiracies, all large gatherings of the people were forbidden. Force was the instrument of submission and authority.[4]

[1] *Cf.*, for instance, *Shabbat* 31a; *Aboth* ii, 4; *Tosefta Berakoth* ii; *cf.* also Chwolson, *Das letzte Passamahl Christi* 74-75.
[2] *Antiq.* xv, 8.5.
[3] *Cf.* Joseph. *Antiq.* xv, 10.4. [4] *Ibid.*

Despite the harsh methods that Herod used in exercising control, there is no doubt that at the same time he promoted the prosperity of his country and the welfare of his subjects. To commend himself to the people he remitted at one time a third[1] of the taxes and at another time a fourth.[2] With unabating zeal he endeavoured to provide relief from the dire distress caused by a famine. To obtain food and clothing for the poor and to supply them with seed-corn Herod sold his furniture and table-plate. As a result of his friendship with Petronius, the procurator of Egypt, the king readily obtained a contract for a supply of corn.[3]

In order to develop trade, new commercial centers were established and cities that were destroyed during the wars were rebuilt.[4] To facilitate commercial relations between Palestine and Egypt, Herod constructed the commodius harbor of Caesarea where ships were secured from the storms, while receiving their cargoes, by a powerful breakwater on which were erected dwellings for the seamen. This town became the chief emporium of southern Syria.[5]

Herod strengthened his Arabian frontiers by establishing a chain of castles and watch towers from which warnings of the movements of the enemy

[1] Joseph. *Antiq.* xv, 10.4.
[2] *Cf.* Joseph. *Antiq.* xvi, 2.5; Marquardt, *Römische Staatsverwaltung* i, 408.
[3] *Cf.* Joseph, *Antiq.* xv, 9.1-2.
[4] *Cf.* Joseph. *Antiq.* xv, 8; 5; *Bell. Jud.* i, 21.2; Strabo, *Geog.* xvi.
[5] *Cf.* Joseph. *Antiq.* xv, 9.6; xvi, 5.1; *Bell. Jud.* i, 21. 5-8; Pliny, *Hist. Nat.* v, 13.69.

could be dispatched to the king.¹ He colonized the districts west of the lake of Gennesaret hitherto traversed only by wandering robber tribes.²

Herod had ingratiated himself with the emperor by giving aid to an expedition sent out under the auspices of Augustus to find the shortest route between Upper Egypt and Arabia.³ Augustus soon determined not to undertake any future oriental transaction without consulting his worthy vassal whom he sought to reward. When Herod sent his two sons to Rome to be educated and expressed his desire to have them come into touch with the members of the Imperial court, Augustus found an opportunity to show favor towards the Jewish king. The emperor personally supervised the education of the youths and had them placed at the Tuscan villa of Asinius Pollio under the care of this learned man and the pedagogue Genellus.⁴ As a further reward for quelling disturbances in the East, Herod obtained from the emperor an additional tract of land so that at this time the vassal's territory extended from Lebanon to Damascus and southward to Mount Alsadamus, "a territory which no Jewish king before had ever possessed"⁵ and in consequence of which he became "the most powerful sovereign of Asia on this side of the Euphrates."⁶

---
¹ *Cf.* Joseph. *Bell Jud.* vii, 6.2; i, 21; 2; Strabo, *Geogr.* 16.2.

² *Cf.* Joseph. *Antiq.* xvi, 9.2 (colony of 3000 Idumeans); *Antiq.* xvii, 2.1-3 (colony of Babylonian Jews).

³ *Cf.* Joseph. *Antiq.* xv, 9; 3; Dio Cassius liii, 29; Strabo xvi, 4.

⁴ *Cf.* Joseph. *Antiq.* xvi, 1.2; Pliny, *Hist. Nat.* vii, 30; xxxv, 2; xxxvi, 5.

⁵ Hausrath, *Neutestamentl. Zeitgesch.* i, 247.   ⁶ *Ibid.*

With Agrippa, the trusted friend and son-in-law of Augustus, Herod was also on friendly terms. The Jewish vassal king had paid Agrippa a visit and the latter at a later period went to Judaea, where he offered a hecatomb in the temple at Jerusalem. The people, enthusiastic over the Roman who showed such a friendly attitude towards the Jews, followed him to his ship strewing flowers along his path and expressing great admiration at his piety.[1] Herod's relations with Augustus and Agrippa were so intimate and the vassal king had attained such a degree of felicity that as Josephus puts it, "whereas there were but two men that governed the Roman empire, first Augustus, and then Agrippa, who was Augustus' principal favourite, Augustus preferred no one to Herod after Agrippa; and Agrippa made no one his greater friend than Herod except Augustus."[2]

Although Herod succeeded in gaining the admiration and even affection of the Romans by his efforts to promote material prosperity in Palestine, his munificence, his introduction of pagan practices and his furtherance of culture,[3] his own people felt nothing but aversion for him.[4] He had succeeded to a certain degree in Hellenizing his realm, but only at the expense of strengthening the national pre-

[1] *Cf.* Joseph. *Antiq.* xvi, 2.1; Philo, *Legat. ad Cajum* sec. 37; Strabo xvi, 2.

[2] *Antiq.* xv, 103; *cf. Bell. Jud.* i, 20.4; *cf.* Weiss, *Die römischen Kaiser in ihrem verhaltnisse zu Juden und Christen*, 8.

[3] Joseph. *Antiq.* xix, 7.3. On the humanistic studies of Herod under the direction of Nicolaus of Damascus, *cf.* " Nicolaus Damascenus " in Müller *Fragm. Hist. Graec.* iii, 350 *sqq.*

[4] *Cf.* Grätz. *Gesch. der Juden* iii, 223.

judices. It was through the generosity of Herod that many benefits were conferred upon the Jews outside of Palestine; it was because of the efforts of this same king that the proconsuls of the Empire refrained from oppressing the Jews lest they incur the wrath of their imperial master's favourite vassal.[1] Herod was well aware that the underlying cause for the apparent discontent and hatred of himself was the fact that he was an Idumaean. The king had burnt the archives of Jerusalem where the genealogies were kept and pretended to be a member of a noted family of Babylonian Jews, but this act did not suffice to erase from the minds of the people the designated term of Hasmonaean slave.[2]

Added to this irretrievable hatred of the people, were the intrigues of Herod's household which embittered the last days of the king. Every member of the royal family seemed to be involved in the network of treachery and suspicion. His own sons conspired against him and though Augustus endeavoured through Nicolaus Damascus to bring about harmony in the family his efforts were in vain.[3] Not content with the execution of his two sons, upon the approach of death, Herod ordered the most distinguished men of Judaea to be brought to Jericho to be imprisoned in the great public

[1] *Cf.* Joseph. *Antiq.* xv, 9.1.
[2] Derenbourg, *Histoire de la Palestine,* 154.
[3] *Cf.* Joseph. *Antiq.* xvi, 10.5-7; 11.1-7; *Bell Jud.* i, 27.1-6. Augustus made the remark that "he would rather be Herod's swine than his son." ("*Melius est Herodis porcus esse, quam filius,*" Macrobius *Saturnius* ii, 4.)

arena that after his own demise they should all be massacred, so that there might be universal mourning at his funeral. The order was never carried out and Herod died unlamented.[1]

The death of Herod was the signal for an insurrection and within a short time the whole of Palestine with the exception of Samaria was in open rebellion. The surviving sons of Herod each sought to have his claim to the throne acknowledged by Augustus.[2] While the decision was pending the emperor sent Sabinus to Judaea to look after affairs there. The procurator was aided by Varus the Syrian proconsul.[3] The latter put down the revolt with an iron hand. Several towns which were in the rebellious districts were destroyed, many Jews were sold as slaves, and as a warning to the rebels, two thousand of them were crucified.[4] A large embassy of Jews was sent from Jerusalem to Augustus, which was supported by the eight thousand Jews then living in Rome, to petition the emperor to deliver them from the family of Herod, and to declare Judaea to be a Roman province united with Syria. Their wish at this time, however, was not fulfilled[5] for finally Augustus divided up the territory in accordance with the last will of Herod. Archelaus was named not king but ethnarch of Judaea; Antipas,

[1] *Cf.* Grätz, *Gesch. der Juden*, iii, 245.
[2] *Cf.* Joseph. *Antiq.* xvii, 9.3-7; *Bell. Jud.* ii, 2.1-7.
[3] Talmudic sources refer to the war under Varus; *cf. Shabbat.* 15a; *Aboda-Sara* 8b; *cf.* also *Seder Olam* (end).
[4] *Cf.* Joseph. *Antiq.* xvii, 10.1-11.1; *Bell. Jud.* ii, 3.1-5.3.
[5] *Cf.* Joseph. *Antiq.* xvii, 11.1-3; *Bell. Jud.* ii, 6.1-2.

tetrarch of Galilee and Peraea; and Philip, tetrarch of the north eastern districts, Trachonitis, Panas, Gaulanitis and Batanaea.[1]

For a brief period each of the three divisions of Herod's territory had its own history.[2] Philip (4-34 A. D.) was regarded with especial favour not only by his own family, but also by the Roman officials.[3] That he was a steadfast friend of the Romans and laid great value upon the favour of the emperor is emphasized by the fact that to the two cities that he built he gave the names of Caesarea[4] and Julias[5] and had the images of Augustus and Tiberius impressed upon his coins. This was the first time that any likeness was engraven on the coins of a Jewish prince.[6] The four pillars on the coins represent the temple of Augustus at Paneas.[7] Our information regarding the character of Philip's reign is derived almost entirely from the reference

[1] *Cf.* Joseph. *Antiq.* xvii, 11.4-5; *cf.* Bohn, *Qua condicione juris reges socii populi Romani fuerint* 9-11; Niese, "Galatien und seine Tetrarchen," *Rhein. Museum,* xxxviii (1883), 583-600.

[2] Brann, *Die Söhne des Herodes* (reprint from the *MGWJ* 1873; pp. 241-256), pp. 77-78.

[3] Hausrath, *Neutestamentl. Zeitgesch.* i, 284; Brann, *op. cit.* 77-87.

[4] To distinguish it from the well-known Caesarea by the sea it was called Ceasarea Philippi; *cf.* Matt. xvi, 13; Mark viii, 27.

[5] *Cf.* Joseph. *Antiq.* xviii, 2.1; *Bell. Jud.* ii, 9.1

[6] This may perhaps be accounted for by the fact that Philip's domain was predominantly pagan. *Cf.* Madden, *Hist. of Jewish Coinage* 100-102; *Coins of the Jews* 123-127; De Saulcy, "Notes sur les monnaies dé Philippe le tétrarque," *Annuaire de la Société francaise de Numismatique et d'Archéologie* iii (1868-1873), pp. 262-265; *cf.* also i, fasc. 3, 1879; p. 181 *sqq.;* Bohn, *Qua condicione juris reges socii populi Romani fuerint* 45-49; Schürer i, 429.

[7] *Cf.* Joseph. *Antiq.* xv, 10.3; *Bell. Jud.* i, 21.3.

of Josephus to his discovery and proof that the supposed sources of the Jordan at Paneas and the lake Phiala[1] were connected, and the statements which the Jewish historian makes in speaking of Philip's death: "He had shown himself a person of moderation and quietness in his rule. He always lived in the country which was subject to him, and used to make his progresses with a few chosen friends; his tribunal also, on which he sat in judgment, followed him in his progresses, and when any one met him who wanted his assistance, he made no delay, but had his tribunal set down immediately, wherever he happened to be, and sat down upon it, and heard the case; and ordered the guilty that were convicted to be punished, and absolved those that were accused unjustly."[2]

Herod Antipas,[3] was anxious to keep up his relations with Rome where he had been educated, but he met with less favor from Augustus than from Tiberius.[4] Like his father, he had a great desire for magnificent buildings. To satisfy this desire, he erected the beautiful capital of Tiberias a place that he had great difficulty in populating. As Josephus points out,[5] Herod "knew that to colonize this place was to transgress the ancient

[1] *Cf. Bell. Jud.* iii, 10.7. Later geographers questioned the correctness of this observation. *Cf.* Guérin, *Galilee* ii, 329-331; Robinson, *Later Biblical Researches* 400.
[2] Joseph. *Antiq.* xviii, 4.6.
[3] *Cf. Luke* xiii, 32; Brann, *Die Söhne des Herodes*, 17-76.
[4] *Cf.* Joseph. *Antiq.* xvii, 1; 3; xviii, 5. 1; 7.1, 2.
[5] *Antiq.* xviii, 2.3; *cf.* Pliny, *Hist. Nat.* v, 15.

Jewish laws, because many sepulchres there had to be taken away to make room for this city of Tiberias and our laws pronounce that such inhabitants are unclean for seven days."[1] Herod indulged in many other expensive enterprises which were out of proportion to the income of his tetrarchy and which aroused the indignation of the teachers of the Law because of his disregard of Mosaic regulations.[2]

Antipas was at heart a pagan. The son of an Idumaean father and Samaritan mother, he was regarded as "a stranger in Israel's gates, and his followers were called 'the Herodians'[3] by the people, as though the tetrarch were merely the leader of a party."[4] Although the mainspring of his reign was the fulfillment of his own personal ambition he was keen enough to keep general public interests in line with his own personal desires.[5]

In the opinion of the people, Antipas was less like his father than his brother Archelaus.[6] The government of the latter was violent and tyrannical.[7] The high priests were deprived of their positions according

[1] *Cf. Numbers* xix, 11-14.

[2] *Cf.* Joseph. *Vita* 12, in which reference is made to the demolishing of a house built by Herod, the tetrarch, because "figures of living creatures" were found in it.

[3] *Mark* xii, 13.

[4] Hausrath, *Neutestamentl. Zeitgesch.* i, 287.

[5] *Cf.* Joseph. *Vita* 54.

[6] *Cf.* Brann, *Die Söhne des Herodes* 1-16; Kellner, *Die römische Staathalter von Syrien und Judäa. Ibid.* art. "*Die kaiserlichen* Procuratoren von Judäa," *Zeitschrift für kathol. Theologie* 1888, p. 630 sqq.; Madden, *History of Jewish Coinage* 91-95; *Coins of the Jews* 114-118.

[7] *Cf.* Joseph. *Antiq.* xvii, 13.2; *Bell. Jud.* ii, 7.3; *Luke* xix, 11-27.

to the pleasure of the ethnarch.[1] The beautiful palace and the useful aqueduct at Jericho and the city which was built and named after himself, did not in any way help the people in tolerating his cruel reign of nine years. The severe penalties which he inflicted on Jews and Samaritans were so oppressive that they forgot their mutual hatred for the time and united against the tyrant. A deputation of the Jewish and Samaritan aristocracy went to Rome and presented their grievances before Augustus.[2] After Archelaus, who had been summoned to Rome by the emperor, had been given an opportunity to plead his cause, he was deposed from his government, and banished to Vienne in Gaul in 6 A. D.[3]

The territorial possessions of Archelaus were attached to the province of Syria, but received a governor of its own chosen from the equestrian order. According to this arrangement Judaea became a Roman province (6 A. D.) and was henceforth to be governed by procurators.[4] When the Jewish deputies requested that Archelaus be removed, they thought that in consequence of this act Judaea would be placed in the same condition as the Phoenician cities which, except in the matter of taxation, had practically the management of their own affairs. They did not

[1] *Cf.* Joseph. *Antiq.* xvii, 13.1.

[2] *Cf. ibid.;* Berliner, *Gesch. der Juden in Rom* i, 22.

[3] *Cf.* Joseph. *Antiq.* xvii, 13.2-3; *Bell. Jud.* ii, 7.3; Dio Cassius lv, 27; Strabo xvi, 2.46.

[4] *Cf.* Joseph. *Bell Jud.* ii, 8.1; Mommsen, *The Provinces of the Roman Empire* ii, 200-203; Derenbourg, *Histoire de la Palestine* 230-247.

realize that the land of the Jews was too extensive, the population too restless and the military position of Judaea too important for such a method of control. Like other dependencies of greater provinces, the territory of the Jews was to be governed by a procurator.[1]

The Jews were, accordingly, greatly disappointed when they found that they were under the direct control of Rome and to be governed by procurators who had little understanding of what was peculiar to the Jewish nationality. Although the rule of the Herods had been undesirable in many respects, they did not wantonly wound the religious susceptibilities of the Jews. Although the emperors were always ready to grant concessions and to exercise toleration, their efforts were often rendered useless because of the perversity of the procurators. These officials, ignorant of the many traditions and ceremonial rites of the Jews and desirous of showing their absolute authority, kindled the more or less burdened and oppressed people to such a degree of excitement that they did not hesitate to enter eventually into a war which meant complete annihilation.[2]

The procurators who governed Judaea during the reign of Augustus were Coponius (6–9 A. D.), M. Ambinius (9–12 A. D.), and Annius Rufus (12–15

[1] *Cf.* Tacitus, *Hist.* i, 11; ii, 16; Arnold, *Roman Provincial Administration*, 109-113; Jost, *Geschichte der Israeliten* ii, 1-90; Seinecke, *Geschichte des Volkes Israel* ii, 216-238; Felten, *Neutestamentl. Zeitgesch.* i, 201-216.

[2] *Cf.* Schürer i, 453-454; Bramston, *Judaea and her Rulers* 291-303; 360-76.

A. D.). Their residence, the *praetorium*, was at Caesarea[1] except during the Jewish feasts when they took up their abode at Jerusalem, in order to better control the vast crowds of people who streamed into the capital.[2] The procurators were to a certain extent limited in their exercise of power by the governor of Syria who had the right, according to his own discretion, to interfere in the affairs of Judaea. The Syrian legate only interfered, however, when a revolt seemed imminent or other serious difficulties impeded the rule of the governors of Judaea. In such a case the ruler of Syria, invested by the emperor with extraordinary powers, took command in Judaea as the superior of the procurator.[3] A further check upon the actions of the Roman officials was the fact that the procurators had to keep the emperor regularly informed of what was occurring within the province, under their immediate control, and before they could take the initiative in any undertaking they had to receive instruction from Rome. The procurators had some judicial control over the Sanhedrin, the Jewish tribunal,[4] and their position against any possible attacks of the Jewish people

[1] *Cf.* Joseph. *Antiq.* xviii, 3.1; xx, 5.4; *Bell. Jud.* ii, 9.2; 12.2; 14.4; 15.6; 17.1; *Acts* xxiii, 23-33; xxv, 1-13; Tacitus, *Hist.* ii, 78.

[2] *Cf.* Joseph. *Bell. Jud.* ii, 14.8; 15.5; Philo, *Legat. ad Cajum* c. 38. At this time the procurators occupied what had been the palace of Herod which was not only a princely dwelling, but a strong castle as well; *cf.* Joseph., *Antiq.* xvii, 10.2-3; *Bell. Jud.* ii, 3.1-4; 17.7-8.

[3] *Cf.* Joseph. *Antiq.* xviii, 8.2-9; *Bell. Jud.* ii, 10.1-5; Tacitus, *Annals* vi, 32; Mommsen, *Provinces of the Roman Empire* ii, 200.

[4] *Cf. infra.* ch. v, p. 187, for exact relation of the procurators to the Sanhedrin.

was secured by the presence of the Roman army in Palestine.[1] When the Roman officials took up their residence in Jerusalem in what was once the dwelling of Herod, the troops accompanying them had their quarters within the walls of this castle.[2] In addition to the command of the troops and judicial authority, the procurators had the administration of the finances of the province and it was the exercise in Judaea of this latter function which, especially, gave rise to tumults of a politico-religious kind.

A few years after the death of Herod, an effort to obtain the valuation of the property of the Jews for the purpose of accurately determining the amount of Roman taxation led to great opposition. In 7 A. D., Quirinius, the Syrian proconsul, was sent by Augustus, to Judaea to take a census of the people of the newly acquired territory, and assess their property in order that taxes might be apportioned according to the Roman method.

The census[3] gave rise to great agitation amongst

[1] *Cf.* Joseph. *Antiq.* xvii, 10.2-3; *Bell. Jud.* ii, 3.1-4; 17.7-8; v, 4.3-4.

[2] *Cf. Mark* xv, 16.

[3] *Cf.* Joseph. *Antiq.* xviii, 1.1; *Huschke, Ueber den Census und die Steuerverfassung der früheren römischen Kaiserzeit;* Lutterroth, *Le recensement de Quirinius en Judée;* Marquardt, *Römische Staatsverwaltung* 204-223; Schürer i, 508-543; Grätz, *Gesch. der Juden* iii, 255.

This census is worthy of note from the fact that it is associated with another, which was taken, according to the third Gospel, shortly before the birth of Christ. Luke (ii, 1-5) mentions a valuation census such as that made by Quirinius, and observed that the Roman taxing was the occasion of Joseph and Mary's journey to Bethlehem and the birth of Jesus in the inn there. The much debated question of the relation of the census mentioned by the evangelist with the only one recorded by Josephus, has given rise to various treatises. Schürer (i, 508-543)

the Jewish people and was regarded by many as the "herald of slavery." Everyone resented the interference in private as well as political affairs. The offensive thing was not so much the method employed in ascertaining the number of the people[1] but rather the Roman taxation as such. According to Schürer,[2] this assumption seems to be implied in the account of the rebellion given by Josephus.[3]

Despite the apparent indignation of the people, Quirinius proceeded to carry out his commission according to prescribed methods familiar to Roman

has examined the question in great detail, giving an analysis of the ideas of the main writers who have dealt with the problem. By exact historical computation it has been shown that there was but one valuation census conducted by Quirinius, and that Luke erroneously set down the valuation that was made in 7 A.D. in the last year of Herod the Great. This conclusion has been reached by Ewald (*Hist. of the Jews,* vi, 44-45), Strauss (*Leben Jesu,* 336-340), Höck (*Römische Geschichte,* i, 2, p. 412 *sqq.*), Keim (*History of Jesus of Nazareth,* ii, 114-115), Mommsen *Res gestae divi Augustus,* 175 *sqq.*) and Schürer (i, 542) and is accepted by the consensus of opinion.

[1] It has been suggested by some writers (Hausrath, *Neutestamentl. Zeitgesch.* i, 294 *sqq.;* Jacobs, "Census," *JE.* iii, 653) that the opposition was due to the fear of the evils incurred in being numbered. They call attention to the punishment inflicted upon King David by God for numbering the people (*cf.* 2 *Samuel* xxiv, 1-15) and indicate that regulations referred to in *Exodus* (xxx, 11-16) or the method, pointed out by Josephus (*Bell. Jud.* vi, 9.3), of ascertaining the number of people in a district by counting the Passover lambs. (For criticism of this method, *cf.* Chwolsen, *Das Ietzte Passamehl Christi* 49-52.) The fear of enumeration, however, can hardly be offered as an explanation for this opposition, for the punishment, in consequence of the sin committed, would fall upon the Romans who did the actual enumeration. There is little likelihood that the Jews were concerned about the evils that might fall upon the Roman official to whom was entrusted the taking of the census.

[2] *Gesch. des judisch. Volkes* i, 532.

[3] *Bell. Jud.* vii, 8.1.

officials. In the first place, the communities were counted either according to houses or according to families, in order to secure a basis for the poll-tax, the *tributum capitis*.[1] This included the income-tax which varied in amount according to the income of the individual, and the poll-tax proper, which was the same in amount for each person. Secondly, Quirinius, endeavoured to divide the fields, survey the separate divisions and ascertain their relative values for the purpose of levying the land-tax, *tributum agri* or *soli*[2] which could be paid partly in money and partly in kind.

The spirit of discontent, however, was widespread and it gave rise to a "religious republican faction who called themselves the Zealots."[3] Two of the leaders of this party, Judas the Galilean and Sadduc advocated open resistance to the efforts of Quirinius to take the census. Both declared that "this taxation was nothing but a direct introduction of slavery,"[4] and that the Jews "were cowards if they would endure paying tribute to the Romans, and after God submit to mortal men as their lords."[5] They proclaimed the principle that conditions could only be bettered by heroic deeds and that God would

---

[1] *Cf.* Huschke, *Census der Keiserzeit* 175 sqq.; Marquardt, *Römische Staatsverwaltung* ii, 193; 197-202.

[2] Marquardt, *op. cit.* i, 193; Huschke, *op. cit.* 39; Bosse, *Finanzwesen im römischen Staats* i, 259.

[3] Grätz, *Gesch. der Juden* iii, 260.

[4] Joseph. *Antiq.* xviii, 1.1.

[5] Joseph. *Bell. Jud.* ii, 8.1.

only come to their aid when they showed that they could suffer and die for the Law.¹

Among the moderate Jews, however, was Joazar, the high-priest. He tried to explain to the people that "the census would not be the precursor of slavery or of the confiscation of property, but was simply necessary in order to control the arrangements for taxation."² Although the agitation on the part of the Zealots was temporarily suppressed³ and the people were persuaded to submit to the taking of the census, the spirit of opposition still finds expression in the declaration of the school of Hillel, which belonged to the moderate party, that it was justifiable to evade being taxed, if possible.⁴ The flame which was kindled at this time lay smouldering in the heart of the whole nation, only to burst forth again sixty years later, in an effort to reassert the principles inculcated during this period.

Although no attempt was ever made again by a procurator to take a census of the Jewish people according to Roman methods,⁵ the people were at this time numbered and at the end of the year all taxes were newly assessed under the supervision of the procurators.

The party of the Zealots still persisted in their

¹ *Cf.* Kuenen, *National Religions and Universal Religions,* 223.
² Grätz, *Gesch. der Juden* iii, 261; *cf.* Joseph. *Antiq.* xviii, 4.3; xix, 6.3.
³ *Cf. Acts* v, 37.
⁴ *Cf. Nedarim* 27b,28.
⁵ Under Nero the census was taken by means of the Passover lambs, according to Josephus, *Bell. Jud.* vi, 9.3.

opposition to the Romans and their indignation was again aroused by another innovation which followed in consequence of the Roman occupation of Judaea. Formerly all public documents and deeds of divorce were dated according to the year of the reign of the Judaean rulers, but now they had to be dated according to the reign of the Roman emperor.[1] The moderate Pharisees who yielded to the demands of the procurator, in this respect, were accused by the Zealots of indifference in matters of religion.

How could such an ignominy, they exclaimed, be perpetrated as to write the words, "according to the laws of Moses and Israel," (the usual formula in the bill of divorce) "next to the name of the ruler, and thus permit the holy name of the greatest prophet to be placed by the side of the name of the ruler.[2]

The direct taxes levied upon the Jews by the Romans consisted of the property tax, in the two forms of a capitation and land tax,[3] the assessment of which necessitated, as we have seen, the taking of the census. In addition to this double tax there was a duty on houses,[4] a duty on market-produce,[5] various customs, duties upon articles on their being

---

[1] *Cf.* Grätz, *Gesch. der Juden* iii, 261. Grätz designates the ruler as pagan, but in the original source, the term "pagan" is not used.

[2] *Ibid.; cf. Yadaim* 4.8.

[3] *Cf. supra* p. 148.

[4] *Cf.* Joseph. *Antiq.* xix, 6.3.

[5] *Cf.* Joseph. *op. cit.* xviii, 4.3; Tacitus, *Annals* i, 78. This market toll in Jerusalem was introduced by Herod, but abolished in 36 A.D. by Vitellius; *cf.* also Joseph. *Antiq.* xvii, 8.4; xviii, 4.3.

exported from the country[1] and tolls levied for the use of roads, bridges and canals.[2]

As Judaea became after 6 A. D. an imperial province its taxes were paid not into the *aerarium* or treasury of the Senate, but into the *fiscus* or imperial treasury.[3] Strictly speaking, Judaea paid its taxes "to Caesar."[4] For the purpose of tax collection Judaea was divided into eleven toparchies.[5] The Roman Government having designated the kind and the amount of the taxes, it remained for the public authorities in the provinces to see that the amount was collected. The Jewish courts seem to have been the places for gathering in the revenue. The produce of these taxes, as for instance the corn,[6] was sent by the Jews to Sidon and from the coffers there, the fixed amount in money was then conveyed to Rome.[7]

The customs were not controlled by officers of the State, but were collected by publicans,[8] who leased

[1] *Cf.* Marquardt, *Römische Staatsverwaltung* ii, 261 *sqq.*; 289 *sqq.*; Herzfeld, *Handelsgesch. der Juden des Alterthums* pp. 159-162; Naquet, "Des impots indirects chez les Romains sous la republique et sous l'empire," *Bursian's Jahresberichte* xix, 466 *sqq.*; Schürer I, 472.

[2] *Cf.* Tacitus, *op. cit.* xiii, 51; Joseph. *Antiq.* xii, 3.3; xiii, 8.3; xiv, 10.6.

[3] *Cf.* Marquardt, *op. cit.* ii, 292 *sqq.*; Schürer i, 473.

[4] *Cf.* Matt. xxii, 17; *Mark* xii, 14; *Luke* xx, 22.

[5] *Cf.* Joseph. *Bell. Jud.* iii, 3.5; iv, 8.1; Pliny, *Hist. Nat.* v, 14.70; Kühn, *Die städtische und burgerl. Verfassung des römischen Reichs* ii, 339; Schürer ii, 229.

[6] *Cf.* Joseph. *Antiq.* iv, 10.6.

[7] *Cf.* Mommsen, *History of Rome*, iv, 159, note 2.

[8] For the period of Hadrian we have a long inscription in Greek and Aramaic which contains the custom-tariff of the city of Palmyra. *Cf.* Reckendorf, "Der aramäische Theil des palmyrenischen Zoll und Steuertarifs," in the *Zeitschrift der deutschen morgenland, Gesellschaft* (1888), pp. 370-415.

the customs of a certain district for a fixed annual sum. Whatever the revenue yielded in excess of the sum they paid, was their gain, if the revenue fell below it, they were responsible for the loss.[1] Often the publicans bought the right to manage these customs by auction and then re-let the profits of these royalties to under-collectors.[2] Since senators and magistrates were forbidden by law to take part in pecuniary and commercial business, the publicans generally belonged to the rank of knights.[3] These capitalists often formed companies to facilitate transactions and the collection of dividends.[4] All charges against publicans had to be brought before one who had been or soon would be a tax official himself. Often tax-collectors advanced money to those unable to pay, thus changing the tax into a private debt upon which a large interest was exacted.[5]

All publicans were by no means necessarily Romans. The lessees of Jericho[6] and of Caesarea[7] were often Jews.[8] Leading and wealthy Jews of Sepphoris were representatives of the Jewish community before the Roman government and in many

[1] Marquardt, *Römische Staatsverwaltung* ii, 289; Rémondiére, *De la levée des impots en droit romain, passim;* Schürer i, 477-478.
[2] *Cf.* Hausrath, *Neutestamentl. Zeitgesch.* i, 161.
[3] *Cf.* Livy xxi, 63; Hausrath, *op. cit.* i, 162.
[4] *Cf.* Tacitus, *Annals* iv, 6; *cf.* Huschke, *Census und Steuerverfassung der römischen Kaiserzeit.*
[5] *Cf.* Hausrath, *op. cit.*
[6] *Cf. Luke,* xix, 1.2.
[7] *Cf.* Schürer i, 478.
[8] The statement of Tertullian, that all tax-gatherers were heathens (*De pudicitia,* c. 9) was rightly contested as early as by Jerome (*Epist. 21 ad Damasum* c. 3), ed. I. Hillberg [CSEL], liv, 111-142.

cases acted as Roman tax-collectors.[1] As members of the town council which consisted of Jews and non-Jews, they were responsible for the full collection of regular and extraordinary taxes and impositions.[2]

The self-interest of the tax-gatherers and the not infrequent extortions[3] that were made by these officials made them as a class hated by the inhabitants. Roman officials living among the Jews often sought out the wealthy and were unscrupulous in getting possession of them. The teachers of the Law warned their audiences not to draw the attention of the tax-gathers to other people's means.[4] The people knew how to vex the farmers of taxes and invented various ways for defrauding the revenue.[5] "Tax-gatherers and sinners"[6] became synonymous terms and in rabbinical literature because of the Jewish scruples about paying taxes, the publicans are put under the category of robbers.[7] Their testimony was not valid at Jewish tribunals.

The oversight of the administration of the large finances of the Temple seems to have been carried

[1] Cf. Büchler, *The Political and Social Leaders of the Jewish Community of Sepphoris in the Second and Third Centuries* p. 5; although Büchler's account refers to the second and third centuries, conditions seem to have been the same during the first century.

[2] *Ibid.* p. 77.

[3] Cf. *Aboda Zara,* 71a; Büchler, *The Political and Social Leaders of the Jewish Community of Sepphoris* pp. 13; 42.

[4] Cf. Büchler, *op. cit.* 41 and note 2.

[5] Cf. *Kelim* xvii, 16; *Kilajim* ix, 2; *Shabbat* viii, 2; Schürer i, 479.

[6] *Matt.* ix, 10; cf. xi, 19; xviii, 17; xxi, 31.

[7] Cf. *Baba Kamma* x, 1.2; *Nedarim* iii, 4; Herzfeld, *Handelsgeschichte der Juden* 161; Schürer, *op. cit.* i, 479.

156   THE TOLERATION OF THE JEWS

out during the period 6–41 A. D. by means of the Roman authorities. During the period 44–66 A. D. it was transferred to the Jewish princes.[1] The care of the money in the Temple as well as the administration of all other possessions, in the sanctuary, was entrusted to the Temple treasurers.[2] One of the functions of these officials was the gathering in of the half-shekel tax.[3]

The withdrawal from the Roman provinces of the large sums of money entailed by the Temple Tax, met with considerable objection. Flaccus, for instance, had ordered the money thus collected in Apamea, Laodicea, Adramyttium and Pergamum to be confiscated.[4] In view of the fact that many provincials desired to retain within the provinces the gold which was sent to the Temple treasury, it is evident that the Jews in several places would have been unable to send the proceeds of the sacred tribute to Jerusalem unless the remission was sanctioned from Rome,[5] itself, no less than from Asia Minor,[6] and unless the Jews had been under the tolerant rule of Roman law.

Despite the apparent discontent of the people with the rule of the procurators, the Jews enjoyed considerable freedom in home affairs and self-administration.[7] As Mommsen points out, they

[1] *Cf.* Joseph. *Antiq.* xx, 1.3; 9.7; Schürer, i, 482.
[2] *Cf.* Schürer ii, 322-328.
[3] *Cf. Shekalim* ii, 1.
[4] *Cf.* Schürer iii, 112.
[5] *Cf.* Philo, *Legat. ad Cajum* c. 23.
[6] *Cf.* Joseph. *Antiq.* xvi, 6.2, 3, 4, 6, 7; Philo, *op. cit.* c. 40.
[7] *Cf.* Schürer, *op. cit.* i, 480.

were given "tolerably free sway in affairs of faith, of manners, and of law, where Roman interests were not directly affected thereby."[1] The transition to the new order of things brought about by the termination of the vassal kingship and the incorporation of Judaea into the empire, necessarily entailed some hardships. This change had been sought by the Jews and in obtaining their request, they obtained with it such arrangements as were ordinarily made by the Roman government when a procuratorial province was established.[2] Conscious of the many advantages granted by Caesar and Augustus, to the Jews living in different parts of the Roman empire, the popular leaders of Judaea repeatedly urged their followers to rid themselves of the Herodian dynasty and seek the immediate rule of Rome.[3]

In bringing about the desired change, the Roman government endeavoured as far as possible to avoid harsh and abrupt methods of procedure.[4] From the point of view of the civil enactments and the orders emanating from the supreme Roman authorities, the Jews could not complain of any lack of consideration.[5] But when it came to a practical application of these orders on the part of the procurators it was a different matter. The average Roman official paid but little heed to Jewish conceptions and feelings and as regards affairs of religion they were only

---

[1] Mommsen, *Provinces of the Roman Empire* ii, 204.
[2] *Ibid.*
[3] *Cf.* Ewald, *History of Israel* vi, 6.
[4] *Cf.* Mommsen, *op. cit.*
[5] *Cf.* Schürer i, 485.

interested in them so far as they had a political side.¹ The procurators received an annual salary from the imperial government and were forbidden to receive bribes or presents from the people whom they governed.² Despite the fact that any governor could be called to account, at Rome, for going beyond the limits of his authority, several procurators of Judaea were guilty of committing acts of tyranny and corruption and to a large extent voluntarily kept alive the disaffection of the Jewish people.³ Although the procurators set up and deposed high priests at their pleasure yet we are told that appointments were not made in a purely arbitrary manner but that respect was paid to the claims of certain families.⁴ The procurators during the reign of Augustus seem to have tolerated Judaism, even so far as to carry the Roman banners through the city without the image of the Emperor.⁵ To Josephus the procurator was only an overseer and the aristocratic Sanhedrin the real governing body. He characterizes the change which took place after the deposition of Archelaus as a transition from monarchy to aristocracy.⁶

Although the Jewish nation had previous to this change, been in a position of vassalage, yet the glamour of Herod's reign produced a semblance of freedom; although the rule of the procurators was

---

[1] *Cf.* Wellhausen, *Prolegomena to the History of Israel*, 534.
[2] *Cf.* Marquardt, *Römische Staatsverwaltung* i, 557-558.
[3] *Cf.* Joseph. *Antiq.* xx, 11.1; *Bell. Jud.* ii, 14.2; *Acts* xxiv, 26.
[4] *Cf.* Schürer i, 480.
[5] *Cf.* Joseph. *Antiq.* xviii, 2.2; 3.1; *Bell. Jud.* ii, 9.1.
[6] *Antiq.* xx, 10 *fin.*

far less oppressive than that of the House of Herod, yet the very presence of the Roman governor in Judaea seemed to strengthen the belief of the pious Jews that the period of freedom had come to an end.[1] According to Jewish ideas, the acceptance of existing conditions was "an insult to all the lofty, divine privileges of the chosen people."[2] The present relations were entirely unfavorable for giving the people that feeling of security in their religious life, without which there could be no peace in Judaea. Religion was the foundation of all relations in life. The Jews had their own Mosiac Code and objected strongly to being tried by any foreign code such as that of the Romans.[3] In consequence of this feeling, religious and secular duties were often brought into direct conflict. The theory inculcated by Judas the Galilean, that it was wrong for a Jew to recognize another lord over him other than God, became deeply enrooted in the hearts of a people who did not fail to attempt a practical application of his doctrine. Already in the Maccabean and the Herodian times, the faithfulness of the people to their religion had been tested and they had become involved in many "conflicts for the existence and perfection of a Kingdom of the true God amongst men."[4]

[1] *Cf.* Wellhausen, *Prolegomena to the History of Israel*, 534
[2] Schürer i, 480.
[3] The same objection finds expression amongst the Christian; *cf.* *I Cor.* 6.
[4] Ewald, *History of Israel* vi, 4.

CHAPTER V

THE LEGAL POSITION OF THE JEWS WITHIN
THE ROMAN EMPIRE

Besides the conflict which arose from the inconsistencies of the demands of religion on one hand and those of the civil government on the other the Jews found themselves at variance with the Romans in still another respect. The tension between the two nationalities became all the more strained, the more the conflict involved each other's peculiarities. The claim of the Romans to universal empire rested on their power as a great conquering nation, while the Jews, as the "chosen people" considered themselves superior to all the others. While the series of events with which we have become familiar overshadowed the Jewish claim, it still lingered in the heart of every pious Jew as an inspiring memory of an earlier period.[1] Regarding himself as "a member of a great, ancient, sacred and unique nation," and mindful of the fact that the Jews had been destined by God for some high vocation, the individual Israelite was continually buoyed by the Messianic hope that in the future his people would control the whole human race.[2]

[1] *Cf.* Ewald, *History of Israel* vi, 3.
[2] *Loc. cit.* vi, 1-5.

But just at a time when the fulfillment of a latent hope seemed possible, the Jews came into direct contact with the Romans as a subject people; a nation strong spiritually, but rendered weak materially by the divisions and class struggles of its own members, encountered the most powerful and ambitious of all nations and one which could naturally show but little understanding for the peculiarities of the Jewish people. The issues which were involved in the collision of the Jewish and Roman nations were probably not apparent to either, but in tracing the history of the Jews from the period of the Maccabees through the reign of Augustus we have already noted many points at which such a collision was imminent and we can readily see that the further development of Jewish events is wholly dependent upon the form which this collision of fundamentally different nationalities and spiritual tendencies assumes.

When Augustus incorporated Judaea into the empire, his action was the natural outcome of a policy which had been pursued in respect to the Jews for many years. Augustus, undoubtedly, supposed that in assuming the direct government of the provinces he would at the same time lessen the anxieties which the restless land of the Herods had caused him. To the emperor it seemed to be of the greatest advantage to Judaea to come under the control of a firm and stable government and the reduction of the nation into such a condition, the only medium of crushing discontent and possible insurrections. Augustus, however, was an advocate of peaceful government and was anxious that the greatest consideration and kindness be shown in effecting the desired change. The majority of the Jews, as we have already seen, were themselves anxious to come under the direct rule of Rome as it seemed the best thing under the circumstances. For the present they were anxious to be independent of the Herodians and thought but little of the future. Although there were many who were indifferent to the material possessions of life and who were intent upon spiritual endeavours, they at the same time realized that the wisest policy to pursue was not one of armed resistance but of patient, peaceful submission. It soon became apparent that the Jews were gaining unexpected advantages in their relations with the Romans.

Three accusations, from a legal standpoint, were brought against the religious worship of the Jews:— their contempt of the gods, their refusal to take part in the imperial cultus and their refusal to participate in the popular festivals.

The charge of $ἀθεότης$, of contempt of the gods, was the burden of the popular prejudice against the Jews and became the weapon of almost all their adversaries from Apollonius Molon and Posidonius to Pliny and Tacitus.[1] The Jews refused to acknowledge any other worship besides their own as legitimate and would not tolerate the gods of other

[1] *Cf.* Apion. in Joseph. *C. Apion.* ii, 6; Posidonius and Apollonius Molon *ibid.* ii, 7; Apollonius Molon, *ibid.* ii, 14; Pliny, *Nat. Hist.* xiii, 4.46; Tacitus, *Hist.* v, 5.

nations. The Romans on the other hand, were willing to tolerate the most diverse forms of religious worship if only the adherents of one cultus would regard the others as legitimate. It was taken for granted that the citizens of the same city should, besides any private worship of their own, participate in the worship of the gods of the city. From the standpoint of the pagans, those who failed to honor the gods or some of the gods whom the city worshipped were exposing themselves to the charge of atheism.[1] In his attempt to meet the reproach that the Jews despised the gods, Josephus points out on one hand, the Jewish idea of God[2] and on the other hand denounces the kind of gods whom others honored.[3]

While the charge of ἀθεότης was often brought against the Jews and in many cities gave rise to conflicts with the non-Jewish citizens, they were not forced by Roman law to participate in the city cultus. The Seleucids had solved the difficulty by simply regarding the Jews as exceptions to the general requirement and the Roman authorities followed the same policy.[4]

[1] *Cf.* Schürer iii, 548; Linsenmayer, *Die Bekämpfung des Christentums* 29, note e; Mommsen, "Der Religionsfrevel nach römischen Recht," *Histor. Zeitschr.* lxiv (1890) 407; *Römisches Strafrecht* 575. For a similar charge against the Christians, *cf.* Tertullian, *Apology* 24; A. Harnack, "Der Vorwurf des Atheismus in den drei ersten Jahrhunderten" *Texte u. Untersuchungen*, n.s. xiii, 3-16; *cf.* also Canfield, *The Early Persecutions of the Christians, passim.*

[2] *C. Apion.* ii, 22.

[3] *Ibid* 33-35; *cf. Wisdom of Solomon*, c. 13-15.

[4] *Cf. infra* p. 194.

Closely connected with the charge of ἀθεότης was the accusation that the Jews refused to worship the emperor. The Jews, and later the Christians, because of the very nature of their ideas regarding divinity could not participate in the practices of the cult of emperor-worship.[1] The Jews regarded the emperor as superior to other men in power but their equal by nature. They considered it a duty to obey and respect him but sacrilege to worship him. Although, except under Caligula,[2] the Jews from the time of Caesar onwards were not required to worship the emperors, the opponents of the Jews were always ready to use their refusal of imperial worship as a proof that they were not loyal citizens.[3] Jewish apologists met this accusation by an appeal to the fact that a sacrifice was offered daily for the emperor in the temple of Jerusalem[4] and that on special occasions hecatombs were offered for the Roman emperor.[5]

Apion (says Josephus) would defame us, because we do not put up images of our emperors, as if these emperors did not know this before, or stood in need of Apion as their defender;

[1] Upon the death of Julius Caesar the Senate decreed to him "every honor at once divine and human" (Suetonius, *Julius Caesar* c. 84; *cf.* Dion Cassius xlvii, 19). Augustus refused to receive divine honors publicly at Rome, though he looked upon the practice of this cult with approval and promoted it in the provinces (*cf.* Suetonius, *Octavianus* c. 52; Tacitus, *Annals* i, 10); *cf.* Wissowa, *Religion und Kultus der Römer*, 318-419.
[2] *Cf.* Philo, *Legat. ad Cajum* sec. 11-15; Joseph. *Antiq.* xviii, 7.2, 8.1; xix, 1.1; Suetonius, *Caligula* 22; Dio Cassius lix, 26.28.
[3] *Cf.* Joseph. *C. Apion.* ii, 6; Tacitus, *Hist.* v, 5.
[4] *Cf.* Joseph. *C. Apion.* ii, 6; *Bell. Jud.* ii, 10.4; *cf. Gittin* 56a.
[5] *Cf.* Philo, *Legat. ad Cajum*, 45.

LEGAL POSITION IN THE ROMAN EMPIRE 165

whereas he ought rather to have admired the magnanimity and moderation of the Romans, since they do not compel those who are subject to them to transgress the laws of their own countries, but receive the honours due to them as it is pious and lawful for those who offer them to pay them. For they do not thank people for conferring honours upon them, when they are compelled by violence to do so.[1]

The attitude of the Jews toward imperial worship did not, however, affect their legal situation. They were not officially required to adore the genius of the emperor and satisfied the imperial authorities by furnishing something like an equivalent in the sacrifices offered in behalf of the emperors.

Connected with imperial worship were the public games in honor of the emperor which were held in almost every provincial town even in the time of Augustus.[2] While Herod had introduced these festal games[3] into Caesarea and Jerusalem,[4] the Jews as a whole looked askance at what they regarded as pagan practices, which tended to cause large numbers of the Jewish population to neglect their own religious observances.[5] It was the attitude which the Jews took towards the games which formed an important

[1] C. Apion. ii, 6.
[2] Suetonius, Augustus 59; cf. Wissowa, Religion und Kultus der Romer, 318-99.
[3] The kinds of games were in general as follows:—(a) in the circus, the chariot race; (b) in the amphitheatre the contests of gladiators and fights of wild beasts; (c) in the theatres plays, properly so called, and pantomines; (d) in the stadium, gymnastic games. For the games in imperial days, cf. Friedländer, Sittengesch. Rom. ii, 293-637; Marquardt, Römische Staatsverwaltung, 468-566.
[4] Cf. supra ch. v, p. 128.
[5] Cf. Joseph. Antiq. xv, 8.1.

part of most of the popular festivals[1] together with the religious rites included in the celebration of them, that gave rise to the accusation that the Jews were disloyal citizens. The refusal on the part of many Jews to participate in the popular festivals was met with the same tolerant attitude on the part of the Roman authorities as in the case of the two other charges which, as we have already indicated, were brought against the Jews.

The tolerant policy towards the Jews was further emphasized by the various privileges which were conceded to them by Julius Caesar, in deference to the requirements of Jewish legalism. This ruler conceived of liberty of conscience in the sense of absolute neutrality on the part of the state, a point of view which he considered to be in the interests of unification and peace.[2] He desired to bring the various cults into harmony with the civil law without protecting, especially, any particular form of worship. Caesar's intelligent skepticism made him liberal.

Of the large number of public enactments, issued by the Senate, the emperors, certain Roman officials or municipal authorities, and collected by Josephus, five can be traced to the influence of Julius Caesar. All of these edicts have as their object the securing to the Jews of the free observance of their own religion and the confirmation of any privileges accorded

[1] *Cf.* "Roman Festivals," *Ency. Brit.* 11th ed., x, 221-222; *cf.* also Fowler, *Roman Festivals of the Period of the Republic, passim.*
[2] *Cf.* Hild, "Les Juifs a Rome," *REJ* xi, 20-23; Renan, *Hist. of the People of Israel,* v, 170.

to them. In one of these decrees, the emperor orders the authorities of Paros not to interfere with the Jews in the practice of their religious observances and adds that any interference was forbidden at Rome itself.[1] Another is a communication to a Roman official from the magistrates of the Laodiceans who assure him that in conformity with his injunctions, the Jews would not be interfered with in the observance of their own religious usages.[2] In a communication from the proconsul of Asia to the authorities and people of Miletus, the latter are informed that they must not forbid the Jews, "to celebrate their Sabbaths and to perform the sacred rites received from their forefathers, and to manage the fruits of their land according to their ancient custom."[3] In a public enactment of the Halicarnassians it is decreed that "as many men and women of the Jews as wish to do so may celebrate their Sabbaths and perform their holy rites according to Jewish laws, and have their places of prayer by the seaside according to the custom of their forefathers."[4] In accordance with a public decree of the Sardians, the Jews were permitted to assemble on the days designated by them, for the celebration of their religious observances and, moreover, the praetors were enjoined to set apart for them a place "for a building and habitation," and that care should be taken that "such sorts of food as they shall esteem fit for their eating may be introduced into the city."[5]

[1] *Antiq.* xiv, 10.8. [2] *Antiq.* xiv, 10.20.
[3] *Ibid.* 21. [4] *Ibid.* 23. [5] *Antiq.* xiv, 10.24.

After the death of Julius Caesar, Dolabella, who supported Antony, sent an edict to the authorities of Ephesus telling them to exempt the Jews from military service on the Sabbath and to permit them to assemble for sacred and religious purposes according to the requirements of their law.[1] Marcus Brutus, the proconsul, who opposed Antony and Octavianus, issued a decree to the people of Ephesus, declaring that the Jews were to be allowed "to act in all things according to the custom of their forefathers without impediment from anybody."[2] While most of these decrees are addressed to the Jews of the East, we know from the statements of Philo,[3] that the Jews living in Rome also shared these privileges.

Among the various privileges[4] conceded to the Jews in deference to the requirements of the Jewish religion was the exemption from actually using arms[5] or marching farther than two thousand cubits on the Sabbath.[6] They were not to be compelled to appear

[1] *Antiq.* xiv, 11-12.   [2] *Ibid.* xiv, 12-12.
[3] *Legat. ad Cajum* sec. 23.

[4] For general accounts of these privileges, *cf.* Schürer iii, 73-74; Goldschmidt, *De Iudaeorum Apud Romanos Condicione* 14-15; Amitai, *Romains et Juifs* 13; Hild, *REJ* viii, 26-37; Vogelstein, *Gesch. der Juden in Rom* 9; Bonnetty, *Religione des Romains* 269; 273; Frankel, "Die Juden unter der ersten römischen Kaisern," *MGWJ* (1854), 410-411; Weiss, *Die römischen Kaiser* 8; Matagrin, *Histoire de la tolerance religieuse évolution d'un principe social* 1-85.

[5] For prohibition with regard to using arms, *cf. Mishnah*, "Shabbat," vi, 2-4.

[6] That is from the city or village where the Jews were at the beginning of the Sabbath. This was called the "Sabbath limit," and a distance of two thousand cubits a "Sabbath day's journey." *Cf. Erubin*

in a court of law on the Sabbath.[1] When a public distribution of money or corn took place on a Sabbath, the Jews were to receive their share of the money or corn on the following day.[2] Instead of oil furnished by the provinces and which the Jews were not permitted to use because it might have contracted uncleanness from unclean vessels used by the Gentiles,[3] they were to receive an equivalent in money.[4]

Besides the assurance that they were not to be interfered with in the observance of the Sabbath, the Jews were guaranteed the undisturbed exercise of their own religious worship. In general the policy of Caesar was unfavourable to free unions or "*collegia*"[5] because in the late republic they were often made use of for political purposes, he therefore "dissolved all '*collegia*' except such as were of ancient foundation," and Augustus enforced the same pro-

---

iv, 3.7; v, 5, 7; *Numbers* xxxv, 1-8; *Acts* i, 12; Joseph. *Antiq.* xiii, 8, 4; xiv, 10.12; *cf.* in general, Schürer ii, 557. On the carrying of arms by the Jews, *cf.* Philo, *In Flaccum* sec. 2; Juster, *Les Droits politiques des Juifs* 32-33; Mommsen and Marquardt, *Manuel des antiquites romaines*, i, 243.

[1] *Cf.* Joseph. *Antiq.* xvi, 6.2, 4.

[2] *Cf.* Philo, *Legat. ad Cajum* sec. 23; on the distribution in general, *cf.* O. Hirschfeld, "Getreideverwaltung in der römischen Kaiserzeit," *Philologus* xxix (1870), 1-96; Esser, *De pauperum cura apud Romanos*.

[3] *Cf.* Joseph. *Antiq.* xii, 3.1; *Bell. Jud.* ii, 21.2; *Vita* 13; *Mishnah*, "Abodah Sara," ii, 6; *Gemara*, "Aboda Sara," 35b.

[4] Joseph *op. cit.*

[5] *Cf.* Liebenam, *Zur Geschichte und Organization des römischen Vereinswesens* 89-97.

hibition.[1] The Jewish communities, however, were expressly exempted and they were permitted to hold meetings or gatherings, "according to the customs and laws of their forefathers."[2] Since, as Marquardt points out, foreign cults were not permitted, down to the second century, within the *pomoerium*,[3] it must be assumed that the Jews were included in this prohibition.

Augustus expressly confirmed and renewed all the privileges granted by his predecessor for the free observance of the Jewish religion and protection from those who endeavoured to suppress it.[4] The views of Augustus regarding toleration were not as broad as those of Julius Caesar. Augustus indicated a reaction towards strictness with a definite leaning towards the Roman worship. He showed great veneration for the remains of the old religion which he hoped to make the basis for a renovated society.[5] He rebuilt the temples which the skepticism or the disorder of the civil wars had permitted to fall in ruins. He made the god Apollo who previously had occupied but a secondary place in the Roman Pantheon, the protector and personification of the empire and with him he connected the legends which

[1] Cf. Suetonius *Octav*. xxxiii, "*Collegia praeter antiqua et legitime dissolvit.*"

[2] Joseph. *Antiq*. xiv, 10.8.

[3] *Römische Staatsverwaltung* iii, 408; cf. Elbogen, *Der jüdische Gottesdienst in seiner geschichtlichen Entwicklung* 449.

[4] Cf. Joseph. *Antiq*. xiv, 10; xvi, 6.

[5] Cf. Suetonius, *Octav*. 30, 31; Ovid, *Fast*. ii, 59; Livy iv, 20.

commemorated the origin of his race.¹ Some of the chief acts of Augustus, resulting from a sense of piety, more or less sincere, were the establishment of the secular games, the committing to the flames of all prophetical books, both in Latin and Greek, with the exception of the Sibylline oracles, and the increasing in number of the priests and Vestal Virgins.² He was a strict observer of the religious ceremonies of foreign nations which had been established by ancient custom but held the others, according to Suetonius, in no esteem.³ The latter, cites as an example the fact that Augustus praised his grandson Caius for not paying his devotion at Jerusalem in his passage through Judaea.⁴

Although Augustus was regarded by his biographers as the most suspicious of men, subject to the most ridiculous fears and strange practices,⁵ which may have given rise to acts of violence under the pretext of religion, the fact remains that he was tolerant in all his relations with the Jews. His policy of toleration may have been strengthened by the tradition of Julius Caesar whose very name still seemed sufficient to protect the Jews. The favor shown to the Jews may have been of a negative character. It may have found its source in what we

¹ *Cf.* Suetonius, *Octav.* 70; Horace, *Odes* iv, 6; Virgil, *Aenid* viii, 704; Hild, *REJ* xi, 22; Preller-Jordan, *Römische Mythologie* 273.
² *Cf.* Suetonius, *Octav.* 31.
³ Suetonius, *Octav.* 93.
⁴ *Ibid.; cf. supra* ch. iv, p. 139, for the attitude of Augustus to his trusted friend and son-in-law, Agrippa, who was on especially friendly terms with the Jews.
⁵ *Cf.* Suetonius, *op. cit.* 90, 91; Pliny, *Hist. Nat.* ii, 7.

might call the philosophical piety of Augustus which finds expression in a general policy showing sincere friendship towards all peoples regardless of their religion.

Augustus showed his favor towards the Synagogue of the *libertini* at Rome.[1] As a mark of respect for Augustus a Jewish synagogue was named after him and another bore the name of Voluminus, a protector of the Jews during the reign of Augustus.[2] Jewish cemeteries as well as synagogues were placed under the protection of the laws.[3] An edict of Augustus places the theft of the sacred books of the Jews in the class of sacrilegious offenses.[4] To protect their graves the Jews, in certain countries, borrowed a device from the pagans. An inscription warned the violator that a heavy fine would be imposed upon him, to be paid altogether or in part either to the municipal or to the imperial treasury.[5] The observance of the dietary laws, the laws of chastity and the rite of circumcison all of which came under the category of the "customs of the fathers," were legally assured to the Jews.[6] Owing to the law forbidding images, Jewish soldiers were exempt from taking oaths on standards bearing eagles[7] and as we

[1] *Cf.* Philo, *Legat. ad Cajum* sec. 23.
[2] *Cf.* Hild, *REJ* xi, 26 and note; Berliner, *Gesch. der Juden in Rom* i, 20; Müller, *Die jüdische Katakombe am Monteverde zu Rom* 108.
[3] *Cf.* Reinach, *op. cit.* iv, p. 564; Elbogen, *Der jüdische Gottesdienst* 450-451.
[4] *Cf.* Joseph. *Antiq.* xx, 5.4; *Bell. Jud.* ii, 12.2.
[5] *Cf.* Reinach, *JE* iv, 564.
[6] *Cf.* Joseph. *Antiq.* xiv, 10.8-17.
[7] *Cf.* Joseph. *C. Apion.* ii, 6; Hild, *REJ* xi, 48. On idolatry, *cf.* the

LEGAL POSITION IN THE ROMAN EMPIRE 173

have already noted[1] the Jews in deference to their religious conceptions were not required to worship the emperors. Judaism attained such a legal standing that it was regarded as a *religio licita* throughout the whole extent of the Roman Empire.[2]

An analysis of the political status of the Jews during the reigns of Julius Caesar and Augustus, indicates the fact that Roman tolerance made many concessions to the Jews in the realm of politics as well as in the domain of religion. With the exception of a few restrictions imposed upon the Jews by imperial legislation and the occasional subjection of Judaism to temporary persecution, the enjoyment of public rights was never materially changed until later times.

At this period it became already apparent that Judaism was a powerful force dispersed throughout the whole extent of the Roman Empire, in fact

special treatise of *Talmud*, "Abodah Zarah"; on the military oath, *cf.* Huschke, *Die multa und das sacramentum in ihren verschiedenen Anwendungen*, p. 368; on the religious significance of eagles as the deities of the legion, *cf.* Seneca, *Epistle* 95; Valerius Maximus vi, 1, 2; Tacitus, *Annals* ii, 17.

[1] *Cf. supra* pp. 164-165.

[2] *Cf.* Schürer iii, 111, note 40. "The expression, 'religio licita,'" as Schürer points out, "is derived from Tertullian *Apologet.* ch. xxi, '*insignissima religio certe licita.*' It does not otherwise belong to the phraseology of Roman legislation. The latter speaks rather of *collegia licita* (Digest xlvii, 22). For the decisive point here lies in this, that to the adherents of any particular worship, permission is granted to organize themselves as a corporation and to meet together for the celebration of their worship. Hence, the formula *coire convenire licet*, which is also of frequent occurrence in the toleration edicts issued in favor of the Jews." [Quoted from Eng. tr. Div. ii, vol. ii, 260, note 132.]

beyond it. To Julius Caesar, as to many of the statesmen of his time, it became evident that the Jewish nation was already a political power, within the State, that could be neither ignored nor overcome. "Judaism was an effective leaven of cosmopolitanism and of national decomposition, and to that extent a specially privileged member in the Caesarian state."[1]

Jewish influence on Roman politics finds expression in the words of the eloquent but intolerant Cicero who, we are told, had learned to hate the Jews from his master Apollonius Molo. He professed to fear, on one occasion, to give vent to his anti-Judaean feelings in a public speech, lest he incite the Jews against him. Cicero attempted to defend the unjust cause of the praetor Flaccus who during his administration of Asia Minor provinces had confiscated the money collected by the Jews with the view of forwarding it to Jerusalem. In the course of his defence, Cicero said:

Next comes that odium about the Jewish gold. . . . You know, Laelius, what a band of them there is, how they crowd together and how strong they are at public meetings. I will lower my voice so that only the judges can hear. For there are not wanting some who would incite them against me and against every prominent man: whom I will not assist so as to make it easier for them. . . Whereas it was customary for gold to be exported yearly, in the name of the Jews out of Italy and all the provinces to Jerusalem, Flaccus by edict forbade its being carried out of Asia. Who is there, judges, that cannot truly praise this? The senate, not only often before, but also in my consulship, determined most decisively that gold

[1] Mommsen, *The Hist. of Rome* v, 419.

ought not to be exported. Is it severity to resist this barbaric superstition? To despise a multitude of Jews, sometimes so fiery at the public meetings, when you are concerned for the good of the commonwealth, was that so very serious an affair?

But it seems, Cneius Pompey, when he had taken Jerusalem, and was victorious, brought forth nothing out of that temple. Now, in the first place this, like many other things, was characteristic of a wise man, leaving no opportunity for a word to be said against him in a city so given to suspicion and evil speaking. For I do not believe that the religion of Jews and enemies was an impediment to the great commander, but modesty. Where then is the guilt? . . . Every state, Laelius has its religion; we have ours. Whilst Jerusalem was standing, and the Jews were at peace, yet the duties of their religious rites were at variance with the splendour of this empire, the dignity of the Roman name, and the institutions of our ancestors; but now, so much the more, because that nation has shown by arms what they thought about our empire, has let us see how far they enjoyed the favor of the immortal gods, by being vanquished, leased out for revenue, and enslaved.[1]

However we may discount the rhetoric of Cicero, his words do nevertheless, indicate the fact that the Jews had some political influence and there existed popular regard and reverence for their religion.[2]

Although the Jewish princes received considerable favor at the imperial court and both Julius Caesar and Augustus were tolerant toward the Jews, the Roman aristocracy remained their chief enemy. The Senate saw in the development of Judaism an opposing force and the recognition of this danger becomes apparent in 59 B. C. when Cicero complains

[1] Cicero, *Pro Flacco* sec. 28.
[2] *Cf.* Berliner, *Gesch. der Juden in Rom* i, 8-12; Vogelstein, *Gesch. der Juden in Rom* i, 8-9; Huidekoper, *Judaism at Rome* 148.

of Jewish influence on Roman assemblies. His defense of Flaccus was the first sign of antisemitism at Rome.[1] A few years before this date Cicero made the proposal that no one should be permitted to exercise a religion, publicly or privately, which had not already been established by the Senate. "Let no one," he said, "have gods separately, nor let men in private worship new gods or foreign ones unless (such as have been) publicly introduced. Let them have in cities the shrines constructed by the Fathers."[2]

The proletariat upon the whole accepted Jewish ideas and opinions more readily than the wealthy. The senate and upper classes were anxious to keep new ideas from penetrating into the lower ranks in order that they might keep these classes under their control. One instrument for controlling those beneath them was the furthering of the public games. The strong opposition of the Jews to these games[3] served to intensify the feelings of the aristocratic class against the Jews.

One member of this upper class, however, was in favor of the Jews. This was Quintus, the brother of Cicero, who advocated some Jewish views. He was appointed successor to Flaccus and was much more acceptable to the provincials than to the aristocracy at Rome. It is probable that his appointment and retention of office for three years were partly due to Jewish influence at Rome.

[1] Hild, *REJ* viii, 20.
[2] *De Legibus* ii, 8.
[3] *Cf.* Joseph. *Antiq.* xv, 8.1.

Although the Roman aristocracy, as a whole, showed little favor towards the Jews, the state authorities throughout the Roman Empire recognized and tolerated the Jewish communities.

The framework of political rights into which the scattered Jewish communities of the Diaspora had to fit themselves varied in different places and at different times. There were three different forms under which the communities of the Diaspora could acquire political recognition.[1]

In many of the great trading cities of the Graeco-Roman world, Phoenicians, Syrians and Egyptians formed what were called settlements of foreigners. These traders not only carried on their business in the great seaports of the Mediterranean but were settled there permanently, and in order to defend their common interests they formed corporations. The members of these corporations lived in the cities as strangers or non-citizens, but their organization enjoyed toleration and recognition from the State authorities. To this class belonged the oldest settlements of the Jews in many places. They formed a colony of foreigners, separate from the political commune. The right of residence was legally maintained. From localities where they were established the Jews could not be expelled except by means of a formal decision issued by the supreme authority of the emperor. Occasionally, at the time of their settlement in a city the Jews had special quarters

[1] *Cf.* Schürer, "Diaspora." *Hasting's Dict. of the Bible,* extra vol., p. 102.

assigned to them as in Alexandria where they were given the quarter called the "Delta"[1] and in Rome the section called the "Trastevere."[2] Their confinement to these special quarters was not strictly enforced and upon the whole they moved about freely. In the quarters inhabited by the Jews they were given the right to erect association halls which were, in fact, their synagogues, for the purpose of common worship and for the reading of the Torah. These synagogues as well as their cemeteries were placed under the protection of the laws.

Another kind of political organizations was the private societies which existed in large numbers in various forms throughout the whole of the Graeco-Roman world. These unions or *collegia* were formed for the furthering of religious or commercial interests. They had their own administration of funds and possessed the right of exercising a certain discipline over their members. Like the settlements of foreigners these organizations maintained an independent position in relation to the political commune but were distinguished from them by the circumstance that for the most part they were made up of natives whether citizens or freedmen, or non-citizens and slaves. Many Jewish communities belonged to this class and the amount of jurisdiction which the Jews of these groups exercised was upon the whole greater than was permitted to other religious or

---

[1] *Cf.* Joseph. *Bell. Jud.* ii, 18.7; *Antiq.* xiv, 7.2.

[2] *Cf. infra* ch. ii, pp. 58-67, for description of Jewish settlements.

trades unions.[1] While, as we have seen, Julius Caesar prohibited in general all *collegia* except those that existed from remote antiquity, the Jewish communities were expressly excluded from this prohibition.[2]

More independent even than the two classes already mentioned were the Jewish communities that were analogous to the corporations of Greeks and Romans in non-Greek or non-Roman countries. These groups were subject neither to taxation by the communes nor to the jurisdiction of the city authorities but formed independent organizations alongside of the communal societies, of the particular cities in which they lived. Such an independent corporation was formed by the Jews of Alexandria and those of Cyrene.

It was especially to Julius Caesar and Augustus that the Jewish communities were indebted for their legal recognition in the Roman Empire. Not only were these communities authorized, at least tacitly, to form autonomous administrative organizations but they were also permitted to exercise financial and judicial functions. The Jews in Italy were permitted by the Roman authorities to collect the Temple tax and transmit it to Jerusalem.[3] The same privilege was granted to the Jews of the East. We have several public documents referring to the right of the Jews to administer their own funds to be sent

[1] *Cf.* Schürer, *Hasting's Dict. of the Bible*, extra vol., p. 102; Mommsen, *Histor. Zeitschrift* lxiv (1890), 421-426.
[2] *Cf.* Joseph. *Antiq.* xiv, 10.8.
[3] *Cf.* Schürer, *Gemeindeverfassung* 10-11.

to Jerusalem. In several of these decrees the municipalities of Asia Minor and Cyrene are enjoined not to interpose any obstacle in the way of the Jews in regard to the collection of this tax.[1] In a communication[2] addressed by the proconsul of Asia to the Milesians, the right to send to Jerusalem the tribute prescribed by Jewish law is confirmed. In another decree Julius Caesar ordained:

> that all the country of the Jews, except Joppa, pay tribute for the city of Jerusalem every year except the seventh year, which thy call the sabbatical year, because therein they neither receive the fruit of their trees, nor do they sow their land. . . . that they pay as their tribute in Sidon in the second year, the fourth part of what was sown . . . that the city of Joppa, which the Jews had originally, when they made a league of friendship with the Romans, shall belong to them, as it formerly did; and that Hyrcanus . . . and his sons shall have as tribute from that city from those that occupy the land, for the country and what they export every year to Sidon, twenty thousand six hundred and seventy-five modii every year; except the seventh year.[3]

Josephus, in speaking of the plundering of the Temple by Crassus, remarks that no one should wonder at the great wealth accumulated in the Temple, since from very ancient times all the Jews throughout the world and those that worshipped God, in Asia and Europe alike, have been sending tribute to the Temple.[4] Philo tells us the way in

---
[1] *Cf.* Joseph. *Antiq.* xvi, 6.2-7; *Bell. Jud.* vi, 6.2; Philo, *Legat ad Cajum* sec. 40.
[2] *Cf.* Joseph. *Antiq.* xiv, 6.8.
[3] Joseph. *Antiq.* xiv, 10.6.
[4] *Antiq.* xiv, 10.6.

which the sacred tribute was collected and sent to Jerusalem.

> The Temple (he points out) has for its revenues not only portions of land, but also other possessions of much greater extent and importance, which will never be destroyed or diminished; for as long as the race of mankind shall last, the revenues likewise of the Temple will always be preserved, being coeval in their durations with the universal world. For it is commanded that all men shall every year bring their fruits to the Temple, from twenty years old and upwards; and this contribution is called their ransom. . . . And since the nation is the most numerous of all peoples, it follows naturally that the first fruits contributed by them must also be most abundant. Accordingly, there is in almost every city a storehouse for the sacred funds to which it is customary for the people to come and there to deposit their tribute, and at certain seasons there are sacred ambassadors selected on account of their virtue, who convey the offerings to the Temple. And the most eminent men of each tribe are elected to this office, that they may conduct the hopes of each individual safe to their destination, for in the lawful offering of the first fruits are the hopes of the pious.[1]

Augustus, Philo tells us, sanctioned the remitting of these sums of money from Rome[2] and later the emperor wrote, "if any one be caught stealing their holy books, or their sacred money, whether it be out of the synagogue, or from the men's apartments, he shall be deemed a sacrilegious person, and his goods shall be confiscated to the public treasury of the Romans."[3] This was a part of the decree which was

---
[1] *De monarchia* ii, 3; *cf.* Mishnah, " Shekalim," iii, 4.
[2] *Legat. ad Cajum* sec. 23.
[3] Joseph. *Antiq.* xvi, 6.2; *cf.* Weiss, *Die römischen Kaiser* 8.

inscribed upon a pillar in the temple of Caesar Augustus.[1]

Although like other Roman citizens, the Jews were subject to personal and patrimonial taxes,[2] they enjoyed, on the other hand, certain privileges in the *prestation* of statute labor and the payment of indirect taxes.[3] The agents of the public treasury, moreover, were forbidden to go amongst the Jews, or to exact from them money or labor during the Jewish holidays or on "the Sabbath-day or on the day of preparation before it, after the ninth hour."[4] No fiscal oath was to be required from the Jews which in any way might offend their conscience.[5]

The Jews were given the further privilege of exercising civil and criminal jurisdiction over the members of their own community. In view of the fact that the Mosaic law concerned itself not only with acts of worship but also with the ordinary affairs of life which were subjected to the regulative principles of divine law, it would have been contrary to Jewish ideas of things to be tried by any other

[1] Joseph. *Antiq.* xvi, 6.2.

[2] *Cf.* Juster, *Les Droits politiques* 92, note 5. The personal taxes were such as the *calefactio balnei publici,* and those for public works and transportation.

[3] Juster, *loc. cit.*

[4] Joseph. *op. cit.* xvi, 6.2; *i.e.,* 3 *p.m.,* according to our reckoning of time.

[5] *Cf.* Joseph. *loc. cit.* xviii, 1.1; *cf.* Ginzberg, "*Eine unbekannte jüdische Sekte,*" *MGWJ* lvi, 427; Juster, *op. cit.* 101-102; *cf. infra* ch. iv, pp. 148-149, regarding the taking of the census by Quirinus; Zumpt, *Das Geburtsjahr Christi,* 200; Wieseler, *Beiträge zur richtigen Würdigung der Evangelien* 95-57.

than Jewish law.¹ Wherever the Jews went they were tried by their own system of law and the employment of their own code in civil processes was everywhere sanctioned by the State authorities. Many Jews who as Roman citizens had the right of seeking redress before the *conventus civium Romanorum* (special tribunals consisting of Roman citizens, which were found everywhere in the provinces) often preferred to bring their cases before the Jewish tribunal for decision.² The Jewish code was simply a little of the Mosiac law with copious commentaries by the rabbis. In civil suits the autonomy of the Jewish courts held only in cases where both parties were Jews; otherwise, even if the defendant was a Jew, the general local tribunal was alone competent, as is evident from the edict of Augustus restraining any court from ordering Jewish litigants to appear before it on the Sabbath.³ In criminal cases the Jewish magistrates exercised a wide disciplinary jurisdiction, including the right of incarcerating and flogging.⁴ A sort of correctional police authority⁵ seems to have been sanctioned by the State authorities. Their jurisdiction, however, does not seem to have been conceded in cases dealing with breaches

[1] *Cf.* Schürer iii, 113-115; *cf. supra* ch. iv, p. 159.
[2] *Cf.* Joseph. *Antiq.* xiv, 10.17.
[3] *Cf. ibid.* xvi, 6.2; *cf.* Reinach, *JE* iv, 567.
[4] *Cf. Acts* ix, 2; xviii, 12-17; xxii, 19; xxvi, 11; 2 *Cor.* xi, 24; *cf.* Mendelssohn, *The Criminal Jurisprudence of the Ancient Hebrews*, 171-172.
[5] Mommsen, "Die Rechtsverhältnisse des Apostels Paulus," *ZNW* ii (1901), 88 *sqq.*

of the common law. At any rate, they were not given the power to inflict capital punishment.

According to Strabo,[1] the ethnarch at Alexandria "governs their nation, and dispenses justice, and sees to their contracts and laws, as if he were the ruler of a free republic." As reference is made in the Talmud[2] to several courts in Alexandria, thus indicating the fact that there was more than one court, the statement of Strabo must mean that the ethnarch as highest political head, was at the same time regarded as the head of the courts. In Sardis, at the order of the Roman proquaestor, the Jews were granted a court of their own.[3]

Throughout the eleven toparchies or administrative districts of Judaea there were local councils or courts, which exercised considerable authority in administrative and judicial affairs.[4] The courts dealing with civil matters consisted of seven members.[5] Those concerned with criminal affairs, were made up of twenty-three members.[6] At the head of the local councils was the Synedrion or as Judaised,

[1] Strabo in Joseph. *Antiq.* xiv, 7.2.
[2] *Ketubot* 25a.
[3] *Cf.* Joseph. *Antiq.* xiv, 10.17.
[4] *Cf.* Joseph. *Bell. Jud.* ii, 14.1; *Matt.* x, 17; xiii, 9; *cf.* also Joseph. *Antiq.* iv, 8.14; *Sanhedrin* i, 6.
[5] *Cf.* Funk, "Die Männer der grossen Versammlung und die Gerichtshöfe im nachexilischen Judentum," *MGWJ*, iv (1911), 34-37; *cf.* also Ginzberg, "Eine unbekannte jüdische Sekte," *MGWJ*, lvi (1912), 564-565.
[6] *Cf.* Funk, *op. cit.* 37-39.

the Sanhedrin of Jerusalem.[1] To this civil council[2] and its high-priest, who was nominated by the procurator,[3] as representative of the imperial master, the Roman government committed the jurisdiction which, in the Hellenic subject communities, was given to the urban authorities and the common councils.[4]

The Great Sanhedrin,[5] which was made up of seventy-one members,[6] included the priestly nobility, with its Sadducaean sympathies and the Pharisaic doctors.[7] It is probable that the members held their position for life and that new members were appointed

---

[1] *Cf.* in general, Büchler, *Das Synhedrion in Jerusalem und das grosse Beth-Din in der Quaderkammer des Jerusalemischen Tempels;* Hoffmann, *Der oberste Gerichtshof in der Stadt des Heiligthums;* Stapfer, " Le Sanhédrin de Jérusalem au premier siècle," *RTP* (1884) 105-119; Schürer ii, 237-267.

[2] Considerable discussion has been raised as to the exact nature of the Sanhedrin. This body must be either a purely civil or an ecclesiastical council. In Talmudic sources it is regarded as an ecclesiastical council, the organ of Tradition; in the writings of Josephus and in the New Testament it is referred to as a civil council. For a confirmation of the Talmudic point of view, *cf.* Hoffmann, *op. cit.* especially, p. 47; for emphasis upon the opposing view, *cf.* Schürer ii, 259.

[3] *Cf.* Büchler, " Die politische Stellung des Hohenpriestens," *op. cit.* 194-218; Langen, " Das jüdische Synhedrium und die römische Procuratur in Judáa," *TTQ* (1862), 411-463.

[4] *Cf.* Mommsen, *The Provinces of the Roman Empire* ii, 204; Kuhn, *Die städtische und bürgerliche Verfassung des Römischen Reichs* ii, 342 *sqq.*

[5] It is difficult to ascertain exactly when the Sanhedrin came into existence. The Jews generally traced its descent from the council established by Moses in the wilderness; *cf. Sanhedrin* i, 6; *Numbers* xi, 16. For discussion of the question *cf.* Schürer ii, 238-248.

[6] *Cf. Sanhedrin* i, 6; *Sebahim* i, 3; *Yadayim* iii, 5; iv, 2; Joseph. *Bell. Jud.* ii, 20, 5; Jelski-Goldin, *Die innere Einrichtung des grossen Synedrions zu Jerusalem* 19-21.

[7] *Cf.* Schürer *op. cit.* ii, 249.

by those holding office or by the important political authorities.¹ According to the *Mishnah* all candidates must be Israelites of pure blood,² and their eligibility to office was tested by the amount of Rabbinical learning which they possessed.³ Pharisees and Sadducees alike had seats in the Sanhedrin.⁴ During the period of our immediate study the former exercised the greatest influence and the Sadducees had to comply with this control "as otherwise the people would not have tolerated them."⁵ According to Josephus the high priest who was the political head of the nation⁶ always acted as the head and president of the Sanhedrin.⁷

Although the civil authority of the Sanhedrin was limited to the eleven toparchies of Judaea proper, this tribunal was the supreme spiritual representative of every Jewish community in the world and its orders were regarded as binding by the whole body of Jews.⁸ Since the Sanhedrin could exercise direct authority only on the communities of Judaea proper, it could not enforce obedience to its orders outside of that domain. When the lower courts were unable to

¹ *Cf.* Schürer *loc. cit.* ii, 250.
² *Cf. Sanhedrin* iv, 2; *Kiddushin* iv, 5.
³ *Cf. Sanhedrin* iv, 4. New members were formerly admitted through the ceremony of the laying on of hands; Lauterbach, "Ordination," *JE* ix, 428.
⁴ *Cf.* The Sadducees, *Acts* iv, 1 *sqq.*; v, 17; xxiii, 6; Joseph. *Antiq.* xx, 1.9. The Pharisees, *Acts* v, 34; xxiii, 6; *cf.* also Joseph. *Bell. Jud.* ii, 17, 3; *Vita* 38.39.
⁵ Joseph. *Antiq.* xviii, 1.4.
⁶ *Antiq.* xx, 10, *fin.*
⁷ *C. Apion.* ii, 23; *Antiq.* iv, 8.14.
⁸ *Cf. Acts* ix, 2; xxii, 5; xxvi, 12.

decide definitely regarding questions connected with the Mosiac Code final appeal was made to the Sanhedrin.[1] All decisions of this tribunal had to be observed by the judges of the local courts on pain of death.[2]

The jurisdiction of the Sanhedrin was not greatly restricted by the authority of the Roman procurator.[3] Not only was this tribunal able to exercise civil jurisdiction according to Jewish law, but it also rendered decisions in criminal matters as well. It had independent authority in regard to police affairs and arrests could consequently be made by officers of the Sanhedrin.[4] It could render final judgment in cases which did not imply sentence of death.[5] While the death sentence had to be ratified by the procurator,[6] the latter, as a rule, regulated his judgment in accordance with Jewish law.[7] The most serious limitation of the Sanhedrin in matters of jurisdiction was the fact that the procurators could proceed independently of the Jewish tribunal. The procurators and even the tribune of the cohorts in Jerusalem could summon a meeting of the Sanhedrin

[1] *Cf.* Joseph. *Antiq.* iv, 8.14; *Sanhedrin* xi, 2.

[2] *Cf. Sanhedrin* xi, 2.

[3] *Cf.* Mommsen, *Römisches Strafrecht* 240; Geib, *Gesch. des römischen Kriminalprozesses* 471-486; Mitteis, *Reichsrecht und Volksrecht in den östlichen Provinzen des römischen Kaiserreichs* 90 sqq.; Schürer ii, 260-261.

[4] *Matt.* xxvi, 47; *Mark* xiv, 43; *Acts* iv, 3; v, 17, 18.

[5] *Acts* iv, 5-23; v, 21-40.

[6] *John* xviii, 31; *Jer. Sanhedrin* i, 1; Lehmann, " Quelques dates importantes de la chronologie du 2ᵉ temple," *REJ* xxxvii (1898), 12-20.

[7] Schürer ii, 261.

in order to ascertain the standpoint of Jewish law upon any matter.[1] For the purpose of supreme jurisdiction the high priest was not permitted to hold a court during the absence or without the consent of the procurator.[2]

According to Josephus the place where the Sanherdrin met was beyond the temple mount.[3] It is difficult to ascertain, definitely, the time of meeting. It is possible that the Sanhedrin came together, like the local courts, on Monday and Thursday of each week.[4] Rabbinic literature implies that the Sanhedrin met every day. No courts were ever held on festival days or on the Sabbath.[5] Because of the regulation that in criminal cases a capital sentence must follow immediately on the same day of the trial,[6] great care was taken that no criminal proceedings should be concluded on the evening before the Sabbath or any festival day[7] since no execution could take place on these days. In the *Mishnah* a description is given of the special form which was prescribed for a trial in which the death sentence

[1] *Acts* xx, 30; *cf.* xxiii, 15, 20, 28.

[2] Schürer *op. cit.* ii, 262.

[3] *Bell. Jud.* v, 4.2; *cf. Sanhedrin* xi, 2; *Middoth* v, 4; *Pe'ah* ii, 6; *Edujoth* vii, 4. According to a passage in the *Mekilta* (*Mishaptim* 4), the Sanhedrin met in one of the chambers of the inner court of the Temple. *Cf. Mishnah* " Sifra," 19a, where the place of the meeting is referred to as the " Tile-chamber."

[4] *Cf. Kethubot* i, 1.

[5] *Cf. Bezah* v, 2.

[6] *Sanhedrin* iv, 1; v, 5. A sentence of acquittal might be pronounced on the same day as that of the trial.

[7] *Cf. Sanhedrin* iv, 1.

was involved.¹ The usual forms of capital punishments inflicted were decapitation, strangling, burning and stoning.² The Sanhedrin, however, was not a sanguinary tribunal and endeavoured whenever possible to obviate the necessity of shedding blood by various regulations.³

Besides the Great Sanhedrin at Jerusalem, there were local councils in other places of Judaea, Galilee and Peraea which like the tribunal of the Holy City could pass sentences involving fines and punishments of imprisonment and death. An appeal to the higher court was only necessary when a decision could not be reached or when the exact interpretation of the Law regarding a particular case was questioned.⁴ These local councils usually met in the synagogues which for the time being were converted into courts of justice.⁵

Our information regarding these local Jewish courts is not very complete. The references in Talmudic literature to the occasional decisions and judgment of individual rabbis in their own schools or by three⁶ scholars which constituted a legal court for

[1] *Sanhedrin* iv, 1; v, 5.
[2] *Cf.* Farrar, *The Life and Work of St. Paul* i, 647-650; 661-664; Bloch, "Das mosaisch-talmudische Strafgerichtsverfahren," *Jahresbericht der Landersrabbinerschule in Budapest,* 1901; Milman, *Hist. of the Jews* ii, 115, note 2; Rabbinowicz, *De la législation criminelle du Talmud, passim.*
[3] *Cf.* Farrar, *op. cit.* i, 647.
[4] *Cf.* Joseph. *Antiq.* iv, 8.14.
[5] *Cf.* Schürer ii, 265.
[6] For a discussion of the exact number constituting a legal court, *cf.* supra, p. 184.

any one occasion, have been collected by Chajes in an interesting review[1] of the subject. A somewhat closer study of the official judges of Galilee has been made by Büchler.[2] The official judges chosen from the nobility were rarely scholars. As they were unfamiliar with Rabbinical law, they made the basis of their decisions and judgments precedent and common sense and, before schools of rabbis were established in the Galilean cities, no one questioned the source of their judgments.[3] The Roman government permitted the Jews to make use of their native civil law but if the parties concerned desired to be judged by non-Jewish law, the judges were obliged to grant them this privilege.[4]

The unsatisfactory condition of the Jewish courts in Galilee finds expression in the complaints of the rabbis, many of which are recorded in the *Talmud*.[5] A large number of the Jewish judges whether appointed by the Roman officials or in the service of the Jewish community were charged with injustice, the acceptance of gifts and other illegal practices.[6] It is difficult to ascertain from Talmudic literature

[1] Chajes, "Les Juges juifs en Palestine," *REJ* xxxix (1899), 39-52.
[2] *Cf.* Büchler, *The Political and the Social Leaders of the Jewish Community of Sepphoris in the Second and Third Centuries* 21-33.
[3] *Cf. loc. cit.* 21-22.
[4] *Cf. loc. cit.* 25-26; I. Lewy, *Verhandlungen der 33. Philologen. Versammlung* (1879), 86, makes clear the fact that Roman courts established in Palestine were accessible to the Jews and in many cases were actually resorted to by them.
[5] *Cf. Kethubot* 105b; *Sanhedrin* 7a; 98a; *Shabbat* 56a; 139a; *Baba Batra* 15b.
[6] *Cf.* Büchler, *The Political and Social Leaders of the Jewish Community of Sepphoris* 25.

exactly who were responsible for the appointment of the Jewish judges. According to one passage, the nomination seems to have been the work of one man who was guided in his choice by considerations of wealth and relationship.¹

Dissatisfied with their official judges, Jewish litigants often urged the rabbis to decide their cases according to the law of the Torah.² Conscious of the irregularities which were prevalent in the Jewish courts the rabbis endeavoured to have the judges removed and the law of the nobility displaced, but their efforts were in vain. The judges were at the same time the political leaders of the community and by means of wealth they could gain the support of Roman authorities.³ As a result of their struggles against the official judges, the rabbis gained the confidence of the lower ranks of society but at the same time they incurred the hatred of the leading classes of the community.⁴

The discontent of the people in regard to the appointment of official judges gives expression to the fact that in judicial matters they were not dominated by Roman authorities. The tolerant policy of Roman rule was further emphasized by the fact that the Jews were given the rights of citizenship and permitted to take an active part in municipal life.

We have already seen that the Jews in a certain number of Greek cities formed communities which

[1] *Cf. Sifre Deut.* 17.
[2] *Cf.* Chajes, *REJ* xxxix, 43 *sqq.*
[3] *Cf.* Büchler, *The Political and Social Leaders of the Jewish Community of Sepphoris*, 32-33.
[4] *Cf.* Büchler, *loc. cit.* 7.

were regarded as private associations of foreign settlers. While certain privileges were conferred upon the Jews of these communities, except, perhaps in the case of a few individuals,[1] they did not enjoy the rights of citizenship and had no control in the direction of municipal affairs.

There, were, however, a large number of towns in which the Jews enjoyed the rights of citizenship.[2] This was especially true of such cities whose constitution had been reorganized or which were newly founded in the Hellenistic period as for instance the capitals of the Ptolemies and the Seleucids, Alexandria and Antioch.[3] As early as 280 B. C. Seleucus I Nicator had conferred the rights of citizenship upon the Jews in all the cities[4] founded by him in Asia Minor and Syria and these rights they continued to enjoy under the Romans as well.[5]

At Antioch the privileges of the Jews were engraved upon bronze stelae.[6] At Alexandria a brass pillar set up by Julius Caesar confirmed the fact that the

[1] *Cf. Acts* xxi, 39, where Paul is spoken of as a citizen of Tarsus. The text, however, is doubtful. *Cf.* Ramsay, " The Jews as Resident Strangers," *Expositor* v (1902), 21-22.

[2] An interesting study of the evolution of the political rights of the Jews in the Roman Empire has recently been made by Jean Juster in his *Les Droits politiques, des Juifs dans l'empire romain. Cf.* also Kuhn, *Die städtische und bürgerliche Verfassung das römischen Reiches.*

[3] Schürer iii, 121-123; Ramsay, " The Jews as Hellenistic Citizens," *Expositor* v (1902), 22-29.

[4] For a list of them, *cf.* Appian, *Syriaca* lvii.

[5] *Cf.* Joseph. *Antiq.* xii, 3.1; *Bell. Jud.* vii, 3.3.

[6] *Cf.* Joseph. *Bell. Jud.* vii, 5.2. *Cf.* the failure on the part of the Antiochians to have the Jews deprived of their privileges at a later period. *Antiq.* xii, 3.1.

Jews were Alexandrian citizens.¹ These rights, Josephus tells us, were conferred upon the Jews by Alexander the Great when the city was founded² and at a later period, after they were for a brief period disregarded, they were expressly guaranteed by Claudius.³ Philo, also, speaks of the citizenship of the Jews of Alexandria.⁴

In Ephesus⁵ and in the rest of Ionia the Jews possessed the rights of citizenship.⁶ During the reign of Augustus, the municipal authorities of Ionia petitioned Agrippa, who then had the administration of the eastern provinces, to exclude the Jews from the enjoyment of the rights of citizenship or, if they were to share these privileges with the Jewish citizens, to compel them to participate in the city religion.⁷ With the aid of Nicholas of Damascus, who spoke in behalf of the Jews, Agrippa maintained intact the rights of citizenship of the Jewish community of Ephesus.⁸ We learn also from Josephus that the Jews enjoyed the rights of citizenship in Sardes⁹ and even outside Asia Minor at Cyrene.¹⁰

[1] *Cf.* Joseph. *Antiq.* xiv, 10.1; *C. Apion.* ii, 4.
[2] *C. Apion.* xix, 5.2; *Bell. Jud.* ii, 18.7.
[3] *Antiq.* xix, 5.2. [4] *In Flaccum* sec. 10.
[5] From Ephesian inscriptions we learn that there was a Jewish community at Ephesus, but no information is given regarding the possession of the rights of citizenship by the Jews. *Cf.* Canon Hick's *Inscr. of British Museum,* nos. 676 and 677.
[6] *Cf.* Joseph. *C. Apion.* ii, 4.
[7] *Cf.* Joseph. *Antiq.* xii, 3.2; *C. Apion.* ii, 4; Ramsay, " The Jews in Ephesus," *Expositor* v, 92-95; Schürer iii, 124-126.
[8] *Cf.* Joseph. *Antiq.* xii, 3.2; xvi, 2.5; Nicholas of Damascus, bks. 123 and 124.
[9] *Antiq.* xiv, 10.24. [10] *Ibid.* xvi, 6.1.

Wherever the Jews in Greek cities possessed the rights of citizenship they found themselves in a self-contradictory position.[1] Owing to the necessity of fulfilling certain religious duties, it was impossible for Jews to be citizens of Hellenic cities in the ordinary way. It was due to the efforts of the Seleucid kings that the essential theory of a Greek city was so widened as to permit a Jew to live in it as an integral part of it. Greek cities were divided into "tribes"[2] and citizenship implied membership of one of these. Every "tribe" was united by a religious bond and its members met to participate in the worship of common deities. This would mean that it was almost impossible for a Jew to belong to an ordinary "tribe." Just as it was made possible for a group of Jews to dwell in a Greek city as resident foreigners and practise their own religious cult in a private association, so it was permissible to enroll a body of Jewish citizens in a special "tribe" which was held together by the bonds of the Jewish religion. The Jews were still confronted by another difficulty. The entire body of citizens were united by a common city cultus in which no Jew could take part. This was solved by Seleucus and his successors by simply establishing an exception to the general principle. It was regarded as perfectly legitimate for a Jew not to participate in the city cultus and he was absolved from all laws and regulations which

---

[1] *Cf.* Ramsay, "Jews as Hellenic Citizens," *Expositor* v, 22-23; Schürer iii, 126.

[2] *Cf.* Fowler, *The City State of the Greeks and the Romans* 37; Greenridge, *Roman Public Life* 66.

were contrary to the dictates of the Jewish religion. It was this failure to honour the gods of the city which became a constant source of complaint on the part of the pagan fellow-citizens of the Jews, and this accounts for the fact that the Jews met with the greatest hatred and opposition just in the very places where they enjoyed the rights of citizenship. Everywhere, it was only the higher authority of the Roman *imperium* that protected the Jews in the maintenance of privileges that were recognized as having been legally given to them.

Besides the local franchise, many of the Jews of the Diaspora had the rights of Roman citizenship conferred upon them. According to Philo, the majority of the Jews living in Rome enjoyed such rights in virtue of the fact that they were the descendants of freedmen.[1] Of the Jews that Pompey brought to Rome and sold as slaves many, on account of their observance of the Sabbath and the dietary Laws, were freed by their own masters and, on obtaining their freedom, the rights of citizenship were conferred upon them at the same time.[2] The descendants of these *libertini* continued to enjoy these rights, and, as we have seen, by the time of Cicero, exercised considerable influence upon Roman politics.[3] All the Jewish citizens in Rome were not of servile origin.[4] Some came to Rome from the

[1] *Legat ad Cajum* sec. 23.
[2] *Cf.* Schürer iii, 84; Juster, *Les Droits politiques* 15.
[3] *Cf. supra* pp. 174-175.
[4] Juster argues that there must have been Jews in Rome before those brought by Pompey, otherwise they could not have exercised within so

East and had received their rights of citizenship by other means,[1] often as imperial favors. Judging from the statements of Cicero,[2] the Jews had seats and the right of voting in the civic councils, although we have no formal source affirming this fact.[3]

Some of the *libertini* must have left Rome and gone back to Jerusalem where they formed a community. It seems to be implied in the *Acts of the Apostles*[4] that this community was made up of Roman freedmen and their descendants.[5] There were, therefore, Jews living in Jerusalem who enjoyed the rights of Roman citizenship. We learn from Josephus that there were Jews in Jerusalem[6] who were Roman knights. During this period there were in Ephesus,[7] Delos,[8] Sardis[9] and in other cities of Asia Minor[10] a considerable number of Jews who

short a period the influence indicated by Cicero. (Speech of Cicero in 59 B.C.; return of Pompey 63 B.C.) The presence of Jews in Rome at a previous period is indicated by the Maccabean account (2 *Macc.* ii, 27), but we have no definite information regarding any permanent settlement of the Jews at that time. *Cf. supra* ch. ii, pp. 27-28; Reinach, "Quid Judaeo cum Verre"? *REJ* xxvi, 36-46.

[1] *Cf.* Girard, *Manuel élementaire de droit romain* 115.
[2] *Pro Flacco* sec. 66; "*scis quanta sit manus, quanta concordia, quantum valeat in concionibus.*"
[3] *Cf.* Juster, *Les Droits politiques* 53; Mommsen, *Manuel des antiquites romaines* vi, 2.25.
[4] *Acts* vi, 9.
[5] *Cf.* Schürer iii, 128, for references to literature in which this matter is treated in detail.   [6] *Bell. Jud.* ii, 149.
[7] *Cf.* Joseph. *Antiq.* xiv, 10.12, 13; *C. Apion.* ii, 4.39.
[8] *Ibid.* xiv, 10.14.   [9] *Ibid.* xiv, 10.14, 24.
[10] *Ibid.* xiv, 10.16, 18, 19; *cf.* Julius Caesar, *Civil War* 3.4; Grätz, "Die Stellung der kleinasiatischen Juden unter d. Romerherrschaft," *MGWJ* xxxv (1886), 329-346; Juster, *Les Droits politiques* 12; *Examen critique* 76.

possessed Roman citizenship. In the case of a few individuals[1] we know that Roman citizenship was conferred upon them as a favor from Julius Caesar but we cannot ascertain exactly how the other Jews of the various cities obtained similar rights.[2]

Many advantages accompanied the possession of the rights of Roman citizenship on the part of the Jews. The possessors living in the provinces were subject only to the jurisdiction of Roman courts, the civil cases being disposed of by a jury made up of Roman citizens,[3] and those of a criminal nature by the Roman procurator as governor. It was only in the *civitates*, recognized as *liberae*, that the Roman citizens as well were subject to the jurisdiction of other than Roman authorities.[4] The one possessing Roman citizenship was exempt from degrading punishments such as scourging and crucifixion.[5] He

[1] Citizenship was conferred upon Antipater and Philo of Alexandria as a favor from Julius Caesar; *cf.* Joseph. *Antiq.* xiv, 8.3; xvi, 2.4; *Bell. Jud.* i, 9.5; *Antiq.* xix, 5.1. Doubts regarding Paul's possession of the rights of citizenship were expressed by Renan (*Saint Paul* ch. xiii) and Overbeck (*Erklärung der Apostelgesch.* 266 *sqq.;* 429 *sqq.*), although Ramsay endeavours to prove that he was a citizen (*St. Paul the Traveller and the Roman Citizen*, "The Jews in Tarsus," *Expositor* v, 29-33; vi, 81-92); *cf.* Schürer iii, 129.

[2] *Cf.* Mendelssohn in *Acta soc. philol.* v, 174-176, for a conjecture as to the means of obtaining it. On the various ways, generally, in which the rights of Roman citizenship might be acquired, *cf.* Rein, "Civitas"; Pauly's *Real-Enc.* ii, 392 *sqq.;* Winer, *RWB* i, 220 ("Burgerrecht"). It is possible that many Jews received the rights of Roman citizenship for military services rendered to the Romans, especially Julius Caesar.

[3] Rudorff, *Römische Rechtsgeschichte* ii, 13.

[4] *Cf.* Marquardt, *Römische Staatsverwaltung* i, 75 *sqq.;* Kuhn, *Die städtische und bürgerl. Verfassung des römischen Reichs* ii, 24.

[5] *Cf.* Acts xvi, 37 *sqq.;* xxii, 25 *sqq.*

also had the right[1] not only of appealing against any sentence to the Emperor but could call upon him at the commencement of the process and at every stage of it, to have the examination conducted at Rome.[2]

In virtue of the fact that the Jews had the rights of Roman citizenship, they possessed also the *jus honorum*, the right of holding office.[3] As every official had to take a pagan oath, the Jews could only accept an official position by adjuring their faith. Later, under Septimus Severus and Caracella the Jews were admitted to all offices[4] without finding it necessary to act contrary to the dictates of their religion. This privilege was conceded to the Jews by both pagan and Christian emperors up to the close of the fifth century when public offices were only accessible to the Jews who were baptised.[5]

In the course of time the Jews attained some of the highest positions and distinctions in the Roman empire,[6] but most of these were acquired after the period of Caesar and Augustus. Most of the Jews who held distinguished positions at this period lived in the East, especially in Egypt, where the Jews succeeded in becoming a far more influential element than in Rome.

[1] *Jus provocationis* or *appellationis*. Cf. Geib, *Geschichte des römischen Criminalprocesses* 675 sqq.

[2] Cf. Acts xxv, 10.21; xxvi, 32; Pliny, *Epist*. x, 96; cf. also Geib, *op. cit.* 383 sqq.; Mommsen, *Römischen Staatsrecht* ii, 1, 245.

[3] Cf. Juster, *Les Droits politiques* 56.

[4] Cf. *Digesta* 50, 2.3.3; Juster, *op. cit.* 56-57, note 4.

[5] Cf. *Const. Sirm.* 6 *in fine;* Cumont, "Une formule grecque de renonciation au judaisme," *Wiener Studien* xxiv (1902), 462-472.

[6] Cf. Juster, *Les Droits politiques* 56-102.

LEGAL POSITION IN THE ROMAN EMPIRE 199

Many Jews were in charge of important offices in the private administration of the emperors at Rome, which were equivalent to public positions.[1] At this time all of these subordinate offices were held by slaves, freedmen or soldiers assigned for these specific purposes.[2] Many Jews because of their servile condition or as *libertini* were forced to accept these positions. When these duties became those of especial dignity, at the close of the third century, the Jews were still permitted to assume them.[3] Among these officials were the *urbaniciani* (*praefecti urbi*), the *praefectiani* (*praefecti praetorio*) and the *cohortales, cohortalina militia* (*rectores*).[4]

Jews were often employed to fill important positions at the imperial palace such as *agentes in rebus*, a kind of secret police.[5] Many were official physicians, *archiatri*.[6] It is probable that many Jews were employed as publicans[7] and we find several controlling the collection of custom duties.[8] Among

---

[1] *Cf.* Juster, *Les Droits politiques* 63-67; note 4, p. 63; *cf.* also Bethmann-Hollweg, *Der röm. Civilprozess* iii, 133-161; Kuhn, *Städtische Verfassung* i, 149 *sqq.;* Hirschfeld, *Verwaltungsbeamten* 457-465; Willems, *Le Droit public romain* 560 *sqq.*
[2] *Cf.* Hirschfeld, *op. cit.* 457 *sqq.*
[3] *Cf.* Juster, *op. cit.* 64, note 7; Willems, *op. cit.* 570.
[4] *Ibid.*
[5] *Cod. Theod.* xvi, 8.16, 24; *cf.* Juster, *op. cit.* 66 and note 5; Hirschfeld, "Die agentes in rebus," *Sitzungsberichte der Königl. preuss. Academie der Wissenschaften zu Berlin* (1893), 421-441; Mommsen, *Manuel des antiquités* i, 374 *sqq.*
[6] *Cf.* Juster, *op. cit.* 67, and the literature mentioned there.
[7] *Cf. supra* ch. iv, p. 154; Juster, *op. cit.* 69, note 5.
[8] *Cf.* Juster, *op. cit.* 69, notes 6 and 7; p. 70, notes 1, 2, 3, 4; p. 71, note 1, and the literature mentioned there.

the municipal obligations which were to be fulfilled by all citizens was that of the decurion. As the performance of certain pagan rites was connected with this office the Jews obtained the privilege of exemption from this duty.[1] Certain Jews fulfilled functions of *curator civitatis*.[2] Because of the esteem in which they were held by their fellow citizens some Jews obtained the honorable title of patron.[3] In accordance with the custom of the Romans to give expression in some way to their benefactors or *honores*, we find upon several inscriptions,[4] which are still extant, the names of Jews to whom such honours were accorded, often in the form of the erection of statues, for the benefits they bestowed upon their fellow citizens.[5]

Among the semi-official professions were those of law and the business of hiring out vessels for the transporting of passengers or goods. Jews were permitted to take up the profession of law[6] which at a later period was expressly tolerated by a decree.[7] The *navicularii* formed an administrative corporation[8] which conferred special honours upon its members.[9] Among these *navicularii* were many Jewish

[1] Joseph. *Antiq.* xvi, 2.2; cf. Juster, *Les Droits politiques* 71, note 2; 72, note 1.
[2] *Cf.* Juster, *op. cit.* 75, note 3, and literature referred to by Juster.
[3] *Cf.* Juster, *op. cit.* note 4.
[4] *Cf. CIGr.* 4486; de Vögue, *Syrie centrale, inscriptions sémitiques,* no. 63; Cooke, *Semitic Inscriptions,* no. 116.
[5] *Cf.* Juster, *Les Droits politiques* 75, note 5.
[6] *Cf. ibid.* 76, notes 3-6; Godefroy, *Paratitlon, Cod. Theod.* ii, 10; Pierantoni, *Gli avocati di Roma antica, passim.*
[7] *Cod. Theod.* xvi, 8.24.
[8] *Cf.* Waltzing, *Les Associations* i, 22; ii, 51 *sqq.;* Marquardt, *Das Privatleben der Römer* ii, 24; Juster, *op. cit.* 77-78.
[9] Godefroy, *Paratitlon, Cod. Theod.* xiii, 5.

ship owners who in the East formed a corporation of their own.[1]

The Jews proved themselves to be good soldiers, well disciplined and deeply attached to their rulers in the Roman armies as they had been, previously, in the armies of the Egyptians, Persians and Greeks.[2]

According to Juster the Jews formed military bodies of their own[3] and in describing the composition of the Jewish armies[4] he says they were made up of (1) mercenaries,[5] (2) native pagans who often formed separate alae or wings,[6] and (3) the Jews. He objects strongly to the statements of several scholars, theologians and jurists that the Jews were exempted from military service[7] and claims that the decree of Caesar as given by Josephus,[8] is wrongly interpreted by them. What Juster, we think, fails to make clear and a fact which is probably implied in the explanations of other writers, is not that the Jews were entirely exempt from military service, but that during this period the Jewish soldiers were

[1] *Cf.* Philo, *In Flacc.* sec. 8; Krauss, *Talmud Archäologie* ii, 388; *cf.* ibid 254, note; Grünwald, *Juden als Rheder und Seefahrer.*

[2] Juster, *Les Droits politiques* 78-82; Bertholet, *Die Stellung der Israeliten und der Juden zu den Fremden,* 199 sqq.

[3] Juster, *Les Droits politiques* pp. 79, 81, 82.

[4] *Ibid.* 83-86.

[5] *Cf.* Joseph. *Antiq.* xiii, 8.4; xiii, 6.2; xiv, 9.4; xiv, 11.5; xiv, 13.9; xv, 7.3; xvii, 8.3; *Bell Jud.* i, 4.3; 5.2; 11.6; 20.3; 33.9.

[6] Joseph. *Antiq.* xix, 9.1; *cf.* Schürer i, 458-466.

[7] *Cf.* Bertholet, *Die Stellung der Israeliten und der Juden zu den Fremden* 240 *sqq.;* Schürer iii, 73; Harnack, *Militia Christi, die christliche Religion und der Soldatenstand in den ersten drei Jahrhunderten* 48, note 1.

[8] *Antiq.* xiv, 10.6.

exempt from military service on the Sabbath because of religious requirements. On the Sabbath, Jews were forbidden either to use arms[1] or to march farther than two hundred yards.[2] The practical character of this matter was seen at the time when civil war broke out between Caesar and Pompey and the consul Lentulus, though raising legions, exempted the Jewish citizens from being liable to conscription and issued instructions to this effect to all authorities having charge of the conscription.[3] Six years later Dolabella confirmed this privilege of the Jews of this same province referring to the previous edicts.[4] The same privilege was conceded in Palestine to the Jews by Julius Caesar.[5] Juster refers to the concessions of Lentulus and Dolabella but says they were merely favours and did not arise from any general principles which might actuate decrees of Julius Caesar or Augustus.[6] One other exemption in deference to Jewish legalism that was made at this time might be mentioned in this connection. Jewish soldiers were not required to take an oath on the imperial images on the ensigns carried in the armies[7] and governors disobeying this command were severely rebuked.[8]

[1] *Cf. supra* p. 168, note 1.
[2] *Cf. ibid.* note 1; Hild, *REJ* viii, 28; xi, 48.
[3] *Cf.* Joseph. *Antiq.* xiv, 10.13; 14, 16, 18, 19; *cf.* Mendelssohn on this passage in *Acta soc. phil.* v, 167-188; *TL* (1876), p. 393; Schürer ii, 264.
[4] *Cf.* Joseph. *op. cit.* xiv, 10.11-12.
[5] *Ibid.* 10.6.
[6] *Cf.* Juster, *Droits politiques* 86, note 9.
[7] *Cf. supra* p. 172.
[8] *Cf.* Hild *REJ*, viii, p. 29.

Although reliable sources regarding the local military service of the Jews is lacking, we can probably draw the conclusion that since all the inhabitants were expected to aid the city in time of danger the Jews were included likewise.[1] At Rome, the Jews as well as all others were prohibited from carrying arms.[2]

In the days of the empire the Roman army[3] was divided into legions and auxiliaries, the former consisting only of those who possessed the rights of citizenship, the latter of provincials who, at least in the early days of the empire, did not, generally, possess that privilege.[4]

As a rule, only auxiliary troops were found in the provinces governed by procurators.[5] At Caesarea, the seat of the Roman administration of the Jewish province of Judaea, the Roman military force consisted of a moderate number of cavalry and infantry, one *ala* and five cohorts, about three thousand men.[6] This garrison consisted for the most part of Caesareans and Sebastians, that is, the soldiers drafted

---

[1] *Cf.* Juster, *Les Droits politiques* 91; Liebenam, "Exercitus," in Pauly's *RECA* vi, 1608.

[2] Mommsen, *Manuel des antiquités romaines* vi, 1, 243; Juster, *op. cit.* 32.

[3] For a detailed description of the composition and nature of the Roman army, *cf.* Marquardt, *Römische Staatsverwaltung* ii, 307-591; Pfitzner, *Gesch. der römischen Kaiserlegionem von Augustus bis Hadrianus.*

[4] *Cf.* Schürer i, 458.

[5] *Cf.* Marquardt, *op. cit.* ii, 518; Schürer, *Zeitschrift für wissenschaftliche Theologie* xviii (1875), 413-425; Mommsen, "Die Conscriptionsordnung der römischen Kaiserzeit," *Hermes* xix (1884), 1-79; 210-234.

[6] *Cf.* Mommsen, *Provinces of the Roman Empire,* ii, 202.

in the region of Sebaste or Samaria.¹ In Jerusalem, even during the festivals, the garrison did not exceed one cohort.² There seems to have been, according to a passage in the *New Testament*, a small company of soldiers, probably native Jews, under a captain, whose function it was to aid the high priest in preserving order in the Temple.³ According to a decree enacted by Julius Caesar and sanctioned by Augustus, "no one, either governor, or general, or ambassador, may raise auxiliaries within the bounds of Judaea, nor may soldiers exact money of them for winter quarters or on any other pretext, but they are to be free from all sorts of injuries."⁴ This decree, the interpretation of which has been a matter of considerable dispute on the part of historians,⁵ probably meant that no compulsory military service could be required from the Jews but, as Muirhead suggests,⁶ to be under arms in the service of the Temple may well have been

¹ Cohorts and *alae* were commonly named from the district or nation from which they had been recruited. *Cf.* Joseph. *Antiq.* xx, 8.7; Schürer i, 459; Mommsen, *Provinces of the Empire* ii, 202. According to Schürer, *op. cit.* i, 460; Mommsen, *op. cit.* ii, 202, note 1, and Hirschfeld, "Die agentes in rebus," *Sitzungsberichte der Berliner Akademie* (1899), 433, there were no *alae* and *cohortes Iudaeorum*. These historians support their statements by the decree of Caesar which is found in Joseph. *Antiq.* xiv, 10.6. Juster (*Les Droits politiques* 85), however, endeavours to prove that the Jews were not exempted from military service; *cf. supra* p. 201.
² *Cf. Acts* xxi, 31-37.
³ *Cf. Acts* iv, 1; Joseph. *Antiq.* xx, 5.3; 8.11; *Bell. Jud.* ii, 2-1; Schürer, *op. cit.* i, 464.
⁴ *Cf.* Joseph. *Antiq.* xiv, 10.6.
⁵ *Cf. supra* pp. 201-202.
⁶ *The Times of Christ*, 44.

considered as a pious duty and not the fulfillment of an unjust demand on the part of the procurator.

In taking a retrospective glance at the condition of the Jews in the Roman Empire, during the reigns of Julius Caesar and Augustus, we have found that upon the whole it was a period of marked toleration. From a political standpoint, despite the occasional oppression of the procurators, despite the fact that the new form of government necessarily undermined some of the precepts of the Law and brought about a natural conflict between the ambitious aims of Jews and Romans, the former, nevertheless, enjoyed a considerable measure of freedom in self-administration and as a close analysis of events has shown, the advantages of Roman rule overbalanced its disadvantages. Although the Roman authorities had a perfect right to interfere in the legislation and in the administration of the law in non-autonomous communities, they took but little advantage of this right in the case of Judaea.[1] In fact, many concessions from the point of view of law were granted to the Jews. In one case the Jews were given the privilege of proceeding against Roman citizens according to Jewish law. If at any time one who was not a Jew intruded into the inner courts of the Temple, in Jerusalem, he could be sentenced to death by the Jewish court, even though he were a Roman.[2] The

[1] *Cf.* Schürer i, 480-481; Mommsen, *Römisches Staatsrecht* iii, 716-764.
[2] *Cf.* Joseph. *Antiq.* xv, 11.5; *Bell. Jud.* 5.1; vi, 2.4; *C. Apion.* ii, 8; Philo, *Legat. ad Cajum* sec. 31; Mishnah, " Middoth," ii, 3; " Kelim," i, 8. *Cf. CIGr* n. 2222, for the decree of the Roman senate with reference to Chios, passed in 80 B.C and dealing with this concession.

subjecting of Roman citizens to the laws of a foreign city was regarded as an extraordinary concession, and, as a rule, was given only to those communities which were recognized as *liberae*.[1] The Sanhedrin, moreover, was given the right to try Jews from different parts of the empire, even if the offense had not been committed in Judaea, and was purely a question of religious belief.[2] In more than one instance, Roman imperialism had "ensured the priceless boon of public peace."[3] When among hostile foreigners the mere claim of the Jews that they had the rights of citizenship, obtained for them help and security.[4]

We have already seen that in numerous ways great deference was shown by the Romans to the religious opinions of the Jews. The Jewish worship was not only tolerated but, by the passing of various enactments, came under State protection.[5] The synagogue services[6] and the Holy Scriptures[7] were also protected by law.[8] At the death of Caesar

[1] *Cf.* Schürer ii, 262; Kuhn, *Die städtische und bürgerl. Verfassung* ii, 24; Marquardt, *Römische Staatsverwaltung* i, 75. *Cf.* also the decree of the Roman senate with reference to Chios, passed in the year 674 A.U.C. = 80 B.C. (*CIGr* n. 2222).

[2] *Cf. Acts* ix, 2; xxii, 5; xxvi, 12.

[3] Addis, *Christianity and the Roman Empire* 8.

[4] Cicero, *In Verrem* v, 57.

[5] Schürer, i, 482; Hoss, *Das Judentum unter den römischen Cäsaren* 18-19; Wagener, *Extrait des Bulletins de l'académie royale de Bélgique* 3e, ser. xxvii (1893), 343; Bonnetty, *Religion des Romains* 273-281.

[6] Joseph. *Antiq.* xix, 6.3.

[7] Joseph. *Antiq.* xx, 5.4; *Bell. Jud.* ii, 12.2.

[8] Schürer, *op. cit.* i, 482; Milman, *History of the Jews* ii, 132; Addis, *op. cit.* 32.

the parties contending for the control of affairs vied with each other in maintaining the privileges granted to the Jews. Dolabella in support of the Jews sent communications to the authorities of Ephesus apprizing them of the freedom of religious worship conferred upon the Jews of that province by previous governors.[1] By an edict of Marcus Junius Brutus, the Jews were protected in their observance of Sabbath and other sacred usages.[2]

Augustus throughout his reign had continually shown a friendly interest in the Jews and when an embassy of Jews from Cyrene and Asia Minor, complained to him of their ill-treatment by the Greeks, he immediately issued four decrees in favor of the Jewish people.[3] While as we have already pointed out,[4] none of these decrees granted any new privileges, they confirmed the Jews in the possession of those that they already had, secured for them the observance of their own religion, and protected them against the theft of their sacred books, and temple offerings and the prohibition of their assemblies. In consequence of these many decrees, "Judaism acquired such a legal standing that it came to be treated as a *religio licita* throughout the whole extent of the Roman Empire."[5]

In a similar way, imperial legislation protected the Jews in their economic relations of life.[6] Except

[1] Joseph. *Antiq.* xiv, 11-12.
[2] *Cf.* Joseph. *Antiq.* xiv, 10-25.
[3] *Cf.* Joseph. *Antiq.* xvi, 6.2-7.
[4] *Cf. supra* p. 108.
[5] Schürer iii, 69; *cf. supra* p. 173.
[6] *Cf. supra* pp. 179-182.

for the few necessary regulations imposed upon the Jews in matters of taxation, no obstacle was placed in the path of their material development. Conscious of the religious susceptibilities of the Jews, Roman authorities not only permitted them to develop, unhampered, their agriculture, commerce and industry according to their own traditions and customs, but even assured this development against hostile forces.

If we found that the Roman misconceptions of the Jewish religion and the consequent aversion to the customs and manners of the Jews gave rise to adverse criticism on the part of Greek and Roman writers,[1] we must remember that their invectives were mere literary products which affected but little the general position of the Jews; that these adverse opinions were current among the literati rather than the Roman populace and government authorities. A close examination of the social relations of the Jews and the Romans in their daily routine of life makes evident the fact that the spirit of aversion was far less manifested in practice than appears from the literature of the period of our immediate study.

The general policy of toleration finds expression in the attitude of the Jews towards Julius Caesar and Augustus. The Jews had been confederates with Caesar when he fought against Egypt[2] and the emperor did not forget this and other services ren-

[1] *Cf. supra* ch. iii.
[2] *Cf.* Joseph. *Antiq.* xiv, 8; Duruy, *History of Rome* iii, 326.

dered to him by the Jewish people.[1] It is true that the privileges granted to the Jews by Caesar were not a mark of gratitude, exclusively, but were based on political motives as well.[2] Whatever might have been the true basis for the tolerant policy of Caesar,[3] it, nevertheless, was put into practice and won the respect and grateful regard of the Jews for their ruler. The untimely death of Caesar called forth the sorrow and resentment of the Jews throughout the Roman world.[4] Suetonius tells us that in the public mourning in Rome " there joined a multitude of foreigners, expressing their sorrow according to the fashion of their respective countries; but especially the Jews, who for several nights together frequented the spot where the body was burnt."[5]

To Augustus no less than to Caesar the Jews were greatly indebted for their formal recognition within the empire. He confirmed and renewed all the privileges granted to the Jews by his predecessor.[6] While Augustus had no love for Judaism, nor indeed for any religion other than that adopted by the State,[7] he, nevertheless, showed great respect for

[1] *Cf* Bonnetty, *Religion des Romains* 265-282.
[2] *Cf.* Merivale, *History of the Romans,* iii, 284; Weiss, *Die römischen Kaiser* 6-7.
[3] *Cf.* Amitai, *Romains et Juifs* 35; Goldschmide, *De Iudaeorum apud Romanos Condicione* 14-15; Mommsen, *The History of Rome* v, 118-119.
[4] *Cf.* Geiger, *IM* ii, 110; Merivale, *History of the Romans* iii, 41; Duruy, *History of Rome* ii, 420; Grätz, *Gesch. der Juden* iii, 153.
[5] *Cf.* Suetonius, lxxxiv; Berliner, *Geschichte der Juden in Rom* i, 182.
[6] Philo, *Legat. ad Cajum* sec. 40-41; Hardy, *Christianity and the Roman Government* 26; Amitai, *Romains et Juifs* 43; Allard, *Histoire des persécutions pendant les deux premiers siècles* 3.
[7] *Cf.* Suetonius, *Octavianus* xciii.

the religion, the ideas, and customs of the Jews. The imperial family sent golden vases and cups for the use of the Temple[1] and at the request of the emperor a burnt sacrifice of a bull and two lambs was daily offered in honour of the God of Israel. This offering, according to Philo,[2] was provided by Augustus himself, though Josephus[3] asserts that it was made at the cost of the Jewish people. It is possible, however, as Schürer points out, that the Jewish historian was unaware of the fact that the money to pay for the sacrifice came actually from the emperor.[4] In the Diaspora, and possibly in Palestine, as far as the Law permitted, the emperor was remembered in the prayers of the synagogue.[5] On special occasions the Jewish people at their own expense offered a great sacrifice in honour of the emperor.[6] This offering was celebrated by the Jews with pious zeal for it was regarded as a "gauge of Roman tolerance and Jewish submission; a seal of friendship between Rome and Jerusalem."[7]

[1] *Cf.* Weiss, *Die römischen Kaiser* 8.
[2] Philo, *op. cit.* sec. 23; 40.
[3] *Bell. Jud.* ii, 10.4; 17.2-4; *C. Apion.* ii, 6.
[4] Schürer ii, 361.
[5] *Cf.* Philo, *In Flaccum* sec. 7; *Pirke Aboth* iii, 2; *Jeremias* xxix, 7; *Baruch* i, 10-11.
[6] *Cf.* Philo, *Legat. ad Cajum* sec. 45.
[7] Hudson, *History of the Jews in Rome* 56.

BIBLIOGRAPHY

I. GENERAL BIBLIOGRAPHICAL WORKS.

Catalogus scriptorum qui contra Judaeos scripserunt, cum veterum, tum recentium, partim Graecorum, partim Latinorum, alphabeti ordine digestorum. Bibliotheca Theologica Joannis Molani. In *Thesaurus Monumentorum Ecclesiasticorum et Historicorum* (Amsterdam 1725), iv, 816-818.

Index De Judaeis: Compendiose Scilicet ex Patribus Complectens Illorum Historiam et Leges, Haereses ac Scelera, Necnon Poenas et per Gentes Dispersionem ac sub Finem Saeculi Conversionem. Patr. Lat. (*cf. infra*), ccxx, 990 sqq.

New York Public Library. List of Works Relating to the History and Condition of the Jews in Various Countries. N. Y., 1914.

Patrologie by O. Bardenhewer 3rd ed. (Freiburg, 1912).

II. SOURCES.

1. *General Collections.*

Ante-Nicene Fathers (ANF), 10 vols., ed. A. Roberts and J. Donaldson. American reprint of Edin. ed., revised by A. C. Coxe (N. Y., 1890-97).

Bibliothek der griechischen und römischen Schriftsteller über Judenthum und Juden in neuen Uebertragungen und Sammlungen, 4 pts. in 2 vols. (Leipzig, 1865-72).

Bibliotheca Latino-Hebraica sive de scriptoribus Latinis qui ex diversis nationibus contra Iudaeos, vel de re Hebraica utcumque scripsere. . . . C. I. Imbonati (Rome, 1694).

Collection de documents inédits sur l'histoire de France (CDIF), publiés par les soins du ministre de l'instruction publique (Paris, 1835-1914).

Corpus Inscriptionum Atticarum (CIA), ed. A. Kirchhoff and others (Berlin, 1873-).

Corpus Inscriptionum Graecarum (CIGr.), ed. A. Boeckh and others, 4 vols. (Berlin, 1827-77).

Corpus Inscriptionum Hebraicarum (CIH), ed. D. Chwolson (St. Petersburg, 1882).

Corpus Inscriptionum Latinarum (CIL), ed. Mommsen and others, 15 vols. (Berlin, 1863-).

Corpus Juris Civilis (CJC), 3 vols. (Berlin, 1877-99), i (*Institutiones*), ed. P. Krüger, and (*Digesta*), ed. T. Mommsen, ii (*Codex*), ed. P. Krüger, iii (*Novellae*), ed. R. Schoell and W. Kroll. Small 11th ed., 1908. German tr. of whole *Corpus* by K. E. Otto, B. Schilling and K. F. F. Sintenis, 7 vols. (Leipzig, 1831-39). Eng. tr. of *Institutiones* by J. B. Moyle (Oxford, 1883), and *Digesta* by C. H. Monro, vol. i (Cambridge, 1904).

Corpus Scriptorum Ecclesiasticorum Latinorum (CSEL), ed. *Consilio . . . Academiae litterarum Caesareae Vindobonensis*, 62 vols. (Vienna, 1866-1913).

Corpus Scriptorum Historiae Byzantinae (CSHB), ed. B. G. Niebuhr (Bonn, 1828-55).

Die Griechischen Christlichen Schriftsteller der ersten drei Jahrhunderte (GCS), publ. by the "Kirchenväter-Kommission der Köngl. Preuss. Akadamie der Wissenschaften" (Leipzig, 1897).

Inscriptionum Latinarum Collectio, ed. J. K. von Orelli, 3 vols. (Turin, 1828-56).

Monumenta Germaniae Historica (MGH), ed. by Pertz and others. (Hanover, 1826-1913).

Nicene and Post Nicene Fathers (NPNF), ed. P. Schaff and H. Wace, 14 vols. (N. Y., 1886-1890); 2d ser., 1890-1900.

Patrologiae Cursus Completus, ed. J. P. Migne.

———— *Ser. Latina* (Patr. Lat.), 225 vols. (Paris, 1844-1861).

———— *Ser. Graeca* (Patr. Gr.), 161 vols. (Paris, 1857-1866).

Sacrorum Conciliorum Nova et Amplissima Collectio (SCC), ed. J. D. Mansi, 31 vols. (Florence and Venice, 1759-98). Reprint (Paris and Leipzig, 1901-), 41 vols.

Scriptores Historiae Augustae, ed. Peter; Teubner series (Leipzig, 1884); Eng. tr. by J. Bernard (London, 1740).

Texte und Untersuchungen zur Geschichte der altchristlichen Literatur (Texte), ed. O. Gebhardt, A. Harnack and C. Schmidt (Leipzig, 1882-), 40 vols.

Thesaurus Monumentorum Ecclesiasticorum et Historicorum, sive Henrici Canisii Lectiones Antiquae, ed. J. Basnage, 4 vols. (Amsterdam, 1725).

BIBLIOGRAPHY. 213

2. *Individual Works.*

Alexander Polyhistor, περὶ 'Ιουδαίων, fragments 3-24 in C. Müller, *Frag. Hist. Graec.* iii, 211-230.

Appian, *De scriptoribus belli Mithridatici tertii*, ed. F. W. Lauer (Cobet, 1871); Gr. text and Eng. tr. by H. White in *Appian's Roman History* iv, 241-477, in Loeb Classical Library (London, 1912).

Apocrypha and Pseudepigrapha of the Old Testament, ed. R. H. Charles, 2 vols. (Oxford, 1913).

Apollonius Molon, συσκευὴ κατὰ 'Ιουδαίων, Frag. 5 in C. Müller, *Frag. Hist. Graec.* iii, 207.

Apuleius, *Opera Quae Supersunt*, ed. R. Helm, 3 vols. in 4 pts. (Leipzig, 1905-10).

Aramaic Papyri Discovered at Assuan, ed. Sayce and Cowley (London, 1906).

Aramäische Papyrus und Ostraka aus einer jüdischen Militär-Kolonie zu Elephantine, mit 75 Lichtdrucktafeln, ed. E. Sachau (Leipzig, 1911).

Aristo of Pella, in Eusebius, *Hist. Eccles.* iv, 6.3.

Athenaeus, Δειπνοσοφισταί, or *The Deipnosophists or Banquet of the Learned*, ed. G. Kaibel, Teubner series (Leipzig, 1887); Eng. tr. by C. D. Yonge, Bohn Classical Library, 3 vols. (London, 1854).

Athenagoras, *Libellus pro Christianis*, ed. E. Schwartz, in *Texte u. Untersuchungen* iv, pt. 2 (Leipzig, 1891).

Augustine, *Opera* (*Patr. Lat.*), vols. 32-47; (CSEL), 15 vols. (1887-1911); Eng. tr. (NPNF), ser. I, vol. i-viii (New York, 1903-7).

―――― *De Civitate Dei*, ed. E. Hoffman (CSEL), xl, 1, 2; Eng. tr. by M. Dods, 2 vols. (Edinburgh, 1871).

Book of Enoch; 1 Enoch, tr. from the editor's Ethiopic text and ed. with introduction, notes and indexes of first edition by R. H. Charles (Oxford, 1912); 2 Enoch, in *Apocrypha and Pseudepigrapha* ii, 425-469 (Oxford, 1913).

Celsus, *Ad Vigilium episcopum de judaica incredulitate, Patr. Lat.*, 6/49-58 (Paris, 1844); in (CSEL), iii, 3.

Chrysostom, John, *Adversus Judaeos Orationes* and *Adversus Gentes* in Opera in Migne (Patr. Gr.), 47-64; Fr. tr. by Abbé J. Bareille (Paris, 1863-78); Eng. tr. (NPNF) 6 vols., ser 1, vols. 9-14 (New York, 1899-1908).

Cicero, Marcus Tullius, *In Verrem, Oratio de Provinciis Consularibus*, and *Pro Flacco* in *Scripta Quae Manserunt Omnia,* ed. C. F. W. Mueller (Leipzig, 1893-1904); Eng. tr. of the ora-

tions by C. D. Yonge, in Bohn Classical Library, 4 vols. (London, 1867-72).
Clement of Alexandria, *Opera Quae Exstant Omnia*, ed. O. Stählin (GCS), 3 vols. (Leipzig, 1905-9); Eng. tr. by W. Wilson (ANF), 4, 12 (Edinburgh, 1867-69).
Codex Justinianus, ed. P. Krüger, 2 vols. (Berlin, 1877-99); Ger. tr. by Otto, Schilling and Sintenis, 7 vols. (Leipzig, 1831-39); small 11th editon (CJC), ii.
Codex Theodosianus, libri xvi cum constitutionibus Sirmondianis et leges Novellae ad Theodosianum pertinentes, ed. T. Mommsen and P. M. Meyer (Berlin, 1904-5); also ed. J. Gothofredi, 6 vols. in 3 (London, 1765).
Collection of Ancient Greek Inscriptions in the British Museum, ed. C. Hicks (Oxford, 1890).
Cyprian, *Opera Omnia*, ed. G. Hartel (CSEL), iii, 3, pp. 133-144 (Vienna, 1868); Eng. tr. by R. E. Wallis (ANF), 8, 13 (Edinburgh, 1868-69).
Cyril of Alexandria, *Opera quae reperiri potuerunt omnia*, ed. J. P. Migne, *Patr. Gr.* lxviii-lxxvii (Paris, 1864).
Democritus, περὶ 'Ιουδαίων, Frag. in C. Müller, *Frag. Hist. Graec.* iv, 377.
De Altercatione Ecclesiae et Synagogae (Patr. Lat.), 13/1131-1140.
Diodorus Siculus, *Bibliothecae Historicae Libri Qui Supersunt*, ed. L. Dindorf, 5 vols. (Leipzig, 1867-8); Eng. tr. by G. Booth, *The Historical Library of Diodorus the Sicilian in Fifteen Books, with the Fragments of Diodorus out of Photius's Bibliotheca and Others*, 2 vols. (London, 1814).
Dion Cassius, Cocceianus, *Historia Romana*, ed. U. P. Boissevain, 3 vols. (Berlin, 1895-1901); Eng. tr. by E. Cary on the basis of the version of H. B. Foster, 9 vols. (London, 1914).
Eusebius of Caesarea, *Historia Ecclesiastica* (Lat. tr. of Rufinus), ed. E. Schwartz (GCS), ii, 1,2,3 (Leipzig, 1903-9); Eng. tr. by A. C. McGiffert (NPNF), vol. i (New York, 1890).
—— *Chronicorum canonum quae supersunt . . . Hieronymi Chronicon*, ed. R. Helm (GCS), viii (Leipzig, 1913).
—— *Evangelicae preparationis libri xv*, ed. Gr. and Eng. tr. by E. H. Gifford (Oxford, 1903).
Florus, L. Annaeus, *Epitomae libri II*, ed. O. Rossbach (Leipzig, 1896); Eng. tr. by J. S. Watson in Bohn Classical Library (London, 1898).
Fragmenta Historicorum Graecorum, ed. C. and Th. Müller, 5 vols. (Paris, 1841-1883).

Georgius Syncellus, *Chronographia*, ed. Dindorf, Gr., with Lat. tr. (CSHB), (Bonn, 1829).

Gregory of Tours, *Historia Francorum*, ed. W. Arnott (MGH), (Hanover, 1885); Fr. tr. by A. Jacobs (Paris, 1863).

Gregory the Great, *Registrum epistularum*, ed. Migne (Patr. Lat.), 77/441-1328. New ed. P. Ewald and L. M. Hartmann (MGH), *Epistolae*, 2 vols. (Berlin, 1893).

Hecateus of Abdera, Αἰγυπτιακά 14, cited by Josephus in *C. Apion*. i, 22.

Hesiod, *Work and Days*, Gr. text ed. by C. Sittl. 1889; Eng. tr. by A. W. Mair (Oxford, 1908).

Horace, *Carmina*, ed. Gow; Lat. text with Eng. tr. by Conington (London, 1911).

Herodotus, *Historia*, ed. C. Hude, 2 vols. (Oxford, 1908); Eng. tr. by G. Rawlinson, 2 vols. (New York, 1910).

Hippolytus, *Philosophumena, sive omnium haeresium refutatio*, ed. E. Miller (Oxford, 1851); Eng. tr. by J. H. MacMahon (ANF), v, 1-153 (New York, 1896).

Inscriptions Grecques et Latines recueille en Grèce et en Asie Mineure, ed. P. Le Bas and W. H. Waddington, 3 vols. (Paris, 1870).

Irenaeus, *Libri quinque adversus Haereses*, ed. W. W. Harvey (Cambridge, 1857).

Jerome, *Epistola xxi—Ad Damasum* in *Sancti Eusebii Hieronymi epistolae*, ed. I. Hillberg (CSEL), vol. liv, iii-142 (Vienna, 1910-12); Eng. tr. in pt. by G. Lewis and W. G. Martley (NPNF), ser. 2, vol. vi, p. 22 (New York, 1893).

Josephus, Flavius, *Opera*, ed. B. Niese, 7 vols. (Berlin, 1885-95); Eng. tr. by Whiston, revised by A. R. Shilleto, with topographical notes by Sir C. W. Wilson, 5 vols. (London, 1900-1903).

Joseph ben Gorion or Pseudo-Josephus, *Josippon . . . Historiae Judaicae Libri Sex, ex Hebraeo Latine vertit*, ed. J. Gagnier (Oxford, 1706); Fr. tr. by F. de Bellforest in Fr. tr. of the works of Flavius Josephus by Genebrard (Paris, 1609); Eng. tr. of a pt. of the work under the title, *A Compendious and Most Marvellous Historie of the Latter Times of the Jews Common-Weale*, by P. Morwyn (London, 1615); Eng. tr. by J. Howell (London, 1652; 1684; 1699); (Bellows Falls, Vt., 1819).

Julius Africanus, *Epistola ad Aristidem* in Eusebius, *Hist. Eccles.* i, 7-11; Eng. tr. (ANF), vi, 125-127.

Julius Caesar, *De Bello Gallico*, ed. E. S. Shuckburgh (Cambridge, 1901); Eng. tr. by E. P. Long (London, 1911).

Justin, *Epitoma historiarum Philippicarum Pompei Trogi*, ed. F. Ruehl, Teubner series (Leipzig, 1886); Eng. tr. ed. J. B. Watson, *Justin, Cornelius Nepos and Eutropius* (London, 1910).

Justin Martyr, *Apologia*, ed. Otto in *Corpus Apologetarum Christianorum* (Jena, 1876); Eng. tr. by A. Blunt, *The Apologies of Justin Martyr* (Cambridge, 1911).

—— *Dialogus cum Tryphone Judaeo*, ed. J. P. Migne (Patr. Lat.), 6 (Paris, 1857); Eng. tr. by G. Reith and M. Dods (ANF), ii (Edinburgh, 1868).

Juvenal, *Saturarum libri v*, ed. H. L. Wilson (New York, 1903): Eng. tr. by A. E. Cole in Temple Gr. and Lat. Classics (New York, 1906).

Lactantius, *Epitome divinarum institutionum*, ed. S. Brandt in *Opera omnia* (CSEL), xix (Vienna, 1890); Eng. tr. by W. Fletcher (ANF), xxi (Edinburgh, 1871).

Letter of Aristeas, ed. H. St. J. Thackeray in Swete, *Introduction to the Old Testament in Greek*, pp. 519-574, 2nd ed. (Cambridge, 1902); Eng. tr. by H. T. Andrews in Charles, *Pseudepigrapha* 83-122.

Livy, *Historiarum Romanarum libri qui supersunt*, ed. J. N. Madvig and J. L. Ussing, 8 pts. in 4 vols. (Hanover, 1863-73); Eng. tr. of Bks., xxi-xxv, by Church and Brodribb (London, 1901).

Maccabees I-III, in *Apocrypha and Pseudepigrapha of the Old Testament*, ed. by R. H. Charles, vol. i, 59-173 (Oxford, 1913).

Macrobius, *Opera quae supersunt*, ed. L. James, 2 vols. (Leipzig, 1848-1852).

Martial, *Epigrammata*, ed. W. M. Lindsay (Oxford, 1902); Eng. tr. by P. Nixon (Boston, 1911).

Mediaeval Jewish Chronicles, ed. A. Neubauer, ii in *Anecdota Oxoniensia*, Semitic ser. vol. i, pt. vi (Oxford, 1895).

Megillath Antiochus, ed. in Aramic, Heb. and Eng. by Filipowski (London, 1851).

Megillath Taanith, or *Book of Fasts*. Aramic text and Hebrew scholia ed. by A. Neubauer in *Mediaeval Jewish Chronicles* ii, 3-25 (Oxford, 1895); Aramaic text and Fr. tr. by Jos. Derenbourg, *Histoire de la Palestine* (Paris, 1867), 439-446; and M. Schwab in his *La Megillath Taanith ou " Anniversaires historiques"* (Paris, 1897). Same text with Ger. notes, Grätz, *Gesch. der Juden*, iii, 559-577; Dalman, *Aramäische Dialectproben*, 1-3; 32-34.

Midrashim: Mechilta, ed. M. Friedmann (Vienna, 1870); Ger. tr. by J. Winter and A. Wünische (Leipzig, 1909).

Minucius Felix, *Opera,* ed. H. Boenig, Teubner ser. (Leipzig, 1903); Eng. tr. by R. E. Wallis (ANF), iv (1890).

Nicarchus, περὶ 'Ιουδαίων, in C. Müller, *Frag. Hist. Graec.* iii, 335.

Nicholas of Damascus, *Fragmenta,* in C. Müller, *Frag. Hist. Graec.* iii, 343-461.

Nouveau recueil des inscriptions Chrétiennes de la Gaule antérieures au viiie siécle, ed. E. F. Le Blant (CDIF), v (Paris, 1892).

Oracula Sibyllina; Gr. text. ed. by A. Rzach (Vienna, 1891); Gr. text, with Ger. tr., ed. by J. H. Friedlieb (Leipzig, 1852); Eng. tr. in *Apocrypha and Pseudepigrapha* of the Old Testament, ed. Charles, ii, pp. 383 *sqq.* (Oxford, 1913).

Origen, *Adversus Celsum* in *Werke,* ed. Koetschau (GCS), i (London, 1899).

Ovid, *De arte amatoria libri tres,* ed. Paul Brandt, 2 vols in 1 (Leipzig, 1902).

Persius, Flaccus, A., *Saturarum Liber,* ed. H. Nettleship, with Eng. tr. and commentary by J. Conington, 3rd ed. (Oxford, 1893).

Petronius Arbiter, *Satirae et liber Priapeorum tertium,* ed. F. Buechler (Berlin, 1895); Eng. tr. by M. Heseltine in Loeb Classical Library (London, 1913).

Vergil, Maro Publius, *Opera,* ed. O. Ribbeck (Leipzig, 1910); Eng. tr. by J. Jackson (Oxford, 1908).

Philo of Alexandria, *Opera quae supersunt,* ed. L. Cohn and P. Wendland, 5 vol. (Berlin, 1896-1906); Eng. tr. from Gr. text by C. D. Yonge in Bohn Classical Library, 4 vols. (London, 1854-55).

Philo Byblius, also called Herennius Philo, περὶ 'Ιουδαίων (Frag. 5, 6), ed. K. Müller, *Frag. Hist. Graec.* iii, 570-571 (Paris, 1848).

Philostratus, Flavius, *Vita Apollonii Tyaneii,* ed. Lat. text, with Eng. tr. by F. C. Conybeare in Loeb Classical Library, 2 vols. (London, 1912).

Pliny, *Naturalis historiae libri xxxvii,* ed. C. Mayhoff (Leipzig, 1875-1906); Eng. tr. by J. Bostock and H. T. Riley in Bohn Classical Library, 6 vols. (London, 1855-57).

Plutarch, *Moralia,* Greek text ed. G. N. Bernardakis, 6 vols. (Leipzig, 1888-96); Eng. tr. by W. W. Goodwin, *Miscellanies and Essays,* 5 vols. (Boston, 1898).

Porphyry, *De Philosophia ex Oraculis haurienda,* ed. G. Wolff (Berlin, 1856); also ed. C. Müller, *Frag. Hist. Graec.* iii, 712.

—— *Chronica* in Müller, *Frag. Hist. Graec.* iii, 688 *sqq.*

—— *Adversus Christianos,* ed. A. Georgiades (Leipzig, 1891).

Quintilian, *Institutionis Oratoriae libri duodecim,* ed. E. Bonnell, 2 vols. (Leipzig, 1882-89); Eng. tr. *Institutes of Oratory: or Education of an Orator,* 12 bks., ed. J. S. Watson in Bohn Classical Library (London, 1856).

Res gestae divi Augusti, ex monumentis Ancyrano et Apolloniensi, accedunt tabulae undecim, ed. Mommsen (Berlin, 1883); ed. of Mommsen, ed. A. E. Allmer (Vienna, 1889); Latin text, with Gr. tr., ed. by A. E. Egger in *Examen critique des historiens,* 412-456 (Paris, 1844); Gr. and Lat. text. in Suetonius' *Divus Augustus,* ed. by E. S. Shuckburgh (Cambridge, 1896), 177-195.

Rutilius Numatianus Claudius, *De Reditu Suo Libri II,* ed. L. Müller, Teubner ser. (Leipzig, 1870); ed. J. V. Vessereaux (Paris, 1904).

Salvian of Marseilles, *De Gubernatione Dei,* ed. F. Pauly (CSEL), viii (Vienna, 1883).

Sammlung der griechischen Dialekt-Inschriften, ed. H. Collitz (Göttingen, 1883).

Seder olam, or *Seder olam rabba,* ed. A. Neubauer in *Mediaeval Chronicles,* ii, 26-67.

Seneca, *Epistulae,* ed. F. Buechler (Bonn, 1878); Eng. tr. by W. C. Sumners (New York, 1910).

Statius, *Silvae* in *Opera,* ed. A. Klotz and R. Jahnke, Teubner ser. 3 vols. in 4 (Leipzig, 1900-1908); Eng. tr. by D. A. Slater (Oxford, 1908).

Strabo, *Geographica,* Gr. and Lat. text ed. by C. Müller (Paris, 1877); Eng. tr. by H. C. Hamilton and W. Falconer in Bohn Classical Library, 3 vols. (London, 1854-57).

Suetonius, *De vita Caesarum libri viii* in his *Opera,* ed. M. Ihm, vol. i (Leipzig, 1908); Eng. tr. by J. C. Rolfe, *The Lives of the Caesars,* in Loeb Classical Library, 2 vols. (London, 1914).

Suidas, *Lexicon;* Gr. and Lat. ed. I. Bekker (1854).

Sulpicius Severus, *Chronicorum liber,* ed. C. Halm (CSEL) (Vienna, 1866); Eng. tr. by A. Roberts (NPNF), xi (New York, 1893).

Sylvester, Pope, *Opera quae extant,* ed. Migne (Patr. Lat. 8/795-848 (Paris, 1844).

Tacitus, Cornelius, *Historiarum libri,* ed. C. D. Fischer (Oxford, 1910); Eng, tr. by A. Murphy, 2 vols. (New York, 1907).

Talmud: Babylonian, Heb. and Ger. tr., ed. L. Goldschmidt, 11 vols. (Berlin and London, 1897-1909); *Jerusalem Talmud,* Fr. tr. by M. Schwab, 10 vols. (Paris, 1871-90).

Targums (Palestinian) on the *Pentateuch,* ed. Ginsburger (Berlin, 1899; 1903).

Tertullian, *Ad Scapulam* and *De Pudicitia* in *Opera omnia*, ed. Migne (Patr. Lat), 1-2 (Paris, 1844); Eng. tr. by S. Thelwall, (ANF), iii, iv (Buffalo, 1885).
—— *Ad Nationes*, ed. Reifferscheid and Wissowa (CSEL) (Jena, 1890).
—— *De Praescriptione haereticorum* ed. E. Preuschen in *Sammlung ausgewählter kirchen—und dogmengeschihtlicher Quellenschriften* (Leipzig, 1892).
—— *Apologeticus*, ed. G. Rauschen (Bonn, 1906), also ed. Migne (Patr. Lat.), 1/416 *sqq.* (Paris, 1844).
Teucer of Cyzicus, 'Ιουδαϊκὴ ἱστορία ed. C. Müller, *Frag. Hist. Graec.* iv, 508.
The Holy Bible Containing the Old Testament and New Testament, American Standard Version (New York, 1901).
Tosefta, ed. M. S. Zuckermandl (Pasewalk, 1881-82).
Valerius Maximus, *Factorum et dictorum memorabilium libri novem cum Iulii Paridis et Januarii Nepotiani epitomis*, ed. C. Kempf (Leipzig, 1888).

III. SECONDARY MATERIAL.

1. *General Secondary Works.*

Addis, W. E. *Christianity and the Roman Empire* (London, 1893).
Allard, P. *Histoire des persécutions pendant les deux premiers siècles d'apres les documents archéologiques*, 3rd. ed. (Paris, 1903).
—— *Julien l'Apostat*. 3 vols. (Paris, 1900).
Amitai, L. K. *Romains et Juifs. Étude critique sur les rapports publics et privés qui ont existé entre les Romaines et les Juifs jusqu'à la prise de Jérusalem par Titus* (Paris, 1894).
Andree, R. *Zur Volkskunde der Juden* (Leipzig, 1881).
Arnold, W. T. *Roman Provincial Administration* (London, 1879).
Bacher, W. *Die Agada der palästinensischen Amoräer*, 3 vols. (Strassburg, 1892).
Basnage de Beauval, J. *Histoire des Juifs*, 15 vols. (La Haye, 1708); Eng. tr. by T. Taylor (London, 1708).
Beloch, J. *Die Bevölkerung der griechisch—römischen Welt* (Leipzig, 1886).
Berliner, A. *Geschichte der Juden in Rom von der ältesten Zeit bis zur Gegenwart*, 2 vols. in 1 (Frankfurt, 1893).
Bernard, J. L. *The Synagogue and the Church* (condensed from the original work of Vitringa, *De Synagoga vetere*) (London, 1842).
Bertholet, A. *Die Stellung der Israeliten und der Juden zu den Fremden* (Freiburg and Leipzig, 1896).

Bethmann-Hollweg, M. A. von. *Handbuch des Civilprozesses. Justinianisch-römisches Recht* (Bonn, 1834).
Bohn, O. *Qua condicione juris reges socii populi Romani fuerint* (Berlin, 1877).
Boissier, G. *La Religion romaine d'Auguste aux Antonins,* 2 vols. (Paris, 1884).
Bonnetty, A. *Documents historiques sur la religion des Romains, et sur la connaissance qu'ils ont pu avoir des traditions bib-, liques, par leurs rapports avec les Juifs,* vol. i (Paris, 1867).
Bosse, R. *Gründzüge des Finanzwesens im römischen Staate* (Brunswick, 1803-4).
Bousset, W. *Die Religion des Judentums im neutestamentlichen Zeitalter,* 2d ed. (Berlin, 1906).
Bramston, M. *Judaea and her rulers from Nebuchadnezzar to Vespasian* (London, 1882).
Büchler, A. *The political and the Social Leaders of the Jewish Community of Sepphoris in the Second and Third Centuries* (Oxford, 1909).
—— *Das Synhedrium in Jerusalem und das grosse Beth Din in der Quaderkammer des Jerusalemischen Temples* (Vienna, 1902).
Canfield, L. H. *The Early Persecutions of the Christians* (New York, 1913).
Cassel, J. P. *De Iudaeorum Odio et Abstinentia a Porcina Eiusque Causis* (Magdeburg, 1740).
Champagny, F. J. *Rome et la Judée au temps de la chute de Néron, from A.D. 66 to A.D. 72,* 2 vols. (Paris, 1865); *Rome et la Judée* (Paris, 1870).
Clinton, H. F. *Fasti Hellenici, The Civil and Literary Chronology of Greece,* 3 vols. (Oxford, 1834).
—— *Fasti Romani. The Civil and Literary Chronology of Rome and Constantinople from the Death of Augustus to the Death of Justin II,* 2 vols. (Oxford, 1845-1850).
Chwolson, D. *Das letzte Passamahl Christi und der Tag seines Todes,* 2d ed. (Leipzig, 1908).
Cooke, G. A. *A Text Book of North Semitic Inscriptions, Moabite, Hebrew .... Jewish* (Oxford, 1903).
Cumont, F. *Les religions orientales dans le paganisme romain* (Paris, 1907); Eng. tr. Open Court Publ. Co. (Chicago, 1911).
Cunaeus, P. *De Republica Hebraeorum* (London, 1703); Fr. tr. by Basnage, 5 vols. (Amsterdam, 1713).
Dalman, G. *Aramäische Dialectproben* (Leipzig, 1896).

Derenbourg, J. *Essai sur l'histoire et la géographie de la Palestine d'après les Thalmuds et les autres sources rabbiniques;* vol. i, *Histoire de la Palestine depuis Cyrus jusqu'à Adrien* (Paris, 1867).

De Saulcy, L. F. *Étude chronologique de la vie et des monnaies des rois juifs, Agrippa I et Agrippa II* (Paris, 1869).

de Vogüe, C. *Syrie centrale, architecture civile et religieuse* (Paris, 1865-77).

Dezobry, L. C. *Rome au siècle d'Auguste; ou, voyage d'un Gaulois à Rome à l'epoque du règne d'Auguste et pendant une partie du règne de Tibère,* 5th ed., 4 vols. (Paris, 1886).

Diestel, L. *Geschichte des alten Testaments in der Christlichen Kirche* (Jena, 1869).

Duruy, J. V. *History of Rome and of the Roman People from its Origin to the Invasion by the Barbarians,* Eng. tr. (Boston, 1894).

Edersheim, E. W. *The Laws and Polity of the Jews* (London, 1883).

Egger, A. E. *Examen critique des historiens anciens de la vie et et du règne d'Auguste* (Paris, 1844).

Esser, J. J. *De Pauperum cura apud Romanos* (Campis, 1902).

Ewald, H. *Geschichte des Volkes Israel,* 8 vols. (Göttingen, 1843-1859); Eng. tr. by R. Martineau, 8 vols. (London, 1869-86).

Fairweather, W. *The Background of the Gospel; or, Judaism in the period between the Old and New Testaments* (Edinburgh, 1908).

Farrar, F. W. *The Life and Work of St. Paul,* 2 vols. (New York, 1880).

Felten, J. *Neutestamentliche Zeitgeschichte oder Judentum und Heidentum zur Zeit Christi und der Apostel,* 2 vols. (Regensburg, 1910).

Fowler, W. W. *The City State of the Greeks and the Romans* (London, 1893).

——— *The Roman Festivals of the Period of the Republic* (New York, 1908).

Freudenthal, J. *Alexander Polyhistor und die vom ihm erhaltenen Reste jüdäischer und samaritanischer Geschichtswerke,* 2 pts. in 1 vol. (Breslau, 1875).

Friedländer, M. *Die religiösen Bewegungen innerhalb des Judentums im Zeitalter Jesu* (Berlin, 1905).

Friedländer, L. *De Judaeorum coloniis* (Königsberg, 1876).

——— *Darstellungen aus der Sittengeschichte Roms,* 3 vols., 8th ed. (Leipzig, 1910); Eng. tr. of 7th ed., *Roman Life and Manners under the Early Empire*, 5 vols. (London and New York, 1903).

Geib, C. G. *Gesch. des römischen Kriminalprozesses* (Leipzig, 1842).

Geiger, A. *Das Judenthum und seine Geschichte*, 3 vols. (Breslau, 1864-71).

—— *Urschrift und Uebersetzungen der Bibel in ihrer Abhängigkeit von der innern Entwickelung des Judenthums* (Breslau, 1857).

Gfrörer, A. F. *Das Jahrhundert des Heils*, 2 vols. (Stuttgart, 1838). Also under the title: *Geschichte des Urchristenthums*.

Giles, J. A. *Heathen Records to the Jewish Scripture History; containing all the extracts from the Greek and Latin writers in which the Jews and Christians are named* (London, 1856).

Gill, J. *Notices of the Jews and their Country by the Classic Writers of Antiquity*, 2d ed. (London, 1872).

Girard, P. F. *Manuel élementaire de droit romain*, 5th ed. (Paris, 1911).

—— *Textes de droit romain*, 3rd ed. (Paris, 1905).

Glover, T. R. *The Conflict of Religions in the Early Roman Empire*, 3rd ed. (London, 1909).

Goldschmidt, J. *De Iudaeorum apud Romanos condicione. Dissertatio inauguralis philologica* (Halle, 1866).

Grätz, H. *Geschichte der Juden von den ältesten Zeiten bis auf die Gegenwart*, 11 vols. (Leipzig, 1895-1909); Eng. tr., 6 vols. (Philadelphia, 1891-98).

Greenridge, A. H. J. *Roman Public Life* (London, 1901).

Gregorovius, F. *Wanderjahre in Italien;* vol. i, *Der Ghetto und die Juden in Rom*, 4th ed. (Leipzig, 1874).

Gronovius, J. *Decreta Romana et Asiatica pro Judaeis* (Leyden, 1712).

Grünwald, M. *Juden als Rheder und Seefahrer* (Berlin, 1902).

Guérin, V. *Description geographique historique et archéologique de la Palestine*, 8 vols. (Paris, 1868-1880); vols. vi-vii, *Galilée*.

Hardy, E. G. *Christianity and the Roman Government* (London, 1894); 2d. ed., *Studies in Roman History* (London, 1906).

Harnack, A. *Der Vorwurf des Atheismus in den drei ersten Jahrhunderten* in *Texte u. Untersuchungen*, n.s., xiii, 3-16.

—— *Militia Christi, die christliche Religion und der Soldatenstand in den ersten drei Jahrunderten* (Tübingen, 1905).

—— *Mission und Ausbreitung des Christentums in den ersten*

drei Jahrhunderten (Leipzig, 1902); Eng. tr. by J. Moffatt (New York, 1908).

Haubold, C. G. *De Statu Judaeorum publico sub imperio Romanorum* in *Opuscula Academica*, ii, 457-476 (Berlin, 1829).

Hausrath, A. *Neutestamentliche Zeitgeschichte,* 2d ed., 4 vols. (Heidelberg, 1873-1877); Eng. tr. of vol. i in 2 pts. by C. T. Poynings and P. Quenzer (London, 1878-80); vols. ii-iv, by L. Huxley, 2 vols. (London, 1895).

Herzfeld, L. *Handelsgeschichte der Juden des Alterthums; aus den Quellen erforscht und zusammengestellt.,* 2d ed. (Brunswick, 1894).

Hilgenfeld, A. *Die Jüdische Apokalyptik in ihrer geschichtlichen Entwickelung* (Jena, 1857).

Hirschfeld, O. *Untersuchungen auf dem Gebiete der römischen Verwaltungs-Geschichte, 1 Bd: Die kaiserl. Verwaltungsbeamten bis auf Diocletian* (Berlin, 1877).

Hobhouse, W. *The Church and the World in Idea and in History* (London, 1910).

Höck, C. *Römische Geschichte vom Verfall der Republik bis zur Vollendung der Monarchie unter Constantin* (Brunswick, 1841-50).

Hoffman, D. *Der oberste Gerichtshof in der Stadt des Heiligthums* (Berlin, 1878).

Hoss, W. *Das Judentum unter den römischen Cäsaran und die Entstehung des Thalmuds* (Karlsruhe, 1895).

Hübner, E. *Inscriptiones Hispaniae Christianae* (Berlin, 1871).

Holtzmann, H., and G. Weber. *Geschichte des Volkes Israel und der Entstehung des Christenthums.* Also under the title *Judenthum und Christenthum im Zeitalter der apokryphischen und neutestamentalichen Literatur.,* 2 vols. (Leipzig, 1867).

Hudson, E. H. *History of the Jews in Rome, B.C. 160-A.D. 604* (London, 1882).

Huidekoper, F. *Judaism at Rome B.C. 76 to A.D. 140,* 3rd ed. (New York, 1880).

Huschke, E. *Die multa und das sacramentum in ihren verschiedenen Anwendungen.* (Leipzig, 1874).

Huschke, I. G. *Uber den Census und die Steuerverfassung der früheren römischen Kaiserzeit* (Leipzig, 1847).

Jelski-Goldin, I. *Die innere Einrichtung des grossen Synedrions zu Jerusalem* (Breslau, 1894).

Joel, M. *Blicke in die Religionsgeschichte zu Anfang des zweiten christlichen Jahrhunderts* (Breslau, 1880-83).

—— *Die Angriffe des Heidenthums gegen die Juden und Chris-*

ten, in den ersten Jahrhunderten der römischen Caesaren (Breslau, 1879).

Jost, I. M. *Geschichte der Israeliten seit der Zeit der Makkab er bis auf unsere Tage,* 9 vols. (Berlin, 1820-28).

—— *Geschichte des Judenthums und seiner Secten,* 3 vols. (Leipzig, 1857-59).

Judeich, W. *Caesar im Orient; kritische Ubersicht der Ereignisse vom 9 August 48 bis October 47; 1, Historische Dissertation Strassburg* (Leipzig, 1884).

Juster, J. *Examen critique des sources relatives à la condition juridique des Juifs dans l'empire romain* (Paris, 1911).

—— *Les Droits politiques des Juifs dans l'empire romain* (Paris, 1912).

—— *Les Juifs dans l'empire romain: leur condition juridique, économique et sociale,* 2 vols. (Paris, 1914).

Kahn, Z. *L'Esclavage selon la Bible et le Talmud,* pt. ii of *Rapport sur la situation morale du Séminaire Israélite* (Paris, 1867).

Kautsky, C. J. *Der Ursprung des Christentums. Eine historische Untersuchung* (Stuttgart, 1908).

Keim, T. *History of Jesus of Nazareth,* 6 vols. (London, 1873-84).

Krauss, S. *Talmudische Archäologie,* 3 vols. (Leipzig, 1910-12).

Krebs, J. T. *Decreta Romanorum pro Iudaeis facta e Josepho collecta et Commentario Historico-Critico Illustrata. Adjuntum est Decretum Atheniensium pro Hyrcano Pontifice M. Judaeorum factum* (Leipzig, 1768).

Krüger, P. *Philo und Josephus als Apologeten des Judentums* (Leipzig, 1906).

Kuenen, A. *Godsdienst van Israel tot den Ondergang van den Joodschen Staat,* 2 vols. (Haarlem, 1869-1870); Eng. tr. by A. H. May, *The Religion of Israel to the Fall of the Jewish State,* 3 vols. (London, 1874-75).

—— *National Religions and Universal Religions.* Hibbert Lectures (London, 1882).

Kuhn, E. *Die städische und bürgerliche Verfassung des römischen Reichs bis auf die Zeiten Justinians* (London, 1864-5).

Lardner, N. *Jewish and Heathen Testimonies to the Truth of the Christian Religion,* 7th vol. of his *Works* in 10 vols. (Leipzig, 1838).

Latyschew, B. *Inscriptiones Antiquae Orae Septentrionalis Ponti Euxini Graecae et Latinae* (St. Petersburg, 1901).

Lazare, B. *Antisemitism, Its History and Causes,* tr. from the French (New York, 1903).

Lietzmann, H. *Apollinaris von Laodicea und seine Schule* (Tübingen, 1904).
Levyssohn, D. *Disputatio academica inauguralis de Judaeorum sub Caesaribus conditione et de legibus eos spectantibus* (Leyden, 1828).
Liebenam, W. *Zur Geschichte und Organization des römischen Vereinswesens* (Leipzig, 1890).
Linsenmayer, A. *Die Bekämpfung des Christentums durch den römischen Staat bis zum Tode des Kaisers Julian* (363) (München, 1905).
Lutterroth, H. *Le recensement de Quirinius en Judee* (Paris, 1865).
McGiffert, A. C. *Dialogue between a Christian and a Jew*, entitled Αητιβολὴ Παπίσκου καὶ Φίλωνος Ιουδαίων πρὸς Μοναχόν Τινα Greek text, introduction and notes (New York, 1889).
Madden, F. *Coins of the Jews* (London, 1881).
Manfrin, P. C. *Gli Ebrei sotto la dominazione romana*, 4 vols. (Rome, 1888-92).
Marquardt, J. *Das Privatleben der Römer* (Berlin, 1873-78); 2d ed. A. Mau, 1886.
—— *Römische Staatsverwaltung*, 2d ed., 3 vols. (Leipzig, 1885).
Martha, B. C. *Les Moralistes sous l'empire romain* (Paris, 1886).
Matagrin, A. *Histoire de la tolerance religieuse. Évolution d'un principe social.* (Paris, 1905).
Meier, F. C. *Judaica seu Veterum Scriptorum Profanorum de Rebus Judaicis Fragmenta* (Jena, 1832).
Mendelson, S. *Criminal jurisprudence of the Ancient Hebrews compiled from the Talmud and other rabbinical writings and compared with Roman and English penal jurisprudence* (Baltimore, 1891).
Mendelssohn, L. *De senati consulti Romanorum ab Josepho Antiq. xiv. 8.5, relati temporibus commentatio* (Leipzig, 1873).
Merivale, D. *History of the Romans*, 7 vols. (New York, 1863-66).
Mielziner, M. *Introduction to the Talmud* (New York, 1913).
Milman, H. H. *The History of the Jews from the earliest period down to modern times* (London, 1878).
Mitteis, L. *Reichsrecht und Volksrecht in den östlichen Provinzen des römischen Kaisereichs* (Leipzig, 1891).
Mommsen, Th. *History of Rome*, and *The Provinces of the Roman Empire from Caesar to Diocletian;* Eng. tr. by W. P. Dickenson, 5 vols. (New York, 1903-5), revised by F. Haverfield, 1909.

―――― *Römisches Strafrecht* (Leipzig, 1899); Fr. tr. by J. Duquesne, 3 vols. (Paris, 1907).
―――― J. Marquardt and P. Krüger (editors), *Manuel des antiquités romaines*, 17 vols. (Paris, 1891-1895).
―――― *Gesammelte Schriften*, 8 vols. (Berlin, 1907-13).
Morrison, W. D. *The Jews Under Roman Rule* (New York, 1890).
Muirhead, L. A. *The Times of Christ* (Edinburgh, 1897).
Müller, N. *Die jüdische Katakombe am Monteverde zu Rome* (Leipzig, 1912).
Niese, B. *Kritik der beiden Makkabäerbücher* (Berlin, 1900).
Overbeck, F. (editor); de Wette, W. M. C. *Kurtze Erklärung der Apostelgeschichte* (Leipzig, 1870). [In his Kurzgefasstes exegetisches Handbuch zum Neuen Testament I, pt. 4.]
Pollock, F. *Essays in Jurisprudence and Ethics* (London, 1882).
Pfitzner, W. *Geschichte der römischen Kaiserlegionem von Augustus bis Hadrianus* (Leipzig, 1881).
Pierantoni, A. *Gli avvocati di Roma antica* (Bologna, 1900).
Preller-Jordan. *Römische Mythologie* (Berlin, 1881-83).
Pressel, W. F. M. *Die Zerstreuung des Volkes Israel*, 5 pts. in 1 vol. (Berlin, 1888).
Preuschen, E. *Analecta: Kürzere Texte zur Geschichte der alten Kirche und des Kanons* (Tübingen, 1909).
Rabbinowicz, I. M. *De la legislation criminelle du Talmud* (Paris, 1876).
Ramsay, W. C. *The Cities and Bishoprics of Phrygia* (London, 1897).
―――― *St. Paul the Traveller and the Roman Citizen* (London, 1895).
―――― *The Cities of St. Paul* (London, 1906).
Reinach, Th. *Les monnaies juives* (Paris, 1887); Eng. tr. by J. Head (London, 1905).
―――― *Textes d'auteurs grecs et romains relatifs au judaïsme réunis, traduits, et annotés* (Paris, 1895).
Rémondière, L. A. *De la levée des impots en droit romain* (Paris, 1886).
Renan, E. J. *Histoire des origines du Christianisme*, 8 vols. (Paris, 1866-83). Vol. iv, *L'Antechrist* (Paris, 1873).
―――― *De L'Identité originelle et da la séparation graduelle du Judaïsme et du Christianisme* (Paris, 1885).
―――― *Histoire du peuple d'Israel*, 5 vols. (Paris, 1887-93); Eng., tr., *History of the People of Israel*, 5 vols. (Boston, 1885-95).
―――― *Le Judaisme comme race et comme religion* (Paris, 1883).

Reynier, L. *De l'économie publique et rurale des Arabes et des Juifs* (Geneva, 1820).

Rheinwald, G. F. H. *Die kirchliche Archäologie* (Berlin, 1830).

Riggs, J. S. *History of the Jewish People during the Maccabean and Roman Periods* (New York, 1910).

Robinson, E. *Later Biblical Researches in Palestine and in the Adjacent Regions* (Boston, 1856).

Rudorff, A. A. F. *Römische Rechtsgeschichte*, 2 vols. (Leipzig, 1857-59).

Ruppin, A. *The Jews of To-day*, tr. from the German by M. Bentwich (New York, 1913).

Salvador, J. *Histoire de la domination romaine en Judée et de la ruine de Jerusalem*, 2 vols. (Paris, 1847); Ger. tr. *Geschichte der Römerherrschaft in Judäa und der Zerstörung Jerusalems*, 2 vols. (Bremen, 1847).

Schiller, H. *Geschichte der römischen Kaiserzeit*, 2 vols. (Gotha, 1883-7).

Schön, G. *Das capitolinische Verzeichniss der römischen Triumphe* (Leipzig, 1893).

Schuhl, M. *Les préventions des Romains contre la religion juive* (Paris, 1883).

Schürer, E. *Die Gemeindeverfassung der Juden in Rom in der Kaiserzeit mach den Inschriften dargestellt. Nebst 45 jüdischen Inschriften* (Leipzig, 1879).

—— *Geschichte des jüdischen Volkes im Zeitalter Jesu Christi*, 4th ed. (Leipzig, 1901; ii, 1907; iii, 1909; index, 1911).

Schwalm, M. B. O. P. *La Vie privée du peuple juif à l'epoque de Jesus-Christ* (Paris, 1910).

Scott, B. *The Contents and Teachings of the Catacombs at Rome* (London, 1873).

Seinecke, L. *Geschichte des Volkes Israel.* 2 vols. (Göttingen, 1876-1884).

Simonsen, D. "Kleinigkeiten," in *Judaica. Festschrift zu Hermann Cohen's siebzigstem Geburtstage* (Berlin, 1912).

Spence, H. D. M. *Early Christianity and Paganism* (New York, 1911).

Stapfer, E. *La Palestine au temps de Jesus-Christ*, 2d ed. (Paris, 1885); Eng. tr. by A. H. Holmden, 3rd ed. (London, 1886).

Strack, H. L. *Einleitung in den Talmud*, 4th ed. (Leipzig, 1908).

—— *The Jew and Human Sacrifice;* Eng. tr. of 8th ed. of German text, by H. F. E. Beauchamp (New York, 1909).

Strauss, D. F. *Das Leben Jesu*, 4th ed., 2 vols. (Bonn, 1877).

Toy, C. H. *Introduction to the History of Religions* (Boston, 1913).

Van der Chijs, J. A. *De Herode Magno* (Leyden, 1855).

Viollet, P. *Histoire du droit civil francais canonique et indications bibliographiques accompagnée de notions de droit*, 3d ed. (Paris, 1905).

Von Gebhardt, O. *Die Psalmen Salomos zum ersten Male mit Benützung der Athoshandschriften und des Codex Casanatensis herausgegeben* (Leipzig, 1895).

Vitringa, C. *De Synagoga Vetere* (Leeuwarden, 1726).

Vogelstein, H., and Rieger, P. *Geschichte der Juden in Rom*, 2 vols. (Berlin, 1896).

Waltzing, J. P. *Étude historiques sur les corporations professionelles chez les Romains depuis les origines jusqu'à la chute de l'Empire d'Occident*, 4 vols. (Brussels, 1895-1900); 2 vols., 1896-1906.

Weber, F. *Judische Theologie auf Grund des Talmud und verwandter Schriften*, 2d ed. (Leipzig, 1897).

Weiss, A. *Die römischen Kaiser in ihrem Verhältnisse zu Juden und Christen* (Wien, 1882).

Wellhausen, J. *Israelitische und jüdische Geschichte*, 3d ed. (Berlin, 1897).

—— *Prolegomena to the History of Israel*, with a reprint of the art. "Israel," from the *Ency. Brit.*; tr. from the German by J. S. Black and A. Menzies (Edinburgh, 1885).

Wendland, P. *Die hellenistisch-römische Kultur in ihren Beziehungen zu Judentum und Christentum*, 2d ed. and 3rd ed. (Tübingen, 1912).

Wesseling, P. *Diatribe de Judaeorum archontibus ad inscriptionem Berenicensem* (Paddenburg, 1738).

Wieseler, K. *Beiträge zur richtigen Würdigung der Evangelien und der evangelischen Geschichte* (Gotha, 1869).

Wilcken, U. *Zum alexandrinischen Antisemitismus* (Leipzig, 1909).

Willems, P. *Le Droit public romain* (Louvain, 1910).

Wissowa, G. *Religion und Kultus der Römer*, 2d ed. (München, 1912).

Ziegler, G. *Der Kampf zwischen Judenthum und Christenthum in den ersten drei christlichen Jahrhunderten* (Berlin, 1907).

Zumpt, A. *Das Geburtsjahr Christi* (London, 1869).

2. *Articles in Periodicals.*

Abhandlungen der histor. philolog. Klasse der Berliner Akademie aus den Jahren 1816-1817.

Hirt, A. L. "Uber die Baue Herodes des Grossen überhaupt, und über seinen Tempelbau zu Jerusalem insbesondere," pt. iv, pp. 1-24.

Acta Societatis Philologae Lipsiensis, ed. Ritschel [Acta soc. phil.]. 2 vols. (Leipzig, 1871-72).

    Mendelssohn, L. "Senati consulta Romanorum quae sunt in Josephi Antiquitatibus" v (1875), pp. 87-228.

American Journal of Theology, ed. Divin. Faculty of Univ. of Chicago (Chicago, 1897).

    Dobschütz, E. v. "Jews and Anti-semites in Ancient Alexandria," viii (1904), pp. 728-55.

Annuaire de la Société française de Numismatique et d'Archéologie, 19 vols. (Paris, 1866-95).

    De Saulcy, L. F. "Notes sur les monnaies de Philippe le tetrarque," iii (1868), pp. 262-265.

Eranos Vindobonensis (Wien, 1893).

    Hula, E. "Eine Judengemeinde in Tlos," pp. 99-102.

Expositor, ed. W. R. Nicoll (London, 1875).

    Ramsay, W. M. "The Jews as Resident Strangers," v (1902), 21 *sqq.*

Extrait des Bulletins de l'academie royale de Bélgique (EBAB), 3rd ser. (Brussels, 1893).

    Giron, A. "La Liberté de conscience à Rome," xxv, pp. 113-141.

    Wagener, A. "La Liberté de conscience à Rome," xxvi, nos. 9, 10, pp. 64 *sqq.*

Hermes, Zeitschrift für Classische Philologie, 48 vols., 1-16 ed. by H. Hübner; 17-36 by G. Kaibel and C. Robert; vol. 37 *sqq.* by F. Leo and C. Robert (Berlin, 1866-1913).

    Niese, B. "Bemerkungen über die Urkunden bei Josephus," xi, pp. 478 *sqq.*

    Mommsen, T. "Die Conscriptionsordnung der römischen Kaiserzeit," xix (1884), 1-79; 210-234.

    Wilcken, U. "Alexandrinische Gesandtschaften vor Kaiser Claudius," xxx (1895), 485-498.

    —— "Ein Actenstück zum jüdischen Kriege Trajans," xxvi (1892), 464-480.

Historische Zeitschrift, ed. by H. von Sybel, M. Lehmann and others (Münich, 1859-1913).

    Mommsen, T. "Der Religionsfrevel nach römischen Recht," lxiv (1890), pp. 389-424.

Illustrirte Monatshefte für die gesammten Interessen des Judenthums (IM), 2 vols. (Vienna, 1865-66).

Geiger, L. "Juden u. Judenthum nach d. Aufassung d. Schriftsteller d Alterthums, ii, Oct. (1865), pp. 13 sqq.
Duschak, M. "Flavius Josephus, seine Zeit und seine Bedeutung als Historiograph," i, pp. 53-59.
Jahrbuch für die Geschichte der Juden und des Judenthums (JGJ) (Institut zur Förderung der israelitischen Literatur.), 4 vols. (Leipzig, 1860-69).
Levy, M. A. "Epigrapische Beiträge zur Geschichte der Juden," ii (1861), pp. 259-324.
Jahresbericht der Landesrabbinerschule (Budapest, 1901).
Bloch. "Das mosaisch-talmudische Strafgerichtsverfahren."
Jahresberichte über die Fortschritte der classischen Alterthumskunde, ed. C. Bursian and I. Müller (Berlin, 1875).
Naquet, Des impôts indirects chez les Romains sous la république et sous l'empire, xix, 466 sqq.
Jahres-Bericht des jüdisch-theologischen Seminars-Fraenckel'scher Stiftung" (JJS) (Breslau, 1884).
Grätz, H. "Die jüdischen Proselyten im Romerreich."
Jewish Quarterly Review, ed. I. Abrahams and C. G. Montefiore, 20 vols. (London, 1888-1908); new ser. (New York, 1910-), ed. S. Schecter and C. Adler.
Abraham, I. "Professor Schürer on Life Under the Law" xv (1899), pp. 626-642.
Adler, M. "Julian the Apostate and the Jews," v, pp. 591-651.
Neubauer, A. "The Early Settlements of the Jews in Southern Italy," iv (1892), pp. 606-625.
Mélanges de littérature et d'histoire religieuses (MLHR), publ. by the Société des Bibliophiles Français (Paris, 1856-).
Boissier, G. "Le jugement de Tacite sur les Juifs," i, pp. 81-94.
Monatsschrift für Geschichte und Wissenschaft des Judenthums (MGWJ), ed. from 1851 to 1868 by Frankel; from 1869-1887 by Grätz; 893—by Brann.
Brann, M. "Die Söhne des Herodes" (1873), pp. 241-56 (Reprint, 1873).
Frankel, Z. "Die Juden unter den ersten römischen Kaisern" (1854), pp. 401-13; 439-50.
Funk, S. "Die Männer der grossen Versammlung und die Gerichtsshöfe im nachexilischen Judentum," lv (1911), 33-42.
——— "Die Kompetenz der Gerichtshöfe," lv (1911), 699-712.
——— "Erwiderung," lvii (1913), 501-506.
Ginzberg, L. "Eine unbekannte jüdische Sekte," lvi (1912). 33-48; 285-307; 417-448; 546-566; 664-689; lvii (1913), 153 sqq.

Grätz, H. "Die Stellung der kleinasiatischen Juden unter der Römerherrschaft," xxxv (1886), pp. 329-346.

―――― "Zur Topographie Palästinas" (1882), pp. 14-17.

Krakauer, G. "Die rechtliche und gesellschaftliche Stellung der Juden im sinkenden Römerreiche," xxiii (1874), pp. 49-61; 97-112.

Rosenthal, F. "Die Erlässe Cäsars und die Senatconsulte im Josephus Alterth. xiv, 10 nach ihrem historischen Inhalte untersucht" (1879), 176 *sqq.*; 216 *sqq.*; 300 *sqq.*

Numismatic Chronicle, ed. W. S. Vaux, J. Evans and F. W. M. (London, 1839-).

Madden, F. W. "Coins of the Jews" (1866), pp. 173-219, pl. vi.

Philologus. Zeitschrift für das Klassische Alterthum, ed, F. W. Schneidewin and E. von Leutsch (Stolberg, Göttingen, Leipzig, 1846-).

Hirschfeld, O. Getreideverwaltung in der römischen Kaiserzeit," xxix (1870), 1-96.

Revue des Études juives. Quarterly publication of the Société des Études juives (Paris, 1880-).

Chajes, H. P. "Les Juges juifs en Palestine," xxxix (1899), pp. 39-52.

Hild, J. A. "Les Juifs à Rome devant l'opinion et dans la litterature," viii, 1 *sqq.*; ix, 125 *sqq.*

Lehmann, J. "Quelques Dates importantes de la chronologie du deuxième temple," xxxvii (1898), pp. 12-20.

Monseaux, P. "Les colonies juives dans l'Afrique Romaine," xliv (1902), 1-28.

Reinach, S. "Inscription Grecque de Smyrne: La Juive Rufina," vii (1883), pp. 161-66.

―――― "Une Novelle synagogue juive à Phocée," xii (1886), 236-43.

Reinach, T. "Inscription juive d'Auch," xix (1889), pp. 219-223.

―――― "Nouvelles remarques sur l'inscription juive d'Auch," xx (1890), pp. 29-33.

―――― "Inscription juive de Narbonne," xix (1889), 75-83.

― "Juifs et Grecs devant un empereur romain," xxvii (1893), pp. 70-82.

―――― "Quid Judaeo cum Verre?" xxvi (1893), pp. 36-46.

―――― "Sur la date de la colonie juive d'Alexandrie," xlv (1902), pp. 161-164.

―――― "Une Inscription juive de Chypre," xlviii (1904), pp. 191-196.

Thiacourt, C. "Ce que Tacite dit des Juifs au commencement du livre v des *Histoires*," xix (1889), pp. 57-74.
Revue de théologie et de philosophie (RTP), ed. M. E. Dandiran and J. F. Astié (Lausanne, 1873-).
Stapfer, E. "Le Sanhedrin de Jerusalem au premier siècle" (1884), pp. 105-119.
Rheinisches Museum für Philologie (RMP), 74 vols. in 75 (Leipzig, 1833-1913). The journal is the successor to *Rheinisches Museum für Philologie, Geschichte u. Griechische Philosophie*.
Mendelssohn, L., and Ritschl, S. "Nochmals der römische Senatsbeschluss bei Josephus, xxx (1875), 419-435.
Niese, B. "Galatien und seine Tetrachen," xxxviii (1883), pp. 583-600.
Ritschl, S. "Eine Berichtigung der republicanischen Consularfasten," xxviii (1883), 586-614.
Sitzungsberichte der Königl-preuss. Academie der Wissenschaften (Berlin, 1893).
Hirschfeld, O. von "Die agentes in rebus," pp. 421-441.
Theologische Literaturzeitung (TL), ed. A. Harnack and E. Schürer (Leipzig, 1876).
Harnack, A. "Memoir of Schürer," xxxv (May 14, 1910), pp. 290-291.
Tübinger Theologische Quartalschrift (TTQ), ed. Grätz (Tübingen, 1819).
Gosser, "Die Berichte des classischen Alterthums über die Religion der Juden" (1868), pp. 565-637.
Langen, "Das jüdische Synhedrium und die römische Procuratur in Judäa" (1862), pp. 411-463.
Verhandlungen der 33. Philologen-Versammlung (Leipzig, 1879).
Lewy, I. "Ueber die Spuren des griechischen und römischen Alterthums im Talmudischen Schriftthum" (1879), pp. 77-87.
Wiener Studien, ed. W. Hartel and K. Schenkl (Vienna, 1879-).
Cumont, F. "Une formule grecque de renonciation au judäisme," xxiv (1902), 462-472.
Zeitschrift der Deutschen Morgenländischen Gesellschaft, ed. R. Anger. . . . E. Windisch (Leipzig, 1846-).
Reckendorf, S. "Der armäische Theil des palmyrenischen Zoll- und Steuertarifs" (1888), pp. 370-415.
Zeitschrift für die gesammte katholische Theologie, pub. by the theological faculty of Vienna, Dr. J. Scheiner. . . . Dr. J. M. Häusle, 8 vols. (Vienna, 1850-57.60).
Auer, "Die Juden in Rom unmittelbar vor und nach Christi Geburt," iv, No. 1 (1852), pp. 56-105.

Kellner, "Die kaiserlichen Procuratoren von Judäa" (1868), pp. 630 sqq.

―――― "Die römischen Statthalter von Syrien und Judäa zur Zeit Christi und der Apostel" (1888), pp. 460-486.

Zeitschrift für die neutestamentliche Wissenschaft, ed. E. Preuschen (Giessen, 1900-).

Mommsen, T. "Die Rechtsverhältnisse des Apostels Paulus," ii (1901), pp. 88 *sqq.*

Zeitschrift für wissenschaftliche Theologie (ZWT), ed. A. Hilgenfeld (Jena, 1858).

Schürer, E. "Die σπεῖρα 'Ιταλική und die σπεῖρα Σεβαστή, xviii (1875), pp. 413-425.

Grimm, W. "Ueber 1 Macc. VIII und XV, 16-21," xvii (1874), pp. 231-238.

3. *Articles in Encyclopaedias and Dictionaries.*

Allgemeine Encyclopädie der Wissenschaften und Künste, ed. Ersch and Grüber (Leipzig, 1850).

Cassel, S. "Juden (Geschichte)," 2d. ser., xxvii, pp. 1-238.

Aramäisch-Neuhebräisches Wörterbuch zu Targum, Talmud und Midrasch, by G. H. Dalman (Frankfurt, 1901).

Biblisches Realwörterbuch, ed. Winer, 2 vols., 3rd ed. (Leipzig, 1847-48), Art. "Bürgerrecht."

Catholic Encyclopedia, ed. C. G. Herbemann (New York, 1907-12).

Pohle, J. "Religious Toleration," xiv, pp. 763-773.

Dictionaire d'archéologie chrétienne et de liturgie, ed. by F. Cabrol (Paris, 1907-); 2½ vols. prepared.

Leclercq, H. "Accusations contre les Chrétiens," i, 265-307.

Encyclopaedia Britannica, 11th ed. (Cambridge, England and New York, 1911).

Johns, C. H. W. "Sabbath," xxiii, pp. 959-962.

Black, J. S. "Feasts and Festivals," x, 220-224.

Encyclopaedia of Religion and Ethics (ERE), ed. J. Hastings (New York, 1908-); 6 vols. have appeared through word "Hyksos."

Barton, G. A. "Circumcision" (Semitic), iii, 679-680.

Carleton, J. G. "Festivals and Fasts" (Christian), v, 844-853.

Gray, L. H. "Incubation," vii, 206-207.

Gallia Judaica. Dictionnaire géographique de la France d'après les sources rabbiniques, by H. Gross, 2d ed. (Paris, 1901).

Hastings' Dictionary of the Bible, 4 vols. (Edinburgh, 1898-); extra volume (New York, 1904).

Schürer, E. "Diaspora," (extra vol.), pp. 91 *sqq.*

Jewish Encyclopaedia, 12 vols. (New York and London, 1901-1906).

de Ricci, S., and Broydé, I. "Paleography," ix, 471-76.

Lauterbach, J. Z. "Ordination," ix, 428-430.
Reinach, T. "Diaspora," iv, 561-62.
Real-Encyclopädie der classischen Altertumswissenschaft (RECA), ed. Pauly and Wissowa; new ed., W. Kroll (Stuttgart, 1893-); 8 vols. prepared.
Liebenam, W. "Exercitus," vi, 1608.
Reim, "Civitas,"
Hamburger Real-Encyclopädie für Bibel und Talmud (Leipzig, 1870-83).
Hamburger, art. "Ordinirung," ii, pp. 882-886.

VITA

Dora Askowith, born in Kovno, Russia, August 30th, 1884. Graduated from the Girls' High School in Boston, Mass., in 1902 and advanced course in 1903. Winner of the Old South Historical Society Prize for the year 1903. Received A. B. degree from Barnard College 1908, with General Honors and Departmental Honors in History and Anthropology. Began her graduate work at Columbia University in the Fall of 1908, taking courses in Mediaeval and Modern European History under Professor James T. Shotwell, and Professor James Harvey Robinson, in Sociology under Professor Franklin H. Giddings and Philosophy under Professor John Dewey and Professor William P. Montague. Received A. M. at Columbia University, 1909. Taught in Public School 18, Bronx, N. Y. 1908-1909. Instructor in History at Morris High School and Wadleigh High School for the years 1909-1912. Curtis University Scholar in Mediaeval History at Columbia University for the year 1910-1911. Temporary instructor in History at Hunter College 1912-1914; assistant instructor 1914-1915.

ERRATA.

PAGE.	LINE.	
XI	14	Nicholaus should read Nicholas.
XII	9	arraignment should read arrangement.
XII	12	4 A.D. should read 4 B.C.
		Tetrachs (4-37 A.D.) should read Tetrarchs (4 B.C.-37 A.D.).
15	32	Meilziner should read Mielziner.
18	23	superunt should read supersunt.
20	30	judgment should read jugement.
22	17	Judaeso should read Judaeo.
24	29	registum should read registrum.
25	8	'Ιουδκίων should read 'Ιουδαίων.
26	32	Actenstuck should read Actenstück.
27	23	consulti should read consulta.
28	29	Axamen should read Examen.
30	13	Makkabaer should read Makkabäer.
30	28	Gratz should read Grätz.
32	28	Judee should read Judée.
43	28	Apacrypha should read Apocrypha.
51	26	Vespasion should read Vespasian.
61	29	Gregerorius should read Gregorovius.
71	30	illusion should read allusion.
77	34	Wortebuch should read Wörterbuch.
81	8	usage should read usages.
95	19	copinus should read cophinus.
96	12	Camonae should read Camenae.
112	18	affect should read effect.
115	14	freemen should read freedmen.
122	26	kinship should read kingship.
122	28	Phillipi should read Philippi.
123	32	im Judas should read in Judäa.
128	31	De Sauley should read De Saulcy.
131	14	syncophants should read sycophants.
131	22	devolved upon should read devised.
142	30	dé should read de.
149	30	Ietzte should read letzte.
150	25	Keiserzeit should read Kaiserzeit.
150	28	Staats should read Staate.
159	12	Mosiac should read Mosaic.
165	26	Romer should read Römer.
185	25	Hohenpriestens should read Hohenpriesters.

www.ingramcontent.com/pod-product-compliance
Lightning Source LLC
Chambersburg PA
CBHW060117170426
43198CB00010B/927